James Young Simpson

Side-Lights on Siberia

Some account of the great Siberian railroad, the prisons and exile system

James Young Simpson

Side-Lights on Siberia

Some account of the great Siberian railroad, the prisons and exile system

ISBN/EAN: 9783744755160

Printed in Europe, USA, Canada, Australia, Japan

Cover: Foto ©ninafisch / pixelio.de

More available books at **www.hansebooks.com**

SIDE-LIGHTS ON SIBERIA

INTERIOR OF A PRISON *KAMERA*.

SIDE-LIGHTS ON SIBERIA

SOME ACCOUNT OF THE GREAT SIBERIAN RAILROAD
THE PRISONS AND EXILE SYSTEM

BY

JAMES YOUNG SIMPSON
M.A., B.Sc.

WITH NUMEROUS ILLUSTRATIONS

WILLIAM BLACKWOOD AND SONS
EDINBURGH AND LONDON
MDCCCXCVIII

All Rights reserved

PATRI MATRIQUE DILECTISSIMIS

PREFACE.

THE following pages record impressions received in the course of a journey in Siberia during the summer of 1896. The limitations under which a study of this kind must necessarily be conducted will suggest themselves to every mind. But so far as controversial subjects are dealt with, the writer can claim to be in great measure free from the limitation of partiality.

Some of the chapters appeared during the course of the past year in 'Blackwood's Magazine,' but with one exception these have been altered and considerably enlarged. The writer would here express his obligations to Professor A. H. Keane's 'Asia' (Stanford's 'Compendium of Geography'); to the second edition of a Russian book, 'Siberia and the Great Siberian Railway,' issued by the Department of Trade and Manufactures in the Ministry of Finance; to various local calendars; and to Professor Thun's able 'Geschichte der revolutionären Bewegungen in Russland,' on which chap. x. is largely based. The statistics everywhere are taken from the Imperial Prison Reports.

Several of the illustrations are from photographs by a Mr Kuznetzov: the remainder are original.

It is a commonplace for those who have travelled in Russia to acknowledge the courtesy of officials with whom they came in contact. To many such officials the writer owes a debt of gratitude, especially to Mr Salomon, Director-in-Chief of Russian prisons, and to State Secretary Kulomzin; as also to his valued friend Prince N. S. Galitzin, who is happily not unknown in this country.

EDINBURGH, *Feb.* 1898.

CONTENTS.

CHAPTER I.

THE LAND AND THE PEOPLE.

Introduction—Area of Siberia—Political divisions—Mountains—Tundra—Taiga—Fertile zone—Amuria—River-systems—The Ob, Yenisei, and Lena — Population — Sub - Arctic races—Buryats and Shamanism — Tungus and Yakutes — Original Russian population 1

CHAPTER II.

THE GREAT SIBERIAN IRON ROAD.

Historical review—Special Commission—Original plan of railway—Progress up to present time—The emigration movement—Regulations for its management—The rush of 1896—Approaching Tchelyabinsk—Kurgan—Omsk—Primitive tools—Crossing the river Ob—Regaining the railway—The workmen employed—Convict labour—A military train—The settlers' camp at Atchinsk—Incidents of the journey—Krasnoyarsk—Careful nature of the work—The section round Lake Baikal—Misovskaya to Srjetensk—Trans-Manchurian branches—North and south Ussuri lines — Changes on the original plan — Coal—Relation of the railway to Russia — The Perm-Kotlass scheme — The monument to Russia's culture in the nineteenth century 16

CHAPTER III.

TRAVEL IN SIBERIA.

On the great post-road—Requirements—Cost of posting—The postmaster's book—To prevent racing—The *yamstchik*—His monotonous life—His management of horses—Post-stations outside and inside—Siberian villages—The public playground—Drunkenness—When the kye come hame—Life on the *trakt*—The Angara—Lake Baikal—The Buryat country—Valley of the Selenga—Fellow-travellers—Tea caravans—Robbery—Incidents and mishaps—Through the flood—Ferries and ferry-boats—River-travel—The Ob—Scenery on its banks—Sunset on the Ob—Taking in wood—The Irtïsh—Difficulties in its navigation 61

CHAPTER IV.

MONARCH OR MONK? A LEGEND OF TOMSK.

Tomsk—Description of the town—"Alexander's House"—The life of Theodore Kuzmitch—His death—The last years of Alexander I.—Did he abdicate? 114

CHAPTER V.

ON THE MARCH.

Departure of a convict gang from the Tomsk Forwarding Prison—The Peresílni Prison at Moscow—Overcrowding—The Russian *mujik* at home—Lodging-houses in St Petersburg—Tiumen Forwarding Prison—A convict barge—Life on the river—Arrival at Tomsk 138

CHAPTER VI.

ON THE MARCH—*concluded*.

Description of the Forwarding Prison at Tomsk—Attitude of the soldiers towards the prisoners—Convict dress—Transference by *étape*—*Étapes* and *polu-étapes*—Allowances on the march—The *brodyaga*—*Étapes* at Mariinsk and near Kansk—Life on the march—*Étapes* in Eastern Siberia—Politicals *en route*—Criticism—Changes effected by the Trans-Siberian Railway . 166

CHAPTER VII.

ALEXANDROVSKY CENTRÁL.

Past opinion regarding Siberia—Evolution of the prison—Statistics—The Siberian exile system—Distribution of ex-convicts and exile settlers—Alexandrovsky Centrál—The *natchalnik*—The Orphans' Home—The church—The prison buildings—Unusual precautions—The outhouses—Capital punishment—The *plet*—Branding—Indoor labour—The Peresílni Prison—The hospital—Local prison at Irkutsk—Contrasted with Alexandrovsky Centrál—Of animal food—The darker possibilities open to a "free command" 194

CHAPTER VIII.

THE SILVER MINES OF NERTCHINSK.

The Nertchinsk penal settlement—How approached—The Chinese in Siberia—The valley of the Shilka—Gorni-Zerentui—Convict labour on the railway—Description of the prison—The children's home—The settlement of voluntary followers—The released convict—Algatchi—Work in the mines—A Tungus village—Akatui—Slavinski the political—Down the mine—Alexandrovsky and its houses of refuge . . . 237

CHAPTER IX.

SAKHALIN AND OTHER CENTRES.

Sakhalin—History of the island—Its climate—Russian population—Native population—Exile settlers—Convict labour—Nertchinsk local prison—A merchants' town—The prison hospital at Tchita—Sunday labour—Local prison at Verkhni-Udinsk—Krasnoyarsk—Tobolsk and its prison factory—The Gubernski prison at Tomsk—Influence of exile settlers upon the Siberians 270

CHAPTER X.

THE REVOLUTIONARY MOVEMENT.

Its birth—Alexander I.—The Decembrists—Alexander Herzen—Tchernishevski—Abolition of serfage—Katkov—Nihilism—Netchaiev's conspiracy—Lavrov and Bakunin—The "going amongst the people"—Failure of the movement—The secret society "Land and Liberty"—Jakov Stepanovitch—The Hundred and Ninety-three—Terrorism—Hunger-strikes—Soloviev's attempt—Campaign against Alexander II.—His assassination—Secret printing-presses and bomb-factories—What the Terrorists achieved . . . 298

CHAPTER XI.

THE POLITICAL PRISONER.

Past opinion—Exile by administrative process—Politicals on the march—An "administrative" in prison—Life in a Yakute *ulus*—A political of the second class—Schlusselburg—The ex-political newspaper editor—Terrorist colonies—Strength of the Terrorist party—Life at Kara—Manifestoes—A girl political—The Netchaiev conspirator—The romance of the political's life—Russia and France—Present-day socialistic movements—Russian justice—Growth of the revolutionary idea—Terrorists and the peasants—The watchmaker and the photographer—Politicals and scientific work—The bright side of their existence—Do they remain in Siberia?—Criticism—The freedom of Russia 328

CHAPTER XII.

CONCLUSION.

Criticism of the Siberian exile system—The future of the country—Its internal development and unity 373

GLOSSARY 377
INDEX . 380

ILLUSTRATIONS.

FULL-PAGE ILLUSTRATIONS.

	PAGE
INTERIOR OF A PRISON *KAMERA* . *Frontispiece*	
AN OLD KARA *PRIJUT*	90
A SETTLEMENT OF VOLUNTARY FOLLOWERS, EASTERN SIBERIA .	152
BRODYAGA BRANDED B . .	178
LOADING A CONVICT WAGGON	192
"FREE-COMMANDS"	200
THE READING-ROOM AT ALEXANDROVSKY CENTRÁL	212
CONVICT BRANDED S K A .	222
OFF TO THE MINES .	238
THE YOUNGEST OF THE GIRLS	250
GUARDING THE PIT-HEAD . . .	252
CONSTRUCTION OF THE PRISON AT ALGATCHI	254
AKATUI . .	258
AT THE PIT-HEAD . .	263
FEMALE CONVICTS, ALEXANDROVSKY	264
BLIND OLD CONVICTS	266
OUTSIDE LABOUR AT THE OLD SMELTING-WORKS, ALGATCHI	276
GRINDING CORN . .	282
THE ROLL-CALL . .	294
IN THE GOLD-MINES AT KARA .	342
FEMALE CONVICT LABOUR AT KARA	352

ILLUSTRATIONS IN THE TEXT.

SETTLERS *EN ROUTE*	31
A BREAK IN THE EMBANKMENT IN TRANS-BAIKALIA	50
LISTVINITCHNAYA	52
YAMSTCHIK AND BURYAT WOMAN	68
OUTSIDE A POSTHOUSE	73
TILL THE MASTER RETURNS	80
RIVER INGODA, EASTERN SIBERIA	93
PENDULUM FERRY-BOAT ON THE NERTCHA	102
FALLEN TREES ON THE BANKS OF THE OB	105
SUNSET ON THE OB	108
VILLAGE ON THE BANKS OF THE IRTÌSH	110
TAKING IN WOOD	112
ON THE OUTSKIRTS	115
THE HOME OF THEODORE KUZMITCH	121
A CONVICT	138
CONVICT-BARGE ON THE OB	154
IN THE CAGE	157
A CONVICT	166
AN *ÉTAPE*, EASTERN SIBERIA	186
ON THE HORIZON	193
CONVICT CHAINED TO WHEELBARROW	195
ALEXANDROVSKY CENTRÁL	203
THE CHURCH AT ALEXANDROVSKY CENTRÁL	207
INSIDE THE COURTYARD	210
PALATCH WITH *PLET*	218
CONVICT CHAINED TO WHEELBARROW, RESTING	221
THE SETTLEMENT OF THE VOLUNTARY FOLLOWERS, GORNI-ZERENTUI	249
THE BEST CABIN	251
MAP OF SIBERIA	*at the end*

SIDE-LIGHTS ON SIBERIA.

CHAPTER I.

THE LAND AND THE PEOPLE.

INTRODUCTION—AREA OF SIBERIA—POLITICAL DIVISIONS—MOUNTAINS —*TUNDRA*—*TAIGA*—FERTILE ZONE—AMURIA—RIVER-SYSTEMS—THE OB, YENISEI, AND LENA—POPULATION—SUB-ARCTIC RACES—BURYATS AND SHAMANISM — TUNGUS AND YAKUTES — ORIGINAL RUSSIAN POPULATION.

SIBERIA is at once the reservoir of the Russian empire and its cesspool. In the latter aspect it has been known of old time; the former distinction has only lately come to light. Alongside of a truer appreciation of the value of the land, based largely upon the unearthing of its hidden treasures and the cultivation of its fertile soil, there has sprung up in the minds of many Russians a recognition of the fatuity of early ideas as to the best use to which the country could be put, and they are quietly working to bring about a change. Hence it has come to pass that to-day the great domain is in a transition stage. The old Siberia, with its unhallowed associations of gloomy exile system, long dark winters, and inhospitable wastes, is slowly passing away before the new Siberia, with its well-organised schemes of emigration, bright summers, and fair expanses of tilled land. Not that there has been any change in the seasons: what has altered is the point of view from which the territory was wont to be regarded.

When one says that the country has a superficial area of nearly 5,312,000 square miles, not only is very little impression of its immense extent conveyed by the figures —this is better done by describing it as about forty-four times as large as Great Britain and Ireland—but it has also to be borne in mind that they are merely an approximation. As a matter of fact, the actual area of Siberia is still unknown. Nansen complained that the charts of the north coast were inaccurate; and the boundary between Siberia and China has still to be strictly defined over many lineal miles. In the interior there are hundreds of square miles where the foot of man has never trod. The *tundra* is little known; the *taiga* is only now coming into consideration. Again, even those districts which have been longest known would seem to be still subject to the caprice of the imperial cartographers. Thus the European Russia of geography should properly lie west of the Urals, but has in part been transferred politically to the other side, so that Siberia is now the poorer for the province of Yekaterinburg, which formerly constituted a part of the Russian dominion in Asia.

Siberia was annexed to the Russian empire in the first instance by the Don Cossack Yermak at the end of the sixteenth century. It may be divided into the following parts: (1) Western Siberia, comprising the Governments of Tobolsk and Tomsk in the basin of the Ob. Formerly these two regions were united under a governor-general, but now their civil governors are subject to the direct control of the Minister of Interior, while the troops in the Government of Tomsk are under the command of the governor-general of the Steppe country. (2) Eastern Siberia, comprising the Governments of Yeniseisk and Irkutsk in the basin of the Yenisei, and the *oblast* [1] of Yakutsk in the basin of the Lena and other lesser rivers, all united under a governor-general resident at Irkutsk. Yakutsk is chiefly remarkable in having one of the poles of greatest cold within its borders. In the district of Verkhoyansk on the upper Yana, $-49°$ C. have been registered in the coldest and $15°$ C. in the hottest month. In the town of Irkutsk the possible range is even greater, as there the maximum and minimum temperatures are $33°·8$ C. (1894) and $-44°·3$ C. (January 1890) respectively. The snowfall diminishes sensibly as you travel from west to east. (3) The Amur *oblast*, to whose governor-general are also subject the adjacent Littoral (Primorsky) territory including Sakhalin, and the *oblast* Trans-Baikalia. The regions covered by these three *oblasts* include the left half of the basins of the rivers Amur and Ussuri, the entire coast-zone bordering on the Japanese, Okhotsk, and Bering seas, together with the peninsula of Kamtchatka, and the territory immediately to the east of Lake Baikal. (4) The Steppe country, comprising the *oblasts* of Akmolinsk, Semipalatinsk, and Semirjetchensk, united under a governor-general. They occupy the upper basins of the Irtish and Ishim, as also the basins of several less important rivers that fall into Lake Balkhash.

[1] An *oblast* (which may be rendered "territory") has not reached the same degree of political organisation as a "government," and has usually as governor an officer still actually in the military service, with the title of "military governor." He has full command of the troops in his *oblast*, but is subject in the last instance to the governor-general.

The Steppe portion proper of this whole region (for Semirjetchensk is essentially a mountainous district) differs from the adjacent plain of Western Siberia in presenting no absolute level. Its ill-watered surface is broken by low but well-marked ridges of crystalline rock containing various minerals, and the oases are so few and far between that it is practically abandoned to the nomadic Kirghize.

Although the better-known western lowlands of Siberia, with their 400 to 600 feet of altitude, have sometimes in popular description and imagination been vaguely extended over a wider area than they really cover, yet it must not be forgotten that there are mountain-ranges in the land of premier importance. Chief amongst these is the intricate Altai system, which, although forming for many miles the natural southern boundary of the country, may be held to run up through it — but by no means continuously — in a north-easterly direction under such names as the Sayan Mountains, and, east of Baikal, the Yablonovoi and Stanovoi chains, as far as the volcanic regions, active and passive, of Kamtchatka, beyond which it gradually descends to the East Cape. Strictly, however, Eastern Siberia is a lofty plateau, of which at least one of these mountain-chains may be regarded as the border-ridge. For peaks perpetually snow-clad, as for the feeding-grounds of glaciers, one has to go to parts of the irregular Altai range, or to the giant of the Sayan—Munku-Sardik (10,700 feet).

From a convenient though not perfectly accurate point of view, Siberia may be regarded as divided into three broad east-and-west zones,[1] of which the one farthest to the north is characterised as *tundra*. This is the name applied to the belt of land that skirts the Arctic Ocean from Novaya

[1] Siberia and the Exile System, by George Kennan, vol. i. p. 57.

Zemlya to Bering Strait, swampy and treeless for the greater part, and extending inland for a distance that varies from 150 to 400 miles. Desolate, inhospitable, treacherous, the surface of the *tundra* is covered in the summer months with myriad meres, rivulets, and marshy places, for the melting snows of winter cannot soak into the frozen subsoil of alternate layers of earth and ice. During the deathless days of June and July the sun shines dimly through the vapour that rises from the mossy bogs; but its heat is sufficient to induce a lusty growth of brown moss and grey lichen, that overspreads the thin unfrozen upper stratum. On the more southern slopes, not so completely waterlogged, the scanty vegetation of the *tundra* is reinforced by dwarf bushes of bilberry, wild raspberry, and cranberry; coarse grasses, dandelions, and poppies too are not unknown. Here and there various species of polar willow, alder, and stunted birch cling to the river-banks or crouch in the lee of some hillock, but it is a larch—*Larix daurica*—that pushes farthest towards the north. In early spring the lonely wastes resound to the harsh screams of cranes, geese, and ducks, swans, grebe, and snipe; while sturgeon, sterlet, nelma, omul, and numerous other fish, ascend the rivers from the sea to spawn. There congregate the reindeer, glad to quit the woods and with them the rapacious gadflies, one representative of the abundant insect life that wakes into being at the breath of the spring.

But in the winter, and more especially throughout those two darkest months when the moon, stars, and northern lights alone illuminate the frigid desert; when the sun brightens the southern horizon for a brief hour as if in unfulfilled promise of a glorious dawn; when the fierce arctic gales plough deep furrows in the trackless snow, and the courses of the frozen rivers are only discovered by a meandering line of dusky scrub; when every living creature has sought the sheltering woods, there to abide until the return of vernal days,—then it is that the *tundra* presents that spectacle of utter dreariness, mysteriousness, nay, otherworldliness, that is peculiarly its own.

The second zone, into which the first imperceptibly passes on its southern borders, is the Forest zone or *taiga*. It stretches from the Urals to the eastern shores of Kamtchatka, and even penetrates far to the north along some of the larger river-valleys. Siberian poplars, with ash-grey stem and quivering leaves; spruces, with their regular isosceles-triangled contour and dark shading; giant larches towering above their fellows; cedars (*Pinus cembra*), whose peculiar branches are crowded with knob-like bunches of green needles; Scotch firs, with cinnamon-coloured upper trunks toning down to sombre iron-grey; the oriental pitch pine, and, towards the outskirts, birches with pure white gentle stems, or moisture-loving alder,—these form the body, while the padding is largely left to the small but graceful Siberian spruce, with smoother bark and darker leaves than the ordinary spruce fir. It is a place of gloom below and silent conflict in mid-air. As little do the life- and light-diffusing rays of the seemly sun penetrate that felted mass of tree-tops, as does the reckless trapper force his way through their stout wall of stems buttressed by the decaying trunks and gnarled roots of heroes that have fallen in the unequal strife with devastating hurricanes, and are now almost buried beneath the accumulated mould of many years. Herbage is wanting in these denser spots: the grey, tenacious, clayey soil is carpeted with moss and lichens. Such is the Siberian jungle, now pierced in part by two thin lines of iron rail.

The third zone, before which the forest belt of lofty trees is slowly retreating towards the north, is the open, fertile, and, in great part, arable zone of Southern Siberia. It practically coincides with the agricultural zone, and is largely inhabited by a settled population; but it includes the whole steppe region, of which only small areas can be brought under the plough. It may be roughly described as lying south of a line drawn from the town of Tobolsk to that of Tomsk, thereafter embracing the southern parts of the Governments of Yeniseisk and Irkutsk. Much of Trans-Baikalia is cultivable, and it is only a question of time till the banks of the Amur and Ussuri become entirely colonised with farmers. Hence in this cultivated tract agriculture is the predominant feature, not only being the fundamental source of the prosperity of those who practise it, but, on the whole, yielding surplus quantities of grain, by the sale of which the population is enabled to pay its taxes and procure supplies. It has been estimated that to every hundred persons of the actual population the following areas are sown with grain:[1]—

	Desiatines.[2]
In the southern districts of the Tobolsk Government	104
In the central part of the Tomsk Government	87
In the agricultural region of the Yeniseisk Government	102
In the agricultural region of the Irkutsk Government	97

That portion of Siberia which, from the name of the river that most contributes to its extensive watering-system, is known as the Amur country, deserves an added word. If the Argun and Kerulen be reckoned as the head-waters of the Amur, then its length is not less than 3070 miles. The excessive humidity of the climate, and the consequent

[1] Siberia and the Great Siberian Railway, second edition, p. 96.
[2] See Glossary.

swampy reed-covered nature of many of the lower mountain-slopes, are by no means favourable to agriculture; still it has not been found impossible to cope even with these drawbacks. The continual burning of the ground vegetation over wide areas of the affected districts has resulted not only in the gradual conversion of the damp soil into fertile land, but has indirectly influenced the climate for the better. The forests, with which much of the regions of the Amur are covered, contain the trees already noted as constituting the *taiga*, with the distinctive additions of the Manchurian cedar, yew, maple, ash, walnut, linden (also found in Tobolsk), and cork-tree. Indeed, owing to its position with regard to the Pacific Ocean, this province has a flora peculiarly rich and unique.

To some minds the river-system of Siberia will be hardly less interesting than the exile system. In the first place, there is no single long river like the Nile, whose tributaries can never be regarded as anything else. Each of the great Siberian waterways may be said to be formed by the junction of two streams of immense volume, as in the case of the Ob-Irtish, Yenisei-Angara, Lena-Vitim, and Amur-Argun systems. A second feature has been stated thus by Professor A. H. Keane: "The land has a general inclination towards the north, so that all the great rivers flowing from the southern highlands pursue a normal and nearly parallel northerly course to the Arctic Ocean. But most of the large tributaries flow rather north-west and north-east to the left and right banks of the main streams, thus affording an almost uninterrupted water-highway from the Urals to the Pacific, as well as from the southern highlands to the Arctic. From the river Ural to Yakutsk, a distance of 6000 miles, this magnificent waterway is broken only by two short portages between the Ob and Yenisei, and between the Yenisei and Lena respectively. The whole country is in this way covered with a network of rivers, affording altogether some 30,000 miles of navigable waters."[1] A third observation applies only to those rivers that flow in a northerly direction. The traveller observes that in each case the river hugs its right bank, which is commonly very steep and lofty, while the left bank is low, sometimes clothed with willow, and merges in the neighbouring plain. At the town of Atchinsk, where the railway crosses the river Tchulim, the embankment rises towards the bridge to a considerable height in order to gain the loftier level of the eastern bank. Appearances suggest that at no very remote date the present western bank formed part of the river's bed—that, in short, the very rivers are joining in the rush towards the east. This displacement of the rivers is due to the rotation of the earth. Since the force with which any moving body on the earth's surface would be deflected to the side under the influence of its rotation is dependent on its velocity, we see that the more quickly moving masses of water in the centre of a stream flowing north will be urged against the right bank more strongly than the slower-flowing parts, so that, on the whole, the current runs more swiftly on that side of the river-bed, and in consequence the erosion there is greater. Penck[2] illustrates this law of Baer by the consideration of a perfectly elastic ball running along a trench with perfectly elastic sides. On coming in contact with the right wall it rebounds, and crosses towards the left wall; but while its motion in that direction is retarded by the earth's rotation, its return journey to the right is accelerated from

---

[1] Asia, vol. i. p. 179.
[2] Morphologie der Erdoberfläche, vol. i. pp. 349-356.

the same cause. This is continually repeated, with the result that, on the average, the right wall is struck more sharply than the left. Where there is no perfect elasticity of the walls, the right suffers tear and wear more than the left. A fourth consideration is that, while the signs of winter are disappearing in the interior and southern parts of Siberia, the estuaries and lower reaches of the great rivers remain frost-bound, occasioning spring floods on all the north-flowing rivers of such dimensions that the Ob, for example, assumes, not so far below Tomsk, the appearance of a great inland sea, whose opposite banks may not be seen from one another.

The basin of this last colossal waterway occupies an area of over a million and a half square miles at the lowest computation, while its length is hardly under 3500 miles. The waters of its chief western head-streams—the Tobol and Ishim—are collected on the left by the Irtish, which, from the fact that it traces its source to the Kobdo plateau in Western Mongolia, should be regarded as "the true upper course of the main stream." The Ob itself rises on the northern slopes of the Altai, and after receiving hundreds of tributaries, of which, on its lower reaches, the Tom, Tchulim, and Ket are the most important, it unites some miles above Troitsk with the more travelled Irtish, and thereafter they pursue a joint course of 700 miles, although indeed in two separate channels—the Great and Little Ob—to Arctic seas. The river Ket possesses a certain commercial interest, as its headwaters have been put in connection with those of the Kas, a tributary of the Yenisei, by utilising an intermediate lake and building a canal some five miles in length. By this enterprise the basins of the Ob and Yenisei are virtually united.

The Yenisei is decidedly inferior to the Ob in respect of the size of its basin, although if, on geological grounds, the Selenga be reckoned as one of its head-streams, its total length is not much less. Both of the great branches take their rise in Chinese territory, and break northwards through the mountain-barriers that separate the two countries. The Selenga, reinforced by the Orkhon, which takes its rise in the veritable Gobi itself, falls into Baikal, the largest fresh-water lake in Asia, of which more will be said later. The outflow of the lake is through the Angara, a considerable, characteristic stream, on which Irkutsk stands. Its confluence with the main river produces a body of water whose breadth is never less than a mile, increasing near that point in time of flood by more than four times that amount, and immediately above its estuary by forty times. One of its chief eastern tributaries, the Nijni (Lower) Tunguska, approaches within fourteen miles of the Lena, which, if we pass over the Khatanga, Anabara, Olenek, Yana, Indigirka, and Kolima, is the only remaining river of any size that discharges its waters into the Arctic. Rising among the mountains to the west of Lake Baikal, it receives upon the right the tribute of the Vitim and Aldan (each of these rivers doubling the volume of the Lena previous to its junction with them), not to speak of the Olekma, and the stately, if somewhat solitary, western affluent, the Viliui. The area of its enormous basin has been estimated at a million square miles, while the length of the Lena proper and the Lena-Vitim system are 2900 and 3280 miles respectively. Unlike the Ob with its large gulf, or the Yenisei with its broad open estuary, the Lena pours its waters into the Arctic by means of a delta some 8000 square miles in extent. Projecting far into the polar seas, its main channel often blocked by floes for weeks in summer, this delta makes the Lena far less accessible than its kindred Yenisei. Of the rivers that flow towards the Pacific, mention need only be made of the Anadir, emptying itself into the Bering Sea, and of the Amur, about which something has already been said. Economically, the latter is by far the most important of all the Siberian rivers. After piercing the Khingan Mountains, which separate Manchuria from the Mongolian plateau, it is joined at Blagovyeshtchensk by the Zeya from the north, and later by the Bureya, while the Sungari and Ussuri swell its volume on the right bank. Before this, however, it has already begun to swerve in a north-easterly direction, and enters the sea opposite the north-west coast of Sakhalin. In connection with the Ussuri is found Lake Khanka, a fresh-water basin of some 1200 square miles in area.

The population of Siberia (including Sakhalin) is given as 5,732,000 by the census of 1897, which, when compared with Koppen's estimate of 2,437,000 in 1851, shows a remarkable increase. The proportion of natives to Russians varies with the locality, being as 1 : 20 in Western Siberia, while in the *oblast* of Yakutsk the figures are nearly reversed.

Of the sub-Arctic races that inhabit the north-east of Siberia, it is sufficient to recall the names of the wandering Tchuktchi, "originally a Manchu or Tungus people," the wild Koryaks, the more hospitable Kamtchadals, the Lamuts and Yukaghirs, all differing in speech and appearance, but still related, however distantly. Their country is in no way adapted to permanent agricultural colonisation. They pass their lives in hunting, fishing, and tending their reindeer herds. Much the same description applies to those purely Finnish tribes, the Ostyaks, Samoyedes, and Voguls, who dwell on the outskirts of the forest zone of Western Siberia, it being a minority in each case that prefers the polar *tundra* zone. Their religion, so far as it exists at all, is mainly shamanistic. The Mongolian stock is indeed represented by some 20,000 Kalmicks who live in the Altai mining region, but more successfully by the Buryats, who, with the Yakutes, alone give any promise of holding their own numerically before the encroachments of a greater race. They are found principally in the country on the two sides of Lake Baikal—although in greater numbers on the east—where they have been settled since the thirteenth century. They are a sober, strong, intelligent people, originally nomadic cattle-breeders, but now showing a tendency to engage in agricultural and industrial pursuits, in which they meet with marked success. Beneath a veneer of Christianity or Buddhism the Buryat still retains a genuine respect for his ancient shamanistic faith. In Shamanism may be traced an element of ancestor-worship; but, as in all Mongolian religions, witchcraft and sorcery play the leading part. The *shaman* is the mediator between man and the spirits, both good and evil. In the execution of his office he is assisted mainly by his ancestors, who are now good spirits. Not only in his attire, but in his twin function of priest and physician, the *shaman* resembles the medicine-man of the North American Indians. The Buryats are very superstitious, and call their more favoured children by uncongenial names, thinking to shield them from malign influences by this artificial depreciation.

Closely allied to the Buryats are the Tungus people who roam all over the great expanse of land lying to the north of the Buryat country between the Yenisei and the Sea of

Okhotsk, except where the Yakutes claim possession. Russians speak of them as reindeer, horse, or dog Tungueses, according to their habits. They are possessed of many noble characteristics, and are intrepid hunters.

The territory of the Yakutes has been in Russian hands since the seventeenth century. It embraces both sides of the middle and lower Lena. Their Turki dialect contains an admixture of Mongolian words. They occupy themselves mainly with cattle-breeding, hunting, and fishing, but their great versatility renders them capable agriculturists and artisans. There corresponds to them in Western Siberia a considerable Tatar population descended from the tribes that composed the ancient Kutchum Siberian kingdom.

If we exclude the more recent peasant immigrants, the original Russian population of Siberia may be said to comprise the following three classes: (1) the Kossaks, who first conquered the country; (2) exiles, political and criminal; (3) dissenters from the Greek Church, who were either banished to Siberia or went there of their own accord. That is to say, the original Russian population of Siberia consists of men and women who were in some way, intellectually or physically, more active or more earnest than their fellow-countrymen and women who remained in European Russia. The result is that to-day the average Siberian is a more vigorous and intelligent man than the average Russian. He picks up a thing more quickly: his life is richer, brighter. Historians tell us that on December 20, 1620, a small body of saddened but determined men—Dissenters too—landed from the Mayflower upon the New England coast, and from that Plymouth colony of Pilgrim Fathers and other like-minded individuals who followed them in later years has sprung much of what is best in the America of our time. The delicate nervous activity and quickness that is more common in the American than in the Englishman — "that added drop of nervous fluid which," as a certain American writer has it, "was bestowed by the Creator upon the descendants of English stock when the final improvement upon it had to be made" — is also found in a lesser degree to be distinctive of the Siberian as compared with the European Russian.

CHAPTER II.

THE GREAT SIBERIAN IRON ROAD.

HISTORICAL REVIEW—SPECIAL COMMISSION—ORIGINAL PLAN OF RAILWAY—PROGRESS UP TO PRESENT TIME—THE EMIGRATION MOVEMENT—REGULATIONS FOR ITS MANAGEMENT—THE RUSH OF 1896—APPROACHING TCHELYABINSK—KURGAN—OMSK—PRIMITIVE TOOLS—CROSSING THE RIVER OB—REGAINING THE RAILWAY—THE WORKMEN EMPLOYED—CONVICT LABOUR—A MILITARY TRAIN—THE SETTLERS' CAMP AT ATCHINSK—INCIDENTS OF THE JOURNEY—KRASNOYARSK—CAREFUL NATURE OF THE WORK—THE SECTION ROUND LAKE BAIKAL—MÍSOVSKAYA TO SRJETENSK—TRANS-MANCHURIAN BRANCHES—NORTH AND SOUTH USSURI LINES—CHANGES ON THE ORIGINAL PLAN—COAL—RELATION OF THE RAILWAY TO RUSSIA—THE PERM-KOTLASS SCHEME—THE MONUMENT TO RUSSIA'S CULTURE IN THE NINETEENTH CENTURY.

WHEN in the years to come men review the greater undertakings of the nineteenth century, it will be hard to find a rival to the Trans-Siberian Railway. Winding across the illimitable plains of Orenburg, traversing the broad Urals, spanning the widest rivers, like the Irtish, Ob, and Yenisei, it creeps round the southern end of Lake Baikal, and mounts the plateau of far Trans-Baikalia. Thereafter, leaving behind it the Yablonovoi Mountains, the line descends into the valley of the Amur, exchanges it presently for that of the Ussuri, and ends at last in Vladivostok. Such is, in brief, the original course of this vast enterprise.

For long, Russia has been feeling her way towards the open ocean. It is as if she were being choked for want of air. The White Sea and the Arctic Ocean enchained in Polar ice, the Baltic similarly blocked for half the year, the Black Sea closed in yet another way, and finally the landlocked Caspian, cannot satisfy her. In face of this, she has been compelled to seek the shores of the Pacific Ocean. As early as the middle of the seventeenth century a handful of intrepid, though predatory, Russian pioneers had gained the barren Okhotsk shore and founded the town that bears that name. But it was only to find that here the same conditions prevailed as on their western Baltic, and the disappointed explorers involuntarily turned their eyes towards the kindlier south. Soon a party of Kossaks and hunters, passing through Trans-Baikalia, took possession of some land on the Upper Amur. Gradually the whole territory on the left bank of that river, and thereafter the region of the Ussuri, came into Russian hands, though it was General Muraviev who in 1854, during the progress of the Crimean war, played the greatest part in the work of annexation. About four or five years later dawned the appearance of Siberian railway effort.

The Trans-Siberian Railway scheme was probably but the development of sundry other lesser projects which had as object the providing of suitable means of communication in and with the newly acquired territories, so that they might be the more easily held, and, in addition, colonised. There are some patriotic individuals amongst ourselves who would have it kept in remembrance that no plan of Trans-Siberian conveyance appeared earlier than that of a certain English engineer. But this had better be forgotten. For when we learn that his proposal to carry a horse tramway from Nijni-Novgorod through Kazan and Perm to some port on the Pacific Ocean was unsupported by any estimate —his name was Dull—we do not wonder that the Government passed it by in silence.

But his was not the only paper scheme. More modest was that of Collins, an American, who wished to unite Irkutsk and Tchita by rail. In 1858 three English projectors—Morison, Horn, and Sleigh—offered to lay a railway from Moscow to the Straits of Tartary, but at the same time petitioned for such privileges as would have retained the exploitation of Siberia and the ensuing profit in other than Russian hands for a number of years. Hence these and all other like vague drafts, based on no preliminary surveys or careful investigation of the needs and trading possibilities of the districts they affected, went no further.

More practical was a Russian project which aimed at connecting the basins of the Ob and Volga. The predominating influence of the Ural mining industry at this time so affected all suggested routes, that of the three which at the end of the "sixties" were alone deemed worthy of consideration every one began at Perm, and two ended at Tiumen. Thus by the smaller work of connecting the Kama and Tura the basins of the larger rivers could be, and latterly were, united. Other men took up the idea of utilising the magnificent Siberian waterways, and showed how far by this means it was possible to traverse the country. By making a canal between one of the tributaries of the Ob and the Yenisei it would be possible to reach the Baikal Lake and ascend the Selenga. Thereafter all that was necessary would be to cross the Yablonovoi watershed and descend into the valley of the Amur.

A mass of details, exact and inexact, had been collected

as the result of the various preliminary surveys bearing on the future Siberian Railway, and since no definite conclusion as to the direction of the route seemed possible under the existing circumstances, a Special Commission was sent out to the Urals and directed to make a final investigation of the question. Their orders were to let the requirements of the Ural mining industry bulk most largely in their deliberations: the Siberian transport trade, although to be kept in view, was always to yield to the other in importance. The principal outcome of this activity was the decision that these two interests were incompatible. Accordingly, for the time being, the idea of a local Ural Railway was preferred to that of a Trans-Siberian trunk line. Government surveys were conducted during 1872-74, and in 1878 the Ural line was opened as far as Yekaterinburg. Four years later it had been extended to Tiumen, through which town it was still felt that the future Trans-Siberian Railway must pass.

Meanwhile, within European Russia there had been considerable railway extension. Orenburg was now in communication with the general system, and if for the moment the idea of a Trans-Siberian Railway had slipped somewhat into the background in the West, yet in the far East no little attention was given to the project, and as early as 1875 there were petitions, *e.g.*, to unite Vladivostok and Lake Khanka by rail, if for nothing else than in view of future relations with China and Japan. The result of all this was, that in 1882 the subject of the Siberian Railway was taken up afresh, and as additional surveys and other considerations showed the inadvisability of continuing the line through Tiumen, the whole matter had to be gone into again from the beginning.

About this period Ostrovski, a Russian engineer, propounded a scheme which, although but an extension of an older and more precise suggestion, still attracted considerable notice. He rather depreciated the idea of a continuous line of rail throughout Siberia,—he saw no need for it at the moment. Develop and facilitate internal communication, he said, and outlets will follow naturally in due time. And in demonstration of this plan he proposed that rails should be laid between Perm and Tobolsk, thus uniting the Kama and the Irtish; between Tomsk and Krasnoyarsk, thus connecting the Ob and Yenisei; between Omsk and Barnaul, to link the Irtish with the Ob far above their natural union. To the last line he attached special importance. It would bring the rich Altai mining district nearer civilisation, and furthermore would strengthen the trade that, by way of Biisk and Kobdo, was being carried on with China. And like some old-time prophet, he looked forward to the day when Moscow and Irkutsk would be the termini of a far-reaching iron road, and even went the length of sketching its route in the following succinct terms: "The road should pass through Riazan, Spassk, Ufa, and thence through Zlatoüst, Tchelyabinsk, Petropavlovsk, Omsk, Kainsk, Tomsk, Mariinsk, Atchinsk, Krasnoyarsk, Kansk, Udinsk, and Balagansk to Irkutsk. It will thus, throughout its whole extent, meet all the chief administrative and trading centres of Siberia, will nowhere quit the zone of densest population, and will traverse almost exclusively the fertile *tchernoziom* tract, from the Volga to the Yenisei." This outline is little different from the course that the railway takes to-day. Greater impetus was, however, afforded by sectional schemes petitioned for by such outstanding men as the Governors-General Korf and Ignatiev. The easternmost or Ussuri line was made the subject of a Special Commission in 1890, which advanced from that detail to discussion of the Trans-Siberian Railway as a whole. Strategical considerations, although always kept in view, were sometimes even subordinated to those of a commercial nature, so great was the desire to bring Siberia into close economic intercourse with European Russia. The questions as to which route should be followed, how the construction of so long a line of railway could be most conveniently parcelled out, and whether it would be advisable to carry it right across Siberia, were eagerly debated. The last point was decided in the affirmative, mainly owing to a marked change for the better in financial prospects about that time. As to whether the railway should be a continuation from Tiumen on the Ural line, from Miass on the Samara-Zlatoüst line, or simply of that which runs to Orenburg, was less easy to decide. But after long study, in which the respective advantages and disadvantages of these three directions were carefully weighed and balanced, it became evident that one in particular held very strong commendatory claims; and eventually in February 1891 it was resolved to lay a track from Miass to Tchelyabinsk, and to carry on the survey from that town to Tomsk. It only remained to determine whether it would be sufficient to make a commencement in any one place merely, or whether, on the contrary, it would be advisable to begin operations at different points. In the latter case the construction of the middle portion of the Siberian Railway might be hastened by two years, and there appeared a possibility of entering on that of the Trans-Baikal portion even before the rails could be laid to Irkutsk. In view of these considerations, the Commission declared in favour of simultaneous commencement at different points.

This is a Russian project with which the reigning Tzar has a close and peculiar connection. During his journey through Siberia in 1891, while yet Tzarevitch, he became personally acquainted with every aspect of the undertaking. The execution of this colossal project is largely due to his great interest and enthusiasm in the matter. An imperial rescript given in his name on the 17th (29th) of March 1891 assured the accomplishment of the task. At Vladivostok the work was formally inaugurated. Nicholas II. wheeled away the first barrowful of earth and placed the first stone in position. Thereafter a start was made from either end.

To carry on the undertaking, a Committee was appointed by the late Emperor Alexander III. It was to consist, amongst others, of the Ministers of Interior, of Agriculture and State Domains, of Finance, of Ways and Communications, of War, and of the Director of the Admiralty. The present Emperor was elected its first president by his father; and when, somewhat later, he had to ascend the throne, he insisted on holding this position in spite of his other arduous duties. The Committee had no executive power, —it was simply administrative, and when in difficulty was required to refer to its imperial founder. It met for the first time on February 10th (22nd) 1893.

The first natural instinct was to hand over the execution of the project to the Direction of the Government railways. Later, it was thought that the gigantic nature of the undertaking would exhaust the resources of that department, and accordingly in June 1893 the actual construction of the railway was taken out of the hands of the Minister of Ways and Communications, and a separate branch of his department was instituted to carry the matter through. This new branch was thus, in a sense, under the Minister of Ways and Communications, and had power to see to the purchase of the rolling-stock, as well as to arrange direct contracts, without being limited to any sum. It could also change the period of contracts and terms of agreement.

The total length of the railway from Tchelyabinsk to Vladivostok along the main line is 7083 versts. Twenty-nine additional versts included below represent branch lines to the principal rivers that intersect the main road.[1] It has been divided into seven sections for convenience in working: these are—

1. Tchelyabinsk to river Ob, 1328 versts; total estimated cost, inclusive of rolling-stock and rails, 47 million rubles.

2. Ob to Irkutsk, 1754 versts; estimated cost, 73 million rubles.

3. Irkutsk to Misovskaya, 292 versts; estimated cost, 22 million rubles.

4. Misovskaya to Srjetensk, 1009 versts; estimated cost, 53 million rubles.

5. Srjetensk to Khabarovsk, 2000 versts; estimated cost, 117 million rubles.

6. Khabarovsk to Grafskaya, 347 versts; estimated cost, 18 million rubles.

7. Grafskaya to Vladivostok, 382 versts; estimated cost, 17 million rubles: being in all, roughly, 350 million rubles.

Such, at least, is the *original* plan and estimate, since subject to considerable modification. For while on the simple

[1] Calculating the verst as ⅔ mile, and the ruble as 2s. roughly, we find that the following figures represent the length and estimated cost of the different sections respectively: (1) 885 miles, £4,700,000; (2) 1169 miles, £7,300,000; (3) 195 miles, £2,200,000; (4) 673 miles, £5,300,000; (5) 1333 miles, £11,700,000; (6) 231 miles, £1,800,000; (7) 255 miles, £1,700,000. Total length and estimate—4741 miles, £34,700,000.

initial section the actual cost has been some nine million rubles less than the estimate, on the second section, which involves cutting a way through the Taiga or forest zone, the estimate will be exceeded. It is probable that the latter condition of things will eventually be found to be true of the grand estimate as well. The third section will be the most difficult, and, comparatively, the most costly, as the road will have to be cut through cliffs which rise from the margin of Lake Baikal to a considerable height. As late as 1897 detailed surveys were being conducted on the southern coast-line of Lake Baikal, round which it is still intended to carry the railway if the new estimates do not prove to be too high.[1]

By the 15th June 1895 one quarter of the line had been laid; in the autumn of the following year passengers were set down at Krasnoyarsk. The year 1897 saw the railway open as far as Nijni-Udinsk, and it is expected that by the summer of 1898, or at latest by spring of the succeeding year, not only will Irkutsk and St Petersburg be connected by rail, but steam communication will have been established between the capital and Vladivostok. That is to say, after crossing Lake Baikal by boat, the passenger will resume train as far as Srjetensk, whence Khabarovsk, which is already joined by rail to the Pacific port, will be reached by steamer. Fourteen days is optimistically given as the duration of such a journey between the extreme points, which will be reduced to ten, or even nine, when everything is in working order and the Manchurian line completed. But it is difficult to see how the original plan can be carried out before 1903. The following figures show the

[1] The cost of the construction of one verst of the railway has so far fluctuated between 35,500 and 64,500 rubles.

numbers of workmen employed during 1895 on the West, Middle, Trans-Baikalian, and Ussuri divisions of the line: 36,629 navvies, 13,080 carters, 5851 surfacemen, 4310 carpenters, 4096 stone-masons, 2091 riveters,—in round numbers, 62,000 men. To meet the demand for official servants and experts, technical schools of engineering have been opened in the towns of Omsk, Krasnoyarsk, and Khabarovsk.

The other Departments of State have combined to lend helping hands. Thus the Ministry of Agriculture and State Domains supplies and delivers gratis whatever timber may be required. The War Department has employed many of its men in survey and map-making, especially on the Amur, so as to get the best line through Khabarovsk. In short, it is a work on which official Russia is quietly priding herself. She is looking forward to the time when she will have a railroad twice as long as that which now unites New York and San Francisco. So much for the past.

. . . .

The train, which, passing along the continuation of the Samara-Miass line, conducts the traveller on his way towards far Siberia, starts on its journey at Tula. Here it was that the writer first came into contact with the eastern emigration movement that during the summer of 1896 was at once so sad and so remarkable.[1]

One of the platforms was literally crowded with a mass of homeless humanity, drawn mostly from the southern and more thickly populated parts of Russia. It was nearly midnight, and the emigrants had clustered in small family

---

[1] It must be distinctly understood that what is related here and on p. 47, with reference to the emigration movement, deals with the summer of 1896 only — steps having since been taken to prevent the recurrence of such congestion.

groups round their few belongings, which were stowed away in sacks, baskets, and wooden boxes. Over their little heaps of worldly goods they had spread sheepskins or blankets of coarse texture. Piled up on these the children lay asleep, wrapped in their *shubas* (sheepskin coats), with the white hide outermost. Commonly one parent rested by them and the other watched, and it was hard to find a group without a babe. Some of the adults wore a timid air, born of sheer helplessness. Most of the men had the dull dogged look of driven cattle: an intelligent face might have more easily been found amongst their wives. Thus they reclined and slept, or talked in low subdued voices, while behind them loomed the dark red waggons with their significant inscription, " 8 horses—40 men," that were to carry them from the land of their nativity. Meanwhile labourers were at work on these mobilisation cars, fitting up an internal arrangement of boards, in order to render them more fit for human habitation during the week or so of railway journey to the East.

As this emigration question assumed somewhat alarming proportions during that summer, and is important in relation to the future of the country, it merits further attention.

For several years the movement to the East has been in progress. In some very slight form it may also be said to be in operation all the year long; but May, June, and July are the months during which the pressure has commonly been most severe. Its origin is not absolutely clear. In some slight form the movement has been in vogue since the end of the seventeenth century. Its course has not been uniform: there were distinct lulls during the Crimean war, and again for some months about the time of the abolition of serfage. A sudden rise in the figures for the year 1892 has led some to suppose that the great famine of 1890-91 brought the Russian Government seriously to face the necessity of providing means for drafting off the surplus population of the south; but a more important factor was the formation about this time of the Committee for the construction of the railway, with which the question of colonisation has been always intimately associated. Indeed, one of the most important reasons for building the railway at all was to unite those numerous though often widely removed areas in Siberia that had already been colonised. Prior to this period certain restrictions had been placed upon emigration; but from this time these were removed in part, and inducements were held out of which the overtaxed peasants living in such a province as Poltava, where the population is very dense and the holdings proportionately small, were only too glad to avail themselves. Latterly, as will be seen, the movement has been checked and restrictions again imposed, as it was found that the population in many centres of agricultural labour was being positively depleted. In many ways the Government has offered encouragement to intending settlers: they are taken as passengers at rates reduced enormously below the third-class fares — the actual price which they pay being 3 rubles per 1000 versts.[1] Those who come from the more northerly parts are conveyed by steamer from Kazan to Perm for half that sum. In cases of dire extremity, grants of money without interest up to 100 rubles are made; while during the first three years the settler is exempt from taxes. The plan commonly followed is, that on arrival at Tchelyabinsk, on the farther side of the

[1] *I.e.*, less than 1*s.* per 100 miles.

Urals, the settlers are arranged into parties and sent under superintendence to the locality that is to be colonised by them. A formal permission is indeed required in the case of every peasant, for which he may have to wait some time; but this measure is solely to hinder debtors from absconding. Once this has been obtained, the arrangements permit of even the poorest peasant emigrating.

The substance of the regulations that underlie the emigration movement may here be briefly outlined. In the governments of Tobolsk and Tomsk a grant of 15 *desiatines* of suitable land is made to every man, and in some cases an additional grant of not more than 3 *desiatines* of forest. In the Governments of Yenisei and Irkutsk the extent of the grant is determined by the quality of the land. This land is conveyed to the settlers on letters of allotment, and, whilst remaining State property, will be for their perpetual benefit. Its sale and mortgage are forbidden, and all such transactions are defined as of no effect. Maps were early prepared at considerable cost, showing the population and physical features of each region.

Owing to the very slender population of the Amur district, regulations have been drawn up to permit of the sale of the State lands in that territory. The principal idea underlying these regulations is to ensure that the State lands pass as private property only to those people— Russian subjects—who really wish and have the capacity to work them. The maximum quantity of land that can be sold to one buyer under the new regulations is not defined: all that is stated is, that while allotments not exceeding 400 *desiatines* are to be made by the military governor, petitions for sale of land in larger quantities are to be presented with reasons to the chief of the district. Those who receive an agreement for a sale have to deposit one-half of the sum in the local treasury, whereupon an arrangement is made for the delivery of the land for three years' use and profit. To obtain full proprietorship, the following further condition is obligatory—viz., that in the course of three years the buyer shall expend, in the working of the land and in furnishing the necessary plant, a sum, for an allotment not exceeding 100 *desiatines*, of not less than the cost of it on the price of purchase. For allotments of from 100 to 400 *desiatines* the sum thus expended must be not less than twice the cost; above 400 *desiatines*, four times the cost. Upon the non-fulfilment of these conditions the allotment is taken back, and the money received is kept as rent. The price fixed in 1895 was 6 rubles the *desiatine* within 20 versts of the large towns in Eastern Siberia and in certain specially fertile places. At other points the land is sold at the rate of 3 rubles the *desiatine*, while a small addition is made for survey expenses.

That the numbers had been gradually rising each year[1] was in no way remarkable; but the sudden increase that marked the spring of 1896 was quite unlooked for. It partook of the nature of a stampede. How it affected the average Russian may be judged from the following incident. A gentleman personally known to myself, while staying at his country residence, was informed one morning that his cook and coachman desired to speak with him. These two men, who had been long in his service and were the recipients of no mean wage, astonished him by quietly intimating that they were leaving for Siberia.

[1] The figures for the year 1892 were, roughly, 100,000 ; for 1893, 150,000 ; for 1894, about 180,000 ; for 1896, about 250,000.

Having known them many years he ventured to expostulate with them, but his suggestion that perhaps they were discontented with their wage and present circumstances was instantly scouted as quite out of the question. He then communicated to them what he knew about the general disorganisation that had overtaken the movement during the early part of May of that year, with its sad attendant circumstances, telling them in all the truth, not so much from any wish to retain them in his service as from his personal interest in them. It was in vain; their only reply was, "Every one is going, and we must go too."

That year the tide set in early, and between the months of January and May 170,000 people had already passed through Tchelyabinsk—in May alone, 100,000: for a period of about a month the daily number of incomers was 2000. The population of the above-mentioned town is 17,000, and on a certain day in May there were just as many settlers camping out around the station and along the railway-line, waiting for further transportation. The result was that the organisation of the young Siberian railway was quite unable to cope with this immense human flood. There were neither rolling-stock nor officials sufficient to conduct the settler-companies to their destination. In time more waggons were got out from Russia, the question was faced, and very soon that large population was moved on—not, however, before cholera, typhus, and other epidemics had broken out and many had died. The question assumed so serious an aspect that a Secretary of State was sent out to inquire into this matter. Having arrived on the spot, he at once gave orders for the cessation of all emigration, and proceeded personally to make fuller investigations and arrangements. As a result, by the end of the summer practically the whole government of Tobolsk had been settled, and the Taiga or virgin forest there is being surveyed and examined with a view to bringing under cultivation land occupied by it. The Secretary's son described to me the interest he had in seeing the different settlements in various stages of growth —some with only four-and-twenty hours of history, others

Settlers en route.

three or four days old, and others again whose existence dated from several weeks back. Those emigrants who wish to go to the Amur perform the journey by sea (forty-five days) from Odessa; but there were families settled in the Tobolsk government that summer which had come back overland from that distant country dissatisfied with the grant allotted them. In one case a family, after spending all they had (3000 rubles) on the journey to the Amur district and back, had settled in Tobolsk penniless.

The journey from Tula towards Siberia cannot be called interesting. A painfully flat landscape, monotony of scenery, everywhere the tracks of the settler: that is all. Thus at Riajsk one side of the platform presented the same picture of frightened incarnations of misery, huddling together against the heavy rain, and crossing themselves at every lightning-flash and thunder-peal. We leave them, and the outlook is replaced by a broad sweep of land that extends on either side to the horizon,—hedgeless and brown where the soil has lately been upturned, but verdant also where one may distinguish the young corn. Occasionally we pass through a strip of wood whose trees exhibit a greenness that may almost be felt. It is the beginning of the Russian spring. Thereafter we traverse wide plains through which the railway track has been so simply led; the telegraph wires decrease in number, and one admits that the world is being left behind. There also, at distances of about 100 yards apart, is stacked in 10-feet lengths the wooden hoarding that in winter serves to shield the line from the fierce drifting of the snow.

Quickly we fly through the government of Penza, to whose prosperity a multitude of windmills testifies. Acres of rye creep close up to the railway track and extend unbroken out of sight. At length we reach the Volga, Russia's "most kindly nurse." The great waterway seems dark and muddy from the height of the noble iron bridge that through 600 *sajens*[1] spans her breadth. The low left bank, flooded at parts and thickly wooded with small shrubs and trees that hug the river's brink, seems to dis-

[1] *Sajen* = 7 English feet; the actual length of the bridge is 4375 feet.

appear, in contrast with the other bank, in height 300 feet or so, covered with luxuriant vegetation; and you may even see a scrap of sandy beach from which the river has retreated, lying beside the dark current.

We pass a village. Its most conspicuous object is the church, with whitened walls and two green domes. You notice that it holds a central place: you might almost fancy that the village had grown up around it as nucleus. The wooden huts, with their brown roofs of thatch, lighter in colour where the straw is of more recent date, stand separate in disconnected lines. The roads on which they abut preserve in part their primitive affinity with the surrounding plain — grass-covered where in their breadth they have not yet been trampled under foot, black where some heavy wheel has rudely cut them up. A few youngsters in bright red shirts lend colour and activity to the scene. On the outskirts of the village each peasant owns a tiny plot, enclosed by stakes which form the basis of a wall of wickerwork. Inside, you see, perhaps, two horses or a cow, or even only straw. At the corner you will note a little dovecot raised on a pole, surmounted by a branch of birch. This welcome home is for blackbirds and the sparrows in the winter-time. Nor is this all, for on the extreme border of the small community, separated by a trench from the outer world, is an unkept square extent of land dotted with crosses, blue, black, or white, sometimes of iron, or, again, reduced to a short wooden post. Thus does the peasant reverence his dead.

The rate of speed of our naphtha-stoked train is 30 versts an hour, and in process of time we leave Samara behind us. The "elevators" form an important feature at the stations in this neighbourhood. These are large metal granaries, in which the produce of the surrounding country is stored. They are often of great height, and in them the grain is tossed about and mechanically sifted, so as to prevent over-heating. Beyond Samara we pass through gently undulating country, which now and again opens out on broader patches of damp reedy ground, occasionally monopolised by copses of stunted willow, birch, and oak. The only signs of habitation over long stretches are the lone cabins of the surfacemen. Sunk in the soil, with low roof sloping backwards, their weak walls buttressed on every side by plank-imprisoned earth, these humble homes strangely testify to the advance of civilisation. Ufa proclaims that we are nearing Asia. As on the Volga, one sees on the river Ufa many house-rafts, capable of supporting a large floating population. Here and elsewhere we pass trainfuls of settlers returning homeward disillusionised.

At length we come in sight of the Ural Mountains, which figure so largely on our maps. The first sense is that of disappointment. Although they extend a considerable length from north to south, and their breadth is fully borne in upon the mind by the slowness of the train, it is yet a remarkable fact that the highest peak only reaches 5200 feet. Languidly the train ascends 100 feet of thickly wooded hill-country. Geological inquiry discloses the truth that we are traversing two folds in the earth's crust. Occasionally we pass through deeper dynamite-blown cuttings, and issue out of them only to look up to pine- and fir-clad heights. We strike a muddy river—Yuresan—born in these cooler altitudes. We follow it, and on either side at times the beetling brows give way to meadow-land, in which are set at intervals quiet hamlets. The tiny stations have a desolate appearance, and towards evening a sublime silence reigns, which is only broken by the tinkling of faint cowbells, the plaintive cuckoo's cry, or the occasional hum of human voices. Thus we pursue our way over varying heights, now riding through a cloud of butterflies that are resting by the wayside, now raising frightened wild-duck from some part of the river's shaded banks.

It was early morning when we steamed into Tchelyabinsk. The country had now reverted to the flatness that characterises the western side of the Urals. Birch and beech were still the prominent trees. It was this town that saw the worst features of the emigration fever; but now, in the middle of June, scarcely 300 remained as witnesses to the past. The platform presented a motley group of interested human beings, — swarthy Tartars, sallow Russians, brisk Siberians, benign Bashkirs, those renowned horse-stealers, and stolid Kirghize, relieved by the presence of the everlasting officer and sundry other petty *tchinovniks*. The Bashkirs, like the Kirghize, were originally a nomadic people, but have now somewhat settled down, and make excellent agricultural labourers.

Leaving Tchelyabinsk, we pass through country that indicates considerable population. Much has been reclaimed, much is under cultivation. Still more is level steppe, occasionally broken by strips of shrubby copse or statelier trees. Short posts in black and white, with the imperial eagle, help to mark off the boundaries of the land reserved on either side for the railway. The soil, where it is exposed, proclaims itself to be the far-famed *tchernoziom* or black earth; beneath it in section one makes out the widespreading *loess*. The villages are of course at a considerable distance from the line: this is the genius of all Russian railways.

Everything becomes simpler as we move farther east.

Soon the stations resolve themselves into plain log-houses, surrounded by regular piles of sawn birch, that serve as fuel for the locomotives.

Kurgan is the first town in Siberia proper at which we stop. From what one can see of it from the station, it has the appearance of being mainly composed of wooden houses; but, characteristically, two white churches with their green domes and roofs obtrude themselves upon the notice of the passer-by. Here we witnessed the first meeting after ten years of a well-known political exile with his parents, and with a younger brother whom he now saw for the first time. A man selling models of convicts at work also recalls the peculiar associations that this country has for the civilised world. We have opportunity to stroll about and look around, for the train lingers an indefinite period at each stopping-place. To the Russian time is not money, still less to the Siberian. You might, for that matter, partake of a protracted repast at every station if there was the wherewithal; but only at special points is provision made. An ominous diagrammatic wine-glass before the name of a station in the time-table indicates the presence of a buffet there. At such a place one is commonly allowed twenty minutes; while elsewhere you will notice a line of tables at a fixed distance from the railroad, behind which stand a number of peasant women in picturesque attire, with milk, kvass, bread, butter, and other viands for sale.

Omsk is situated in a bare plain, on two rivers, the Irtish and the Om. As a result the town can be descried from a great way off. At this distance the barracks, Cadet Corps College, and the Church of St Nicholas are the most prominent objects. The bridge across the Irtish is of the type commonly met with along the line—iron girders supported on stone piers. Its length is 2100 feet. The embankment at this point is between 35 and 40 feet high: even yet a staff of men is almost constantly at work keeping it in repair. This was also found to be the case over great lengths of the line farther to the east: the heavy rains are continually washing away in part these huge structures. It is obvious that, in addition to what we may call the temporary demand for workmen, such an immense railway will require a permanent contingent of labourers to clear away snowdrifts and repair the line. To secure this object, it was proposed to introduce navvies from European Russia: steps have been already taken in this direction, and experiments are being carried out successfully. The only distinguishing feature about Omsk station, which was in process of building, is that here one sees half-a-dozen lines of railway. This is, of course, a provision for the future; the three trains weekly in either direction scarcely require them meantime.[1] For the moment, except on the main line, all was in possession of a crowd of settlers who numbered 8000 at one time. Omsk is the centre of distribution in this region. Here the emigrants present their papers to the authorities and are told whither they must go. The wiser heads first make a visit of inspection, and then return to Omsk to fetch their families and goods if the allotment has proved satisfactory.

We have already noticed the numbers of men who are engaged on this vast undertaking. In the heat of the midday sun it was assuredly hard work, and one was not surprised to see the somewhat deliberate fashion in which any particular task was carried through. The great majority of the labourers were toiling in white (or what had once been

[1] There is now at least a daily service.

white) cotton shirts and pantaloons, barefoot, bareheaded. Some of their tools and implements were primitive—*e.g.*, the wheelless barrow shoved along a plank. One saw the evolution of the spade in a single party, for while some were employing long-handled wooden shovels, all of one piece, others had the edge of the blade protected with a thin binding of tin, while yet others had the ordinary one with iron blade. Another tool looked like half a pick, with the back of the head flattened hammer-wise. They also made use of giant sledge-hammers of wood—a vast bole with a stout handle driven into it, making a very formidable weapon. Utilising a thick beam as lever, they would prise up great lengths of rail attached to the sleepers, and so fill in more ballast. One noticed also the absence of what are commonly known as "chairs": the broad-based rails are simply laid on the notched sleepers, and held in position there by a small species of clamp on the inside only. Great care is being exercised in the regulation of this railway. Every hundred yards or so appear white boards indicating the gradients, which occasionally alter very considerably over quite short ranges. Also at extremely short intervals are posted the usual men in charge of the line, green flag in hand, to signify that their section at least is clear. Throughout its length the line is continuously accompanied on either side by excavations of varying size, from which the soil was taken for its construction. At those points where over long distances the embankment remains a considerable height, these trenches increase greatly in breadth, but not so much in depth. The cause of this is simply that the ground is frozen at about 6 feet below the surface till towards the end of July, so that the upper stratum alone is workable. These broad ditches fill with water, and become the spacious nurseries of myriads of mosquitoes and other objectionable forms of insect life. Beyond these lie immense expanses of verdant plain, whose uniformity is interrupted at intervals by irregularly set thickets of stunted birch. Occasionally some Kirghize boy betrays our laboured progress by forging ahead of the train on his hardy pony. Shaggy, sure-footed, speedy, they are the true Siberian travellers; shrewd also, for when the sun has dipped below the western horizon and the evening air seems to exist for nothing but mischief-making mosquitoes and their inhuman clan, mark how by yonder small encampment in the lee of a birch coppice the patient burden-bearers stand beside the fire, facing the wind, and hold their heads in the smoke to be relieved from their pestiferous associates. Animal life otherwise is not much in evidence. Occasionally a startled hare dashes from his "form" too near the track of progressive man. Perhaps a mallard rises from some weeded brake, and overhead a towering hawk recks not but for his prey: save for these we are alone.

In time we come to Krivoschekovo, having just crossed the Barabinsky steppe. We are now 2058 versts from Moscow, 1325 from Tchelyabinsk. The river Ob is at this point to be spanned by a bridge of over 2500 feet; but as the wooden scaffolding was burned down, the construction of it has fallen much behind that of bridges farther on, and as yet only one girder unites two of the five stone piers.[1] Here again we notice a gathering of settlers, who are, however, not allowed within the unfenced precincts of the station. A goodly number of log cabins may be seen in the vicinity, but these do not form the village, which is 4 versts off across the river. What one sees is simply the natural upgrowth of two years of railway

[1] It has since been completed.

labour. It follows that the original Krivoschekovo will decline in importance, and its place be taken by this upstart village: thus does the railway make and unmake places. To drive to the river, the only available conveyance is a country *tarantassik*. The first impression is that of a large basket supported on four wheels. More careful inspection discloses two stout axle-trees connected by six poles—branches unhewn and lying in the horizontal; a seventh, stronger than the rest, finds place below the other six. On this arrangement, only placed well forward, is perched the wicker basket, across which is set a board held in its place by ropes, and on this two men may sit with fear and trembling. Straw lines the bottom. A smaller board, most wonderfully balanced on the front edge of the basket, and also held in place by ropes, accommodates the driver. Behind the coble there remain about 3 feet of the horizontal framework, on which heavy baggage may be settled: it is an embryonic *tarantass* without the hood. The wheels have a run of 6 inches on the axle, which is so long as to prevent all chance of a capsize; along this they perpetually wobble. The shafts are two young birch-trees, with the unlopped stumps of the branches still much in evidence. Between them is a small unshod Siberian pony, of a dun shade, in size and appearance not unlike a Shetlander; the traces are two half-inch ropes. It is supported by an outrunner trotting abreast, and retained by two as slender ropes, while a strap attaching his apology for a bridle to that of his neighbour hinders him from running at an angle of more than 45° to the line of progression. We start, how? The driver simply whistles to his pair, and off they bound. It is early morning, but here many of the people are already astir. The baker's shanty is thronged by simple hungry peasants. Already in an open shed the butcher quarters his unsavoury lamb before an eager assemblage.

Now we are off, but how the dust flies! The little tracehorse holds his head out to the left and runs for dear life. The track is cruelly rough: every few minutes we shoot into a hole, and are as quickly jerked out. Soon we reach the brown turgid Ob. On its farther bank the red *rubashkas* of the men and the brightly coloured dresses of the women stand out against the dull yellow huts that crowd the bank, and against the dark pine-trees behind. We arrive at the ferry-boat and board it. But notice its primitive simplicity. Two barge-like boats are joined by a large platform deck that is common to them both. At one end of this platform a wooden cogged wheel works on a stout beam to which the tiller is attached. More complicated is the contrivance by which this paddle-boat is made to move by a literal three-horse power. On the outside of either boat is a paddle-wheel with wooden blades; these are connected also with a large cogged wheel which lies in the horizontal. Outside this wheel is a trotting-ground, where the three ponies perform perpetual circles, being attached by horizontal poles to one large vertical axle leading through the centre wheel. The upper end of this axle turns in another thick beam that stretches across over all, being supported on either side outside the pony-track by a wooden pillar. Two of the ponies had attendant boys, who continually walked behind them and kept them moving. The third driver was a tall fine-looking peasant with a mop of curly yellow hair and a bushy unkempt beard. In his magenta shirt and much-patched black velveteen pantaloons, whose ends were buried in tall boots, he looked an imposing figure; and it seemed a pity that a man who had to stoop each time he passed under the high crossbeam already alluded to, should have to spend his days doing such menial service.

The clayey road creeps irregularly up the bank through the straggling huts that comprise the village. A tributary of the Ob has cut deeply into the bank, and the wooden bridge with its loose planks shakes and rattles ominously as we fly across, to bury ourselves in the sweet pine-woods. The dusty road winds and twists through verst after verst of placid pine and trembling aspen: its roughness causes us to make acquaintance with every corner of the oscillating basket. The back seat is no longer tenanted; it simply serves as something to which to cling. We pass two *telyegas* filled with various household stuffs: behind them are walking three barefooted peasant women with bright merry faces, a little girl with a handful of wildflowers, and four or five men. My companion salutes them: they are from Periyaslav in South Russia, and are proceeding to their new home, some forty miles away. Still we go on; and then another turn of the road brings us face to face with a second slow procession. In the first wicker cart sit two young men clad in grey, with bare heads and clean-shaven faces: on their knees is the coffin of a little child, dressed out in pink and wildflowers. In the second cart rides the father, with haggard downcast look, wearing the unbleached cotton coat that proclaims him to be something more than a peasant; and by his side is a young boy. The third cart contains two women. One is the mother—you see it in her face.

At last we come to the station in the wood; it is called Ob. A cluster of buildings is growing up; it looks as if some day it will be a place of importance. As yet, however, nothing is open save a waiting-room; the ticket office is in a fourth-class waggon on the train, and still there are settlers, still the crowd of interested peasants.

But now the country changes: up to the Ob, plain had predominated. What seems rather like an unending park, planted with silver birch, the beauty of the Siberian forest, now supervenes. The orange-tinted *Trollius asiaticus*, so expressively called in Russian what we might render as "little fire," colours the open ground in part, growing more plentifully, however, in the shade of individual trees. The wild rose also abounds, and brackens usurp what remains. Along the railway-line, which winds in long-drawn sigmoid curves, navvies are now in greater evidence. The Direction takes on practically all who offer, as the supply is not in excess of the demand. The unusual daily wage of $1\frac{1}{4}$ ruble is paid; labour cannot be got cheaper. On the western half of the line the men are mainly Russians, Siberians, and in a few instances Italians; farther east you find convicts, Chinese, and Koreans. During the summer they lie out at night or rear a simple dwelling by means of sleepers, much as a child makes a house of bricks.

The question of criminal labour on the railway presents some interesting features that may be briefly narrated here. Once it was resolved to employ convict labour, the problem that presented itself to the Ministry of the Interior was how, out of the criminal prisoners from European Russia, the lazy local population of the Siberian prisons, and the political exiles, to form a disciplined army of railway workmen. It was, however, solved so brilliantly that the convicts working on the Mid-Siberian road by their labour and irreproachable conduct attracted the attention of the august President of the Committee of the Siberian Railway. Convict labour was at first directed to the construction of the Ussuri Railway, where, on the contrary, it far from verified expectations, and the convict party was soon sent back to the island of Sakhalin. On a larger scale the experiment was repeated in the construction of the Mid-Siberian Railway. In order to make the work attractive, and so include convicts of all categories, a regulation was made for those who came under the Governor-General of Irkutsk, that eight months' railway work should count as one year of imprisonment or hard labour, according to circumstances. For the exiles the term required to enable them to be registered as peasants was to be reduced, in return for labour on the railway, in the proportion of one year for two. For those who more than two years before had been transported for life, the period during which they should have to wait before permission would be granted to choose a dwelling-place was reduced by one-half; and for those compelled to live in far Siberia, the term of deportation was to be shortened by counting one year as two.

The success attending convict labour on the Mid-Siberian Railway gave rise to the idea of again extending these regulations to the other farther eastern section of the railway. With this object the same privileges were granted to prisoners and exiles coming under the surveillance of the Governor-General of the Amur as to those under the Governor-General of Irkutsk.

For the supervision of the exiles the Minister of the Interior appointed special officers, and for the supervision of the common criminal labourers, inspectors and orderlies. The former enjoy a position of district country control, with the added right of calling out a military escort. Each individual controller has 200 versts of the road allotted to him. The inspectors and orderlies have the privileges of the lower police ranks, and are disposed at every 50 versts of road-construction.

Again we have exchanged our wooded park for the open plain, along which we ride now somewhat timidly, and at last reach the banks of the river Tom, where the unfinished bridge once more renders the ferry-boat indispensable. Later we saw the testing of the bridge previous to opening. On each span a train consisting of four locomotives and four laden waggons had to remain for two hours; thereafter the train traversed the bridge several times, increasing the rate of speed at each passage.

Tomsk, the third largest town in all Siberia, is not situated on the main line; a branch line of 90 versts from a point called Taiga runs thither. True to all traditions, the Tomsk terminus is 3 versts from the town. When we passed eastwards in June, Taiga was represented by a few piles of logs, and the branch-line was in process of construction. Three months later, not only was the usual large stone waterreservoir standing sentinel, pagoda-like, over a neat array of log-houses, varying in colour and appearance, but the buffet was capable of supplying a champagne lunch in honour of an event of local interest.

The new train on the far side of the river Tom is entirely composed of trucks filled with iron rails and tools, except for two or three carriages reserved for the inspector and director of that division of the line: one of these we share. There is, however, one fourth-class waggon full of labourers. At Mariinsk we pass a military train—part of the general movement of Russian troops towards her eastern frontiers. In their white cotton jackets with red epaulettes, dark-green trousers, black waist-belts, long boots, and white peak caps, the men look in the best of spirits, as if they were enjoying themselves to their hearts' content. At the station they descend, form up, and then march off, singing awhile some of their strange folk-lays. In about an hour the sound of a measured tramp of feet accompanying a lively chorus betokens their return, and each man may be seen swinging along with a large brown loaf of rye-bread under his arm.

Now we enter a distinctly hilly and wooded country. The floral wealth is very great—purple cypripedia, aconite, blue potentillas, wild geranium, equisetum, and a hundred other varieties. Two lovely lilies now demand attention owing to their quantity,—the graceful yellow *Hemerocallis*, set like so many golden stars in a firmament of emerald, smiles back to the drooping purple *Lilium martagon*.

On occasions the train comes to a standstill, and the workmen who accompany us rush out and pull up the wild rhubarb. Scotch fir, spruce, Siberian poplar, alder, and birch predominate. Approaching Atchinsk, however, we again come on the open plain. As our waggon creeps nearer the town on a side-line, we observe that we are gradually working into the midst of a large band of settlers. Suddenly there is a violent jerk, then the train stops, and we find that we have left the rails: thus we are conveniently situated for study right in the middle of the settler colony.

It was already evening, and the cool night wind had begun to blow. Reviewing the temporary camp pitched upon either side of us, we could perceive that it contained perhaps 300 souls. It was only natural to find that they had mostly come from Southern Russia, but had been waiting where we found them six long weeks, in hope of further transport to the neighbourhood of Yeniseisk. They had much of which to complain, and recounted how they had suffered numerically from epidemics. Cholera, typhus, and other loathsome enemies of mankind had walked—were walking—at their ease amongst them; 30 per cent had died. Most had ensconced themselves in the lee of the embankment, which at this point began to rise to meet a bridge that spans the small river on which Atchinsk stands. Beside them were the railway trenches water-filled; clouds of mosquitoes filled the air. These the colonists attempted to drive away by smoking, or by sitting closely round the fires that formed the centre of each family circle; or again, some plucked short half-charred sticks out of the fire, and blew on them, so that they served by the engendered heat to protect their faces; while others, again, sought refuge in shawls and handkerchiefs, so wrapping up their heads that only an eye remained visible. Not far removed, in little heaps, lay their worldly possessions,—a square box or two wrapped in sacking forming the groundwork, on and around which were bags and bundles tied with rope, untied, split, bursting, empty. A few branches bent hoopwise, with either end stuck in the ground, and interwoven with yet other leafy branches, formed their rude dwellings. Some, more fortunate, had improvised a tent of dirty cloth, into which they could just crawl. Others had adopted the device of the surfacemen, and appropriated sleepers for hut-building purposes. See them squatting there, in weariness of soul, killing time as best they may around a samovar, perhaps a family heirloom that once saw better days. Thus, then, they sat by the low fires in darkbrown homespun *kaftans*, fleecy *shubas*, or padded jackets. And as they sat they talked I know not what about, perchance some memories of home, while far to the west the last rays of the declining sun were filling the heavens with a purple glow. We sat by the car-window and watched them in the stillness of the night: now and again they would start up when there was borne from some remoter group keeping late vigil one of those soft, weird, minor melodies that are the priceless possession of the Russian folk. And when the dying strains of the song soared to a high-pitched note held by the female voices, while the men prolonged it an octave lower, it seemed like some sad musical interrogation, Why had they left Poltava to die on the Siberian steppe?

Next morning we left our helpless waggon, crossed the river by the ferry-boat, and started off on the last possible railway-stretch in a fourth-class car. One night the coupling-irons gave way on a somewhat steep incline, and the detached portion of the train began to roll backwards. Fortunately the man in charge of the only brake awoke at this moment, and in a few seconds the retreat was stopped. He confessed, however, that it was more owing to the rough state of the line than to the efficiency of the brake that the runaway portion was so quickly controlled. But this was not all, for first the engine deserted the track, and later on another waggon followed its example, so that in all we spent exactly four days in covering what was performed in thirty-six hours on the homeward run. As we carried workmen with us, however, it was only a case of waiting till the necessary repairs were accomplished, except in the case of the coupling-irons. The Taiga has been cut down for about 40 yards on either side of the embankment, making a broad clearing of 100 yards or so at parts. Along the rough roadway, seldom devoid of gradient, the weary engine toils: at times it almost seems as if a steeper bit of incline would be too much for it, when suddenly with a jerk the difficulty is overcome, and we resume our seven miles an hour, the slow rate being in part a precaution for safety.

One fine morning at 3 A.M. we enter the hill-encircled plain where lies the town of Krasnoyarsk. Piles of wood, stone, and rails indicate that here, at any rate, is to be a station of some dimensions; and when towards the end of summer we passed through again, an imposing building had been reared in red sandstone. The bridge over the Yenisei will be one of the masterpieces of the line. Built, like them all, in the lattice-girder style, it will have a length of over 3000 feet, and will not be open before the autumn of 1898. The bridge over the Tom, with three spans, is only about half as long as this will be, and it cost half a million rubles. After crossing the Yenisei, the line skirts the heights that overlook the town of Krasnoyarsk; thereafter, ascending practically all the time, it traverses the valleys of the Berezovka and Sitik till a point is reached nearly 1000 feet above the level of the Yenisei bridge, and comes out finally at Kansk. Between the latter station and that of Nijni-Udinsk the embankment sometimes rises to a height of 70 feet, while between Nijni-Udinsk and Irkutsk there are bridges over at least four rivers whose breadth exceeds 700 feet.

Although when coming back we joined a special waggon at a point 103 versts east of Krasnoyarsk, yet from this town we had to begin driving on the way out. We constantly passed little patches of embankment, either finished or in process of construction, or again as yet merely represented by three sticks standing in the tree-cleared vista, of which the outer two indicated the extreme limit of the breadth of the embankment, while the third marked its height at the middle point. And as we drove on through

D

the forest we would suddenly come on the birch-bark huts of the workmen nestling in the shade of the trees. The labourers, variously attired, but with a preference for the red *rubashka*, sit round their fires: a few *teleygas* still heaped with goods, the hobbled horses, all proclaim that work has not long commenced at this point. In the distance the over-

A break in the embankment in Trans-Baikalia.

seer is riding away on his horse to the nearest village, now that the day's work is over.

It is difficult to estimate the enormous amount of labour that has been expended on this railway. Consider how, to begin with, all the sleepers have been sawn tediously by hand. The log rests at a considerable elevation upon two props; one man stands upon it, working the saw downwards to another man below. Then in the construction of any high embankment the supporting piles are driven in by a primitive contrivance, also of wood, in the form of a giant tripod, from the top of which there hangs a pulley. Over this runs a rope, to one end of which is attached a heavy stone, with level base, while the other end is led on to a wheel at the side, by means of which the weight is raised. This arrangement is fixed over *each pile* in turn, so that the descending stone may strike it: thus after a generation the pile is driven home to the required depth. Again, one was impressed with the extremely finished nature of the work: thus the side of the large brown embankment was often covered with an infinite number of small squares of turf, each of which was held in position by two little pegs of wood.

One other point may be briefly touched upon. With one or two exceptions, Siberia is not in the possession of good roads—at least, not of such as could be utilised for the transport of rails, fixed or rolling stock. The natural course was therefore to employ her splendid waterways, and one of the first acts of the Committee of the Trans-Siberian Railway was to authorise the expenditure of over a million rubles on the improvement of water-communication on the rivers of Western Siberia, and on the exploration of the Amur. How much required to be done in the way of deepening channels, cutting down trees which threatened to fall into the water, retaining rivers in their beds, and marking dangerous places, can only be understood by those who have seen it for themselves. How much has been done is only in keeping with the really remarkable speed at which this whole enterprise is being carried through.

Owing to the manifold difficulties attending the construction of the section of the railway that embraces the southern end of Baikal, a temporary branch is meantime being built from Irkutsk to Listvinitchnaya on the western shore of the lake. From this port a steamer of 4000 tons will transport the train bodily across the lake.[1] A model of this boat was on view at the Nijni-Novgorod Exhibition of 1896. It was intended that it should make its own way across the ice-bound lake; but instead of working on the American principle of, as it were, climbing up on the ice and so breaking

Listvinitchnaya.

it down by sheer weight, in accordance with the idea of a Russian engineer the model represented the vessel as provided with a screw in the bow, which, by its action near the surface of the water, might be supposed to weaken the ice. This scheme was latterly condemned, for however well it might succeed with a foot of ice, it seemed to be a very

[1] At any rate in summer. The latest scheme for winter is an electric railway on the ice.

inefficient method of coping with the thicker Baikal ice. There was a twin screw-propeller at the stern; and the bow was modelled to have the same appearance above water as the stern. Four funnels, disposed in corners of an imaginary square, served to give the steamer, on the whole, a very imposing appearance.

It was impossible to see anything of the work round the south end of the Baikal lake, as the direct route leads one naturally to traverse it by steamboat. Further, it seems needless to give any details of the projected work on that section, as they are liable to be changed by the more recent surveys—in fact, will be changed if the line is to be laid at all. For when one learns that the original plan included, amongst other feats, the boring of a tunnel over 12,500 feet in length on a continuous incline, so that it could only be attacked from one end, embankments sometimes 112 feet in height with proportionately high retaining-walls laid in cement, and endless cuttings in granite, gneiss, and sandstone, one is not surprised that the Committee shrank from entering on this stage before the matter had been gone into once again.

From the port at Misovskaya on the south-east shore of the lake the railway proceeds afresh, at first following the coast line, only shortly to leave it and enter the valley of the Selenga by creeping round the Khamar-Dabansky hills. This river is spanned by an iron bridge some 2100 feet in length, now in process of construction, from which one will be able to catch a glimpse of the town of Verkhni-Udinsk, situated near the junction of the Uda and the Selenga. The line now enters the valley of the Uda, traversing fertile regions inhabited by the industrious Raskolniks or Dissenters, and at a distance of about 600 versts from Baikal commences to ascend in good earnest the eastern slope of one of the branches of the Yablonovoi Mountains. At the summit the line is 3410 feet above the sea. Here the difficulty of working is enhanced by the extreme changes in temperature even in midsummer. Thus in June and July a difference of 30° C. has been registered between the readings during the day and at night, the effect of which can be well imagined. The subsoil is perpetually frozen, and in summer the ground thaws only to a depth of 2 feet. Thereafter the railway course descends into the basin of the Pacific Ocean, passing through Tchita about 700 versts beyond Baikal, and 270 versts farther on crossing the river Nertcha, when it reaches the town of Nertchinsk, where the station will be some 6 versts distant from the town. Although the next stretch along the valleys of the Ingoda and of the Shilka to the town of Srjetensk, which stands on the right bank of the latter river, is of no great length, still the difficulties here connected with the earth and constructive works are formidable. Both valleys are narrow and wind considerably — that of the Ingoda, indeed, throughout its entire length — being shut in by mountains whose steep rocky slopes leave little free space between them and the water, thus necessitating heavy cutting, while the floods of the Shilka are notorious. This means that where these free spaces have been utilised in the service of the railway the periodic inundations which cover them (as in the summer of 1897) do considerable damage to the line on this river as well as on the Amur, thus introducing a further annual outlay that had not been foreseen.

The railway, which, inasmuch as it keeps to the left bank of the Shilka, only as a matter of fact comes to the village of Matakan opposite Srjetensk, was thence planned to continue down the valleys of that river and the Amur for a distance of 2000 versts to the town of Khabarovsk. Upon this route, which traverses sparsely populated *taiga*-covered country, no serious detailed surveying had ever been done; and beyond the general idea that the railway could be shortened by diverting it from the valley of the Amur, even although this river must eventually be crossed by a bridge 8400 feet in length, little was said or done. The reason of this became apparent when, in December of 1896, the terms of the Cassini Treaty between Russia and China were published, whereby the former Power acquired the right of adding a Trans-Manchurian branch to its Trans-Siberian railway. In consequence, the latter can no longer claim to be called Trans-Siberian, for although those in highest quarters still speak of some time uniting Srjetensk and Khabarovsk by rail on the lines of the original plan, yet this project has been so indefinitely postponed that meanwhile, at least, it may be considered as abandoned. In place of it a line will break off from the Trans-Siberian Trunk at the station of Onon just below Nertchinsk, enter China at Old Tsurukhaitu, traverse Manchuria by way of Tsitsihar and Ninguta, and rejoin the original line at Nicolskaya on the South Ussuri section. This Trans-Manchurian branch will be 1280 miles in length, 946 of which lie in Chinese territory, and will mean a reduction of at least 350 miles on the original plan. The other line, projected to run directly from Vladivostok to Hunchun, and thence through Kirin, Petune, Tsitsihar northwards to Aigun and Blagovyeshtchensk, is less important, and is not likely to be taken up for some time to come.

Upon the political importance of this move, as well as on the other terms of the treaty, we cannot dwell at any length. They practically mean Russian administration of the whole of Northern China, probably ending with its acquisition. They open up to Russian capital and enterprise a country renowned for its gold and rich in fine pasture-land. Finally, in connection with certain purely Chinese railways that are being constructed, they bring us within measurable distance of the time when the Trans-Siberian railway will find its Eastern terminus, not at Vladivostok, but on the milder shores of the Gulf of Pechili, which is the ultimate goal in the vision of Russian railway extension.

The last two sections of the Trans-Siberian Railway comprise what is known as the Ussuri line, running from Khabarovsk to Vladivostok, a distance of 715 versts. They are known respectively as the North and the South Ussuri lines; and while the latter was in working order by February of 1896, it took a year longer before the Northern, and consequently the whole system, was open to the public. In connection with the Northern half, two surveys were made—the first in 1891, the second three years later. The chief results of the final survey were—(1) that the length of this section (formerly 347 versts) was curtailed by 16 versts, which entailed an estimated saving of 800,000 rubles in the construction, and of 40,000 rubles in annual outlay; (2) that the line is now strategically safe. Originally it was planned to lie along the valley of the river Ussuri, which forms the frontier line between China and Siberia, and consequently it would have been exposed at several points. Its direction has been so changed that for over 100 versts it entirely deserts the valley, and although never far from the river, does not approach nearer than at Muraviev-Amursky (the older Grafskaya), where it is still 3 versts away. It remains within 5 versts of the Ussuri over 72 versts, or 21 per cent of its length: for the rest, it bends away eastwards at a distance of from 5 to 30 versts. Again, the stretches where damage from floods might have been expected have been greatly reduced in extent, as also the deep cliff-cuttings that the nature of the ground demanded.

The Southern section is now considered to begin at Iman, 387 versts from Vladivostok and ten versts north of the Grafskaya of the first survey (1888), whose name has now been changed to Muraviev-Amursky, in honour of the man who made the country Russian. The final surveys were completed in 1892, and the following year part of the line was open for traffic. The railway still keeps on the right bank of the Ussuri, till at the 328th verst from Vladivostok it crosses it by an iron bridge 840 feet in length. Thereafter it traverses the Khanka plain at a distance of from 20 to 40 versts from the lake. At its south-east corner it enters the valley of the Lefoo, crosses the watershed between that river and the Suiphun, a stream that falls into the Gulf of Amur, and enters its valley in turn. It only remains to skirt the sea-shore of the Gulf and come to rest in Vladivostok, where it would seem that all difficulties connected with a frozen port have now been overcome by means of ice-cutters.

The principal result arrived at by this study is, that the plan of 1888, with which we started, will be profoundly modified before the railway is completed. Its length from Tchelyabinsk to Vladivostok now stands at 6858 versts, including 2000 versts, as allowed by the original estimate, from Srjetensk to Khabarovsk. But, with the Trans-Manchurian branch, a further reduction of 600 versts must be made from that number, leaving the total length at 6258 versts. Even this enormous undertaking is not sufficient for Russian energy, and already plans are made for a branch line in the direction of Biisk, while it can only be a question of time till another connects Kiakhta with the Grand Trunk.

In connection with the geological expeditions that have also been at work on behalf of the railway, some excellent results have been obtained. Hitherto the fuel used has been wood, and a recent discovery of coal at Pavlodar had not been regarded with any great interest. More lately, however, in the Mid-Siberian district, there have been two remarkable discoveries of anthracite or stone coal, but of very good quality, at points within 20 versts of the railway. Also in Trans-Baikalia, in the valley of the Selenga, and other places, valuable deposits have been found, some of the seams averaging 35 feet in thickness.

In its relation to Russia, it is obvious that the new railway as an exporting agency may not be altogether an unmixed blessing. The route from Europe to Siberia through the Kara Sea is still too uncertain a course to come into anything like general usage. Meantime an expedition is engaged in hydrographical work in these regions; and the lapse of a few years may make a great change in the point of view from which this passage is regarded at the present moment. But Siberia requires some cheap convenient way even now by which to export her produce. The yearly excess of grain available for export is 9 to 12 million *puds*. A moment's thought will serve to show how the great railway, mainly in its function of populating the country, will soon augment this large quantity. At the same time, to flood the already crowded Russian markets with Siberian corn would be fatal to the agricultural world of the former, where prices are at a minimum.

To obviate this, a proposal was laid before the Committee of the Trans-Siberian Railway to join by rail the basins of the Ob and northern Dwina. The projected line was to start from Perm, and, passing through Viatka, to strike the Dwina near the village of Kotlass, whence a run of 641 versts down the river, whose depth here varies from 14 to 28 feet, would bring one to Archangel. During the summer of 1895 upwards of seventy steam craft were plying on that stretch of the river. It has been estimated that the cost of delivery of grain cargoes in London would be about $1\frac{3}{4}$ to $2\frac{1}{4}$ kopeks the *pud* cheaper from Tiumen, and $3\frac{1}{4}$ to $6\frac{1}{2}$ kopeks from Barnaul, through Archangel, than through St Petersburg. In time, with the improvement of the navigable condition of the Dwina and other rivers, as also by the lowering of the freights, it is supposed that this difference would be yet more increased to the advantage of Archangel. The cheapening of grain in the Archangel market will mean the fall of prices on all the White Sea coast, and will provide the possibility in the widest measure of increasing the sea industry, which is now declining year by year, and passing into the hands of the Norwegians. The estimated cost of this railway is 35 million rubles (£3,500,000). A commencement was made in 1895, and it is improbable that the line will be brought into direct connection with the other branches of the Russian railway system in order that it may perform its function successfully, while Archangel is joined with Vologda by rail. At the same time, it must be remembered that the principal exports from Siberia will just be such bulky raw produce as grain and timber, which demand cheap transport and cannot be expected to provide royal revenues.

On the other hand, it is hoped that other returns will be

increased. Thus, while at Odessa the duty on imported tea, regardless of quality, is about 21 rubles the *pud*, at Irkutsk it varies from 13 rubles on the best qualities to 2½ on brick tea. This artificial reduction is made solely in favour of the *trakt* or great post-road—to keep this commercial route open. With the railway all necessity for such a lowering of dues disappears, and the estimated additional revenue from this source alone is nine million rubles annually.

One feature about the railway and its influence is very noticeable. Russians are just beginning to find out what they have got in Siberia, this Greater Russia. The seeming indifference of the Russian people to the new exploit is really remarkable. If any English-speaking race were in the position of Russia at the present time, it is inconceivable that one would not meet with a host of individuals of all sorts and conditions rushing out to take possession of this land of promise—clerks, tradesmen, speculators, prospective hotel proprietors, saloon-keepers, bankrupts, members of the Salvation Army,—and what did one find in Siberia? Not a single Russian travelling to spy out the land from mere love of it, and few anxious even so much as to visit this country of the future.

Such, then, is the great monument to Russia's culture in the nineteenth century. Strategic,—how otherwise, to begin with, could she defend her 13,000 versts of Chinese frontier? —political, economical, its influence will be felt in the succeeding centuries. For some three hundred years, indeed, Siberia has been considered a Russian possession, but when the first train runs its unhindered way from St Petersburg to Vladivostok, then only will the work of Yermak have been completed.

CHAPTER III.

TRAVEL IN SIBERIA.

ON THE GREAT POST-ROAD—REQUIREMENTS—COST OF POSTING—THE POSTMASTER'S BOOK—TO PREVENT RACING—THE *YAMSTCHIK*—HIS MONOTONOUS LIFE—HIS MANAGEMENT OF HORSES—POST-STATIONS OUTSIDE AND INSIDE—SIBERIAN VILLAGES—THE PUBLIC PLAYGROUND—DRUNKENNESS—WHEN THE RYE COME HAME—LIFE ON THE *TRAKT*—THE ANGARA—LAKE BAIKAL—THE BURYAT COUNTRY—VALLEY OF THE SELENGA—FELLOW-TRAVELLERS—TEA CARAVANS—ROBBERY—INCIDENTS AND MISHAPS—THROUGH THE FLOOD—FERRIES AND FERRY-BOATS—RIVER-TRAVEL—THE OB—SCENERY ON ITS BANKS—SUNSET ON THE OB—TAKING IN WOOD—THE IRTÎSH—DIFFICULTIES IN ITS NAVIGATION.

It is, however, in its simple primary function of transportation that the new railway affects the traveller most. Few pages in the annals compiled by those who have in time past crossed Siberia are more graphic than the ones in which they describe their varied experiences by water and by land. One shares with them the tedium of days and weeks lost on the Ob and Yenisei in miserable steamers that seemed only to fulfil their destiny when they ran aground. Occasionally in October, towards the end of the season, some luckless vessels are overtaken in mid-voyage by the relentless frost, and forced to winter on the spot where they are captured, while passengers and crew are glad to seek their destination overland. Or, again, in the perusal of a paragraph that relates the story of conveyance by *tarantass* over some stretch of ground more rough than usual, one shuts one's eyes expectant of the next bump, which to the traveller signified painful acquaintance with the leathern hood, as the sturdy Siberian ponies ran, like the herd of swine, down a steep place violently, even to the length of plunging into some mountain torrent that had enlarged the borders of its conduit and buried the road under two feet of water! Soon, very soon, all this will be but a memory. True, there still remains an illimitable sweep of country north and south of the long avenue that leads from Europe to Vladivostok, but as yet the tracks are few, and there is little to attract humanity except in the person of the explorer. And should any contingent circumstance arise, such as still greater discoveries of gold, or even coal, than have been already made, and the alluring spot bid fair to become a resort of men, it is only reasonable to surmise that the enterprise that is laying the thin metal lines across the continent will not shrink from putting the new centre in communication with the main artery. Since, then, transport by steam-boat and by *tarantass* will suffer to some considerable extent by this most recent introduction, it may not be out of place to dwell on them a little at this stage.

In order to travel by the well-organised Siberian post, it is no longer necessary to provide oneself with a *podorojnaya* or order for post-horses, but those who have the right procure that special form of paper which is granted to persons on Government service, giving them the first claim to whatever horses at a station are available. Further, letters from the governor of the province to be traversed, or from the Postmaster-General, are still more satisfactory, as furnishing one with a complete title to the provision of the stable, and so enabling one to go from station to station at maximum speed. Every person who can afford to do so drives in his own *tarantass* or *kolyaska*, in which case it is only necessary to change the team and *yamstchik* at the several posthouses. The alternative is to travel *na perekladnikh*, which involves the additional change of conveyance at the end of each stage; and as the vehicles supplied on many occasions cannot with clemency be even eulogised as decrepit *tarantasses*, progression in this fashion is as upsetting an experience in every sense of the word as one can well imagine. The whole system is, like most things Russian, fenced by a long series of regulations which are only made never to be observed; or, rather, those simply are regarded that appeal to common-sense. But there is an unwritten code commanding infinitely greater respect than any of the burdensome dictates that in print adorn the station walls.

Amongst ordinary passengers, the claim to horses at any station is decided by the order of arrival. The passage of the post is the one great hindrance to the eager traveller, as it leaves so many empty stalls behind it, and every one must give precedence to it. Tables are hung up on the station wall showing when it is timed to reach that particular halting-place; hence the postmasters know exactly when to expect it, and for three hours before reserve the required number of horses. Moreover, the complement of horses kept at each station averages twenty-one, so the feelings of the traveller may be imagined when he sees the post drive in, consisting, as it often does, of five *tarantasses* in charge of one or two armed officials. This means fifteen at least of the available stock swept away at once, and if the station is crowded there are heart-burnings as one or two favoured individuals drive off with the remaining teams. It must be very annoying to arrive at a point a few hours in advance of the mail only to learn that there are a score of horses ready, but not for you. It is, however, possible to make up for the dearth by outside help, and in obedience to your official letters the postmaster must go and find some peasant who is willing to let you have horses on hire, if indeed some one of the crowd around the posthouse door has not already done so, perceiving your difficulty. Many people never employ any other than these *volni* (free) horses, as they are then masters of the situation, and are not so likely to suffer much detention. But the peasants are naturally inclined to overcharge. One Tatar refused to provide a *troika* for a 20-verst stage under 7 rubles. Or, again, look at that skulking peasant with a pipe between his teeth, one of a group of loafers, who proceeds to shuffle towards you as you stand about the station realising that no horses are obtainable for the next short stage of 18 versts. He removes his cap, and sheepishly inquires if *barin* wishes horses. You ask him how much he wants for a *troika*, and he replies "4 rubles." The post fare for the distance only amounts to 1 ruble 92 kopeks. You offer three, but he turns away with a smile, and you have to wait three hours. But after two hours—and this is very characteristic—another peasant, who knows what has passed already, comes up awkwardly and offers you horses for 5 rubles. After vainly endeavouring to explain to the man that he is a sublime fool, and that since you have been delayed two hours you may as well remain the third, you feel a certain anxiety to learn what attitude of mind could possibly have prompted his action. He frankly confesses that he believes you are so tired and worried with waiting two hours that you will now be glad to take horses at any price. But it is you who smile this time as the peasant marches off.

Otherwise, the regular cost of posting is ridiculously low. The charge for a horse varies with the locality, from $1\frac{1}{2}$ to $4\frac{1}{2}$ kopeks per verst, but 3 kopeks is the figure constant over the greatest area. A rough calculation fixes the tariff at $1\frac{1}{2}$ kopek the verst in Western and 3 kopeks in Eastern Siberia. In addition, there is a Government tax of 10 kopeks per horse over each stage. The number of horses required for each style of conveyance is also carefully regulated with due regard to the number of passengers and the weight of baggage.

Further, the postmaster keeps a book wherein he notes each traveller's name, the place from which he has just come, as likewise his immediate destination, the hour of his arrival at the station, together with his *yamstchik's* name and the number of horses engaged by him. And when the new-comer starts on his way again, the information regarding him is completed by filling in the moment of his departure, the size of his team, and the approximate time at which the same horses shall on their return, and after three hours' rest, again be ready for service on the road. As this register is always open to inspection, the traveller can see at a glance how many horses are out, and how many yet remain in the stable. Residents in a town can start on a journey with post-horses from their own door, the main restriction in their case being that they must not keep them waiting more than one hour. On these long stretches, little matters, such as the greasing of the wheels, come into great prominence: this operation is repeated every 100 or 150 versts.

To prevent racing, the order in which travellers left the last station, rather than that in which they arrive at the succeeding one, is the point taken into consideration, so that, except in cases of accident or wilful delay, any person who has been passed on the road, but who succeeds in gaining the next station before his rival resumes his journey thence, can claim the horses which the latter party may already have actually in harness. If, then, one has obtained a good start, it is advisable to maintain the lead, while the comparative progress that one makes when in pursuit of a friend or enemy can always be calculated from the postmaster's entry-book. Where, however, it is a case of an equal start for every one, as, *e.g.*, after getting off the Baikal steamer, the horses are handed over to travellers in the order in which they make demand for them at the station. This occasions a scramble of minions from the ship's side to the post-station.

Still, in addition to letters, much tact is required if one wishes to make any great progress. It is a rule that the rate of speed on the highroad should be maintained at 12 versts an hour, neither more nor less; but this is one of those typical mandates that cannot always be put into practice. People suffer in various ways. At one station we passed two gentlemen from Moscow who had succeeded in making only 69 versts in thirteen and a half hours. The *pisar* would have every one believe that his chief end in life is to save his master's horses, but the wary traveller soon discovers that it is rather to get money out of him by pretending that no teams are available, when such is not the case. He often announces to the new arrival that it will be necessary to wait for several hours, but after a time he comes back and reports that the horses can be had sooner through his exertions, and the fool gives him money, whereas he ought to have looked in the register. It is always preferable to try gentleness first: many a traveller spoils his chances of progression by adopting too lofty a tone in his dealings with the *pisar*. Unless he is really some one of great importance in other than his own estimation, to go upon this tack is of little use, as one daring postmaster went the length of saying in my hearing, " The Governor-General is nothing to us."

But we have only now come to the most important factor in post-travel—the *yamstchik*. Regular uniform he has none, although there are one or two badges of office which are more or less constantly worn. Of these the principal is a round metal plate with the imperial eagle and inscription wrought thereon. It is generally affixed to the front of the driver's cap, and a duplicate is sometimes worn on the left arm. When a man who was not a regular *yamstchik* was pressed into the service on any occasion, he simply strapped a badge round his arm: it is no easier to borrow a cap in Siberia than at home. The most common form of the latter was the round, flat-topped, astrakhan-bound cap, although as often without the astrakhan as with. Most of the wearers so crush them down upon their heads as to make the upper part of the ear stick out at a right angle. In winter these organs are protected by flaps, and carefully tucked in beneath a yet more oppressive head-gear. The rest of the costume varied with the pecuniary condition of the individual; and if, as sometimes happened, one's *yamstchik* had decked himself out in a heavy cloth coat with plaited skirt, or a black open-breasted *khalat* with velveteen collar, girded about with some light-coloured waistband, he looked an imposing figure mounted on the box. But what was most pleasing in artistic effect was the Kossak driver with jack-boots, black velveteen trousers, coloured sash, and bright *rubashka* with the *yamstchik's* badge attached to an arm thereof, and finally the dark cloth peak-cap with the yellow band that is his proud right.

The *yamstchik's* life is a miserable monotonous cycle. It is spent over an average of 45 versts—*i.e.*, the distance between two stations, there and back. Your first acquaintance is when you see him emerging out of a stable-shed with his two-belled *duga* in one hand, while by the other he leads the centre horse of his *troika;* the other pair follow. He

Yamstchik and Buryat woman.

proceeds to harness, and when everything is ready retires once again into the post-station for the little black leather bag which holds his commission. On this paper, which he receives from the *pisar*, to whom you have previously paid your *progon*, are noted down several particulars, such as the number of horses that he has, and the hour of his departure. Now he gathers the ropes into his hands, and has a race to gain his seat before the mettlesome ponies start; for directly the hardy little creatures feel the restraining hand at the other end of the line, they bound off eagerly while yet the *yamstchik* is scrambling into his place. It is often necessary, in consequence, to hold the animals' heads till the driver has got settled. But when the ponies are of a more serious cast of mind, and are content to start off only when they are bid, a low whistle or an explosive yell constitutes the common signal. After a run of 3 or 4 versts out of the village, the *yamstchik* stops to rests his *troika*, dismounts and walks round them, closely scrutinising their bearing, now tightening the breeching, now loosening a trace, and then comes round to the carriage and asks permission to smoke. This granted, he produces a little wooden pipe with a baby bowl, and fills its grimy hollow with some mixture dug out of a red or brown cloth pouch. Then he retires behind the carriage, strikes up with flint and steel, blows a few puffs, and then carefully redeposits the panacea in his pocket; once more he ascends his throne, and we are off again. When we reach the post-station that is our destination, he gets down, and after handing his despatch-bag to the *pisar*, who makes corresponding entries in the paper, he turns to us and says, what we have already perceived, "Prijechali" ("Arrived"). We retire inside the building, not however before having presented him with his *pourboire*, more particularly described in Russian as *natchai* (for tea). He proceeds to unharness his team, and when, some time after, we again get on our way, we see him starting homewards astride one of his horses, while the others follow, or else lying in the bottom of some *na perekladnikh* vehicle that came in charge of a fellow-*yamstchik*, while his own horses are secured to the back of the conveyance. And if both he and we have waited a little longer, and he be of a particular style of palate, we may see him staggering off intoxicated, to the wonderment of his mute charges; but even then he does not forget to raise his cap, and wish *barin* God-speed on his farther journey.

But over it all, what magnificent management of equine life! Some *yamstchiks* do not employ a whip,[1] while others are content simply to swing it wildly round their heads and do the rest by word of mouth. The driver sustains a conversation with his willing team, coaxing them, calling them by endearing names, cheering them, complimenting them. How they prick up their ears to catch his words! And then perhaps one of their number makes a mistake, or, more rarely, shies, or shows signs of flagging, and immediately there pours out on the astonished animal a torrent of abuse that increases and grows ever wilder and more fierce, till in sheer terror the creature throws back its shaggy head and springs forward with renewed energy, watching awhile the circling *nagaika* out of the corner of its eye. Much depends on the loquacity of the *yamstchik*. Some are by nature sparing in their words; as a class, they are not prodigal of their blows. If you want to understand how far it is possible for man and beast to understand one another, take your seat beside a Siberian *yamstchik* over a long stage, and although you may understand of the actual words employed in the course of the strange monologue even as little as the horse itself, yet in that crooning interspersed with blessing and cursing that will rise and fall more or less during the whole interval between two successive post-stations, and in the response thereto, you will see, as is rarely possible elsewhere, of what the horse is capable.

The *yamstchik's* driving partakes of recklessness. He is sometimes so drunk that everything depends on the horses,

---

[1] The whips most commonly used have short handles, with a curry-comb attached in addition to the stout, long lash.

which can be trusted faithfully to perform their duty in such an emergency, choosing, however, their own pace. If you are alone this is an awkward contingency, especially if it is necessary to sit on the box and sustain the driver. The gallop at which the *yamstchik* sets out is of necessity not maintained over the whole distance, but the fast trot into which it drops never slackens, growing, on the contrary, into an impetuous charge when a hill rises in front, and the steeper the incline the more furious is the assault. When once the eminence is gained, a halt is always made for a few minutes to recover breath. This is the moment that has been seized by highway robbers to attack the post and other travellers. And if the sides of the road are elevated and covered with a thick scrub, then it is possible to pick off every man as he sits in his *tarantass* waiting on his reviving horses, as has been done on more than one occasion. In descending a hill the *yamstchik* never shortens rein in the orthodox manner. He maintains his grasp of the ribbons at the same point, but draws them towards him, so that he is often seen sweeping down a sharp descent with either hand in the region of the corresponding ear. The majority of them wear coarse leathern gloves, as the hempen reins pull heavily on the hand.

The extreme simplicity and freedom that attach to the post system are not unnatural. Thus, the first part of a 36-verst stage happened to be hilly, and we decided to start with five horses in our heavy *kolyaska*. After 25 versts the road became more even, and we considered that four would take us along as quickly as we wanted. We were then driving across the common (these preserves are always miles in breadth) of an intermediate village, and our *yamstchik* unharnessed one of the trace-horses, hobbled and turned it loose, and we continued our journey. No one would touch it,—horse-flesh is too cheap in that country. At the same time the horses of each station—commonly 12 hands, and with a dark stripe running down the back—are subjected to various slight mutilations, usually of the ear, for purposes of identification. Further, if two parties travelling in opposite directions happen to meet on the road about halfway, the *yamstchiks* with their horses may change masters if mutual consent is given, and thus they save a whole stage.

In a journey of any considerable length it is obvious that one had to deal with many interesting types of Jehu. The Buryats make splendid drivers, and are only excelled by the Kossaks in the Far East. But it is not the differences national so much as individual that create an impression. One of our drivers was afflicted with St Vitus's dance. How his horses flew! Another had a violent hæmoptysis. Poor fellow! his undermining cough even made his sympathetic charges look round with wistful eye. As a class the *yamstchiks* are a good set of men. Often drunk, it is true, but capable of moral endeavour even in that state. Once, when, owing to a scarcity of horses at the post-station, we were compelled to hire four peasant horses with their master, who had had to borrow one of them, it happened that the off-horse, which was the loaned one, was not drawing well, and our driver got down to readjust the trace and breechings. Another *tarantass* passed us at the moment, the *yamstchik* whereof seized the occasion to pull up and come to our assistance. He was, however, quite tipsy, and could render little help. Our own driver, growing angry at the refractoriness of the horse, remarked to the other man that, if it did not go better now, he would simply punish it severely, and that it did not matter so much since it was borrowed. But the reeling man turned round, looked the offending brother in the face, and said to him slowly and with marked emphasis, "On that account you ought to take all the better care of it."

The condition of the posthouses varied greatly. The stations that lay on the less frequented byroads differed

Outside a posthouse.

from those on the *trakt* mainly in their smaller size and greater cleanliness. If you happened to be asleep just before arriving at one of them, it is probable that you would be rudely awakened by the pronounced rumbling that accompanies the last 3 or 4 feet of the journey. For the road outside the posthouse door is always laid with wooden planks to preserve it from being converted into a pit, and in the course of time this outside flooring becomes loose, and protests audibly at being run over. Two posts, painted black and white, stand on either side of the door, one of which supports a lamp. On the other is a tablet bearing the name of the station—*Tulinskaya potchtovaya stantziya* (Tulinsky post-station)—followed by those of the nearest town in either direction, with the number of versts that it is distant, and beneath that the names of the nearest post-station on either side with its remoteness likewise.

Inside there is little of note. The post-station is usually the largest log building in the village. The quadrangular yard, in and around which are arranged the stables and other outhouses, is enclosed by a stout stockade. Of the two rooms that look to the front, one is generally reserved by the postmaster himself, and the other is devoted to the travelling public. In some cases more than one apartment may be at their disposal, but the furniture rarely exceeds a few chairs, one or more small tables, and two or three wooden benches, with an occasional lounge or old divan in some of the better houses. The small windows, that rarely light the public rooms satisfactorily, are mostly of the horizontal swinging type. And in mid-summer more than one lazy postmaster has still left in their place his double winter windows, with jars of sulphuric acid between to absorb the moisture. To one table a large folio notebook for the registry of complaints is attached by a sealed string, and it is sufficient to open this book on arrival to see with what kind of postmaster you have to deal. On the side-roads they were sometimes blank throughout. And the homelier simplicity of these less frequented stations was seen in the creepers planted in window-pots and gracefully led by secret strings and tapes all over the ceiling, so that to pass an hour there was like partaking of a pilgrim's rest in some leafy bower after the bare dull rooms of the *trakt* post-stations.

On the wall of the common room will be found lithographic pictures of the heads of the imperial house, of Father John of Kronstadt, whose fame has spread throughout Siberia, and occasionally of scenes from Russian life, while in a corner opposite the door is the indispensable *ikon*. But the traveller by preference studies a printed list of certain articles of food *à prix fixe*, with which the postmaster or postmistress is supposed to be able to provide him. It is an appetising carte, including *ryabtchik* cutlet; but, as a matter of fact, you can count on little more than a samovar with hot water, black bread and milk, more rarely eggs, and exceptionally meat. In winter it is somewhat otherwise, for frozen blocks of *shtchi*, off which you chop a piece and drop it into hot water, together with black bread and the national dish—*pilmeni*—are your mainstay.

. . . .

Of many things the outward appearance is deceptive, giving a really false impression of the strength and real nature of the life within, and in nothing does this come out so strongly as in the Siberian villages, through whose dreary squalid lengths the post-road creeps. At first, when one continues to drive day after day and week after week without remarking any sign of land-ownership other than the village settlements with their unfenced cultivated fields in close proximity, one is tempted to believe that this is a country where a great Socialist ideal has been realised—where the soil belongs to the people, and where you may look in vain for the large landed proprietor. And it is only after a time that the truth dawns upon you slowly, and you see that, on the contrary, you are traversing the domains of an imperialist whose eastern march is the Pacific, and on whose royal estate these villagers are but tenants. For practically all Siberia belongs to the Crown, and the village communes enjoy the use and profit of their acres, but no legal possession. Hence litigation about land is unknown, and neighbouring villages that may have reason to differ about their rights to any particular tract, the desirableness of which is evident to both, still sometimes decide such questions in the most primitive fashion.

Each of these villages in the west is strangely like its neighbour. Indeed they only differ in one respect—their linear extent; otherwise they are all at the same stage of development. In almost every case they consist of a double row of plain single-storeyed log cottages, separated from one another by their side-yards, through the front wall of which you pass by one of three doors (commonly a large centre one for waggons, and two side ones for pedestrians) in order to gain entrance to the habitation. Around this courtyard are disposed the sheds and barns of the cottager, which provide shelter for everything from grain to poultry and horses. He makes use of very thick logs in the construction of his broad-eaved residence, dovetails them at the corners, beyond which they project about a foot in the two directions, and caulks them with moss, while the front wall may also be broken by the similar protruding ends of beams that compose an internal dividing wall. Dark brown or grey to the outward eye, they sometimes do not even stand squarely upon their foundations. The windows, whose framework is picked out in white, are commonly composed of eight square panes, of which some have the power of opening to the outside. In the humblest dwellings, fragments of glass, not sufficiently large to fill up the frames by themselves, are fixed between two layers of birch-bark cut to the required size. Moreover, the windows are provided with outer shutters attached to the white-painted ornamental framework, and closing flush with the wall. Often in the yard may also be found a sunken storeroom, where the milk is kept cool in summer. The interiors of the cottages are unaccustomed to be whitewashed, although the posthouses cannot be included in this characterisation. The chimney may be built of brick and whitewashed, or an old iron tube may serve in that capacity. Often it does not exist at all to external appearance. Almost always you tread the bare wooden floor, which in some cases is concealed beneath a thick layer of straw or rushes.

The well is a prominent feature of each village. The children play with the long pole, balanced at one end by additional blocks of wood or a stone, and watch the bucket-rope as it disappears and drags the other end to earth. But more unusual was the open recreation-space, in which were set up a wooden "horse," parallel bars, sometimes a trapeze, and a long horizontal pole for balancing feats. In the evening the villagers love to sit out on benches, each in the shadow of his house; or the men talk in groups, and the women in companies discuss their little family themes. The Siberians love bright colours, and in towns and villages they indulge in them often without any regard to taste. Some of the peasant women had strength of mind sufficient to carry a green bodice over a strong purple skirt, while red and pink, or heliotropes and browns of every shade, were largely fancied. Their dress is very uniform. Outside of all is an ordinary apron; below that a print skirt, often held up by two bands of the same material passing above the loose bodice, one over each shoulder. The men are content with a brightly-coloured *rubashka*, velveteen or tweed trousers, jack-boots and peak-cap, and a short pea-jacket in the cool evenings.

There is little need to dilate upon the drunkenness of the Siberian folk, but from Tomsk onwards it was not once or twice merely that we passed men lying in the centre of the village road; and often late in the evening, small groups of inebriates stumbled along the uneven track, unduly emphasising with each loss of balance sundry snatches of their weird minor airs. The concertina is a favourite instrument: nearly every evening some one promenades a village, forcing on the inhabitants its wheezing plaint. Moreover, the door of the *kabak* is always the rendezvous for "the lewd fellows of the baser sort." These speedily become a wrangling group, and a strange kaleidoscopic effect is produced as the men in *rubashkas* of red, pink, orange, green, blue, grey, or white move round about and in and out of one another under the influence of *vodka* fumes. How they vociferate! One man contradicts all the others, who are determined to suppress him. Or see that old white-haired man as he staggers home leaning on the shoulders of his daughter, or that little girl as she trots down the village, trolling some peasant air, carelessly carrying a flask of *vodka* beneath her arm. Drink is the curse of Siberia. The land is very rich, and there is a royal waste of everything—of time, of space, of natural products. We have seen peasants who could afford to refuse 10s. for the hire of two *troikas* over a short stage. Their laziness is great. Sunday evening is usually spent in rioting and drunkenness: they rarely work on Monday. This is largely due to outward prosperity. Siberia is almost unique in consideration of the small amount of poverty within her borders; you rarely see a beggar in a town. The land is very fruitful; the peasants have good herds of horses and cattle; fifteen of each are no unusual possession. It remains to be seen what effect the railway will produce upon these lethargic communities. When competition compels them to work, they will perhaps find that they have forgotten the meaning of that sublime word.

As you drive through a village towards the evening, you will notice how each cottage is besieged by a small herd of horses, or cattle, or goats, peering in at the windows or lying down without, while they whisk off the flies with their tails. In the morning the villager opens the gate of his yard, and of their own account his horses and his cattle stream out and join the little bands from other cottages to march off to the pasture-land. The village commons, or the pasture-land immediately surrounding them, are carefully hedged in throughout the many miles of their circumference. Where the fence strikes the post-road a gate is set up, and in a miserable cabin by the roadside vegetates the village idiot or pauper to whom are intrusted the duties of gatekeeper. Late in the afternoon the flocks and herds return without guidance, commonly following some more than usually sagacious member of the fold adorned in consequence with a bell, and wait about their master's cottage till he returns from his day's labour at some other point of the compass, or if he be there already, till of his good pleasure he opens the wooden doors. And if you pass along at the right time, you will see multitudes of horses and mares attended by frisking foals, of cows with calves, and of lesser goats sauntering homewards along the road. Then as each detachment comes opposite its quarters it breaks off, and the diminished body, neighing and lowing and bleating, moves on. An easy-going company, for if any of them feel wearied they simply lie down in the middle of the thoroughfare and obstruct the passage; and when to these at other times of the day are added dogs, sheep, poultry, pigs, and children, it often seems as if all the life of the place were in the street.

The peasant culture of the land is primitive but successful. The regular brown patches on the hillsides in the Far East betoken the agriculturist; but when one passes the lonely ploughman despondently trudging behind his team of a dozen sturdy oxen, who require the constant attention of two

Till the master returns.

youngsters continually rushing from one end of the line to the other plying their goads, it is possible to understand the cost.

The villages on the highroad as far as Lake Baikal become poorer as one journeys towards the east. The continuity of the double row of cottages is broken, in fact is lost: each man settles where he feels inclined. There is also a shrinkage in the size of the individual building. They are more often awry, and covered with damaged roofs, and the live stock that patrol the road are not present in such great force. The village dogs likewise gain in ugliness: in fact it was sometimes difficult to understand where dog ended and wolf began.

. . . .

Life on the *trakt* is a most monotonous experience, and if you insist on travelling by night it may also be most tiring. For days at a time the scenery does not change: you know what you are coming to, what you may look for, except in those cases when escaped convicts prepare some little surprise. One stretch alone can be praised for its beauty—that between Irkutsk and Verkhni-Udinsk. As you leave the former town, you pass under a wooden archway over which is inscribed in great gilt letters, "Doroga k' Velikomu Okeanu" ("Road to the Great Ocean"—*i.e.*, the Pacific). The distance to Verkhni-Udinsk is only 287 versts, but in that short space you encounter an unwonted diversity of surroundings. The road at first follows the valley of the Angara, skirting its right bank, till it reaches the shores of Lake Baikal, out of which this remarkable river falls. The Angara is probably the swiftest river in the world, and its stony bed can be descried through many fathoms of its translucent flood. In the height of summer its temperature is about 10° C. at the surface, and 4° C. below the surface in mid-stream; hence you will hunt in vain for a bathing-box upon its banks at Irkutsk. It does not commence to freeze until the beginning of January. They also say that in its case the anchor or ground ice is the first to form. Lastly, owing to the unusual season at which it freezes, its floods are mistimed, and occur not in the spring but in early winter, when all the other rivers are frost-bound.

Between Irkutsk and Lake Baikal the valley of the Angara is richly clothed with larch, spruce, and birch, while the left

F

bank is consistently higher than the right. Many islands float on the bosom of the rapid current, some of which are wooded, while others are low and treeless, looking like green blotches on the surface of the water. In the neighbourhood of Irkutsk, villages line either bank at intervals; but as the left bank rises up more steeply, though clad with birch, pine, and spruce even to the water's edge at places, the human habitations tend to restrict themselves to the other. As we approach the lake the lower levels of the right bank disappear, the trees shrink in size, and on the opposite shore ravines are cut back into the hills which now close up on the stream. To their summits and higher reaches the trees gradually retreat, no longer brushing the water as it rushes by, while cliffs and promontories stand out boldly into the current. At the same time the valley widens appreciably till it is more than a mile in breadth. We turn a corner, and beneath us are the rapids, the throes of the river's birth, beyond which expands the peaceful surface of Baikal. The cool limpid water seems to hesitate a moment before it leaves the lake, then suddenly makes a fierce dash, tumbles wildly over the rapids, and settles down upon its quiet journey to the Polar Sea. Just at the point where the Angara issues out of Baikal, a curious curved belt of rock extends almost right across the bed of the river, now rising close up to the surface, now breaking through it, especially at the famous Shamanski Stone. The Buryats will tell you how an old Shaman planted this natural monument there in times gone by, and that on it live the *ongoni* or heavenly spirits who reveal themselves through the Shamans. It towers in two grey peaks, around which circle some gulls. On one side of it are the rapids, on the other the placid lake.

The broken water enables you to trace distinctly the

direction of the ledge of rock over which the water pours. Steamers pass it by hugging the left bank, where it is broken. The great dam keeps back the flood, so that practically all the water that descends flows over the top of it, and men say that if it were blown up with dynamite, Irkutsk and the other places in the valley down below would all be carried away. The road skirts the shore of the lake, upon which the hills so crowd that, even if it was desired, there is no other possible form for a village to assume than a long thin double line of cottages, with somewhat restricted road-space between. Such is the little settlement of Listvinitchnaya, whence one takes passage for the other side.

Lake Baikal is no less remarkable than the river to which it gives birth. Spoken of locally by Russians and Mongolians alike as the Holy Sea, it is the deepest known fresh-water lake. The name Baikal probably stands for Baikul, which by interpretation means the Rich Sea, having reference to the abundance of life inhabiting it. Nyanza, Superior, Michigan, Huron, and Tanganyika alone surpass it in size. Six-and-sixty times the size of Lake Geneva, it extends throughout its length of nearly 420 miles, curving, though in no very pronounced fashion, from north-east to south-west. Its breadth varies from 10 to 60 miles. Its shore-line falls little short of 1200 miles, and the surface of its transparent deep blue waters exceeds 14,500 square miles. It has a distinct ebb and flow apart from all changes of level directly due to the earth tremors of volcanic origin that add to the awesomeness of the lake. The average depth is rarely less than 819 feet. But at parts the bottom has been touched only at 4500 feet; one investigator avers to have sounded 4900 feet of depth; the natives believe it to be bottomless. Situated 1561 feet above the level of the sea, it is divided, as it were, into a northern and a southern part known as the Little and Great Baikal respectively, from the circumstance that Holy Cape on the eastern shore and Olkhon Island on the west stretch out in some degree to meet one another. A submerged ridge running parallel to the Irkutsk and Trans-Baikalian coasts, above which the water is at places not more than twenty-eight fathoms deep, is more important geologically, as suggesting that the lake originally consisted of two longitudinal cavities. The supremely picturesque shores, which often take the form of high granite cliffs rising abruptly from the water's edge, apparently do not shelter the lake from the two prevailing winds, which, blowing from the north-east and from the south-west, can lash the erst peaceful surface till it becomes rampant, and regular billows, a fathom and a half in height, effectually forbid all steamboat passage. The surface temperature of the water does not alter more than 10° C.; at the bottom it registers 3·5° C. The lake is frozen by December, when the sledge traffic is instituted, and the ice breaks up again by May. Desolate, buried among ravine-cut hills, hemmed in by undaunted cliffs, ravaged by winter tempests, shrouded by impervious fogs due to intense evaporation, Baikal has inspired the native mind with dread since earliest days. Other-world beings live in its depths; the hills that circle it are the abode of spirits. A small shrine stands on the pier at Listvinitchnaya, where prayer is made by many a voyager: there are those who still fling money and bread into its waters to propitiate the unknown rulers.

On the far south-western side of the lake the waters do not approach so closely to the foot of the hills, which are thickly covered with a dark-green mantle of young spruce, spotted with silver birch. And above this recent growth stretch the tall, grey, lifeless trunks of cedar, larch, and pine, sad memorials of bygone forest-fires. The road, which is not of the same quality as those in the west, skirts the edge of the lake for about 40 versts, and in consequence abounds in sharp rises and falls. As we advance, the wealth of vegetation increases, till it sometimes seems as if we were in the *taiga* once again. Willows, aspen, and cinnamon firs join forces with the trees already mentioned, and the strong undergrowth would stifle him who attempted to pierce its jealous density. At length we leave the pebbly beach upon which the wavelets gently break, and follow the road as it bends sharply inland towards the hills that, retreating from the lake-side, stretch range upon range, peak upon peak, in an easterly direction as far as the eye can see. So a plain spreads out on our left, which may have been under water at some remote period, for it is certain that the Baikal of to-day lies in a diminished basin.

We have now fairly entered the country of the Buryats, and the Government notices, affixed to the telegraph-poles, are printed in their tongue as well as in Russian. The principal wayside flower is the pink willow-herb, which covers whole areas of ground, occasionally giving place to a red Turk's-cap lily; but in the open a long bent has choked off almost everything except where copses of very young birch have sprung up. We pass the post-station of Kabanskaya. It proclaims itself as being 6091 versts from St Petersburg, 5487 from Moscow, 536 from Tchita, and 204 from Irkutsk —sufficiently out of the world for most purposes. A village through which we drive shortly after exhibits a certain freshness and tidiness that were not too noticeable west of the Baikal. The dwellings are at least square on their foundations, if lacking somewhat in symmetry of arrangement;

while the church, whose white plastered walls are surmounted by a steel-grey roof set with gilt stars, has evidently been the original nucleus of the community. To-day that position is held throughout Siberian villages in another sense by the wine-shop. It is a public holiday, being the completion of a fast, and every one is in his best attire. The greater seriousness of Trans-Baikalian village life is evidenced even by the paling that fences round the common. It is a carefully constructed ridge of wicker-work done with birch-branches, and well calculated to prevent horses and cattle from straying. The individual habitations with their pent-houses stand absolutely detached, but a lower stockade surrounding the whole also helps to convey the impression of a freer, easier existence. Towards the outskirts of the village the cottages dwindle into huts.

When we next awoke of a morning we had entered the valley of the Selenga. It is possible to go from Irkutsk to Verkhni-Udinsk by boat, as this river falls into Baikal. At first the valley is narrow, partaking almost of the nature of a ravine, on the left side of which the road is cut. The trees, similar to types already met, attain no height; an alpine poppy of delicate yellow has usurped the roadside. The morning air is fresh, and immediately below us is the swirl of the Selenga. Trans-Baikalia is a fair land of everlasting hills clothed with the social pine, and dark sequestered valleys inhabited by a people of soft graces and pleasant charms, who live alongside of their Buryat neighbours in a state of peaceful amity.

We drove up to a post-station in this neighbourhood that lay high on an escarpment in the lea of the last summit, with no attendant village. Its form was that of a little whitewashed building with the usual offices, in which the sturdy ponies snatch their too short rest before they again unfalteringly convey some other Trans-Baikalian traveller over a stage of his route. On the left of the entrance was the common room, with the *kontora* near by, while on the right were the two rooms of the liveried postmaster. And at the far end of the short passage, curled up on a rude bench, was the little postmistress of some sixteen summers, with the fair hair and blue eyes that are no rarity here, in tasteful bright red gown, set off by a pretty white pattern, diligently reading some Russian tale—a peasant girl amid her mountains. When we came out again a dun falcon wheeled in ever narrowing circles around the lip of the crag that overhung the post-station; but marking as yet nothing for his cruel talons, he soared aloft into the realms of space. When we passed that way again the postmaster's little daughter was dead.

After a time the track descends to the level of the river, but we take our line rather by the four telegraph-wires supported on lanky tripods. The valley begins to open out, the hills decrease in size, and their thick wooding tends to disappear. Soon we emerge on the river-plain, and now that the directive influence of the hills no longer makes itself felt, the Selenga, flowing due north at this point, continually edges eastward, leaving behind it a level willow-covered waste. In a hollow on the right bank of the river Verkhni-Udinsk is cosily settled, somewhat like Krasnoyarsk. To the north rise, shoulder to shoulder, the grey hills, whose granitic composition shows out at many an escarpment. In consequence, especially towards the summit, the pine-trees can be counted individually, and lend the hills the appearance of couchant monsters with bristles erect, jealously guarding the town sleeping below. Brave are these wind-sown pines with a strong grip of life, maintaining a foothold and finding the means of existence in most unlikely ground, as they wind their roots around the lichen-covered rocks. The first hint of the town is given by four spires that seem to start out of the sandy soil; and a little later one notices a large edifice consisting of a central building with two wings, removed at some distance from the town, on a slope facing the south. Its white plastered walls, bright red roof, and light encircling wall shine out gloriously from the dark pine-trees, amidst which it is set. Elsewhere you would take it for a hydropathic: here it happens to be the prison.

It would not be difficult to sum up in a sentence the various parties that one meets upon the road—the post, peasants, fellow-travellers, *brodyagi*, the military trains, and, most formidable but also most interesting, the caravans of merchandise. It is not an uncommon thing for a heavy mist to descend upon the steppe towards evening, so that it seems to be a wonderful matter how the *yamstchiks* know their way. Then a dull red glow emerges out of the gloom, ever increasing in brightness, and the tired traveller thinks that now at last he is within sight of the lamp that is by night lit outside the post-station. But as he approaches the expanding blaze, it gradually descends to the level of the earth, till at one moment it seems as if he were going to be driven right into the midst of it. And he who looked for the welcome door of some post-station is met by what appears to be a serried circle of pikes. These resolve themselves, however, into the shafts supported on their *dugas*, of a multitude of carts that are drawn up in a ring round a roaring fire, beside which squats a picturesque group of strange humanity, for the drivers of the caravans are men of no gentle type. The still night air is disturbed by their loud coarse cries and exclamations as they while away the night in mirth and drunkenness, by which they are left in a state of torpidity throughout the day. And at intervals a milder response pierces the mist from the tinkling bells of their hobbled horses.

The overland tea-trade from China through Kiakhta is too well known to demand more than the mere mention. Add to this the fact that a large part of the supplies of each Siberian town has to be conveyed thither overland by horse, if the railway has not yet reached them, and it is easy to picture to oneself the need for the long caravans of from ten to one hundred and fifty carts of tea and other merchandise that continually pass along the great highroad. The material units of which these serpentine bodies are built up are of the simplest. The broad square wooden axle of the cart is only thinned down where it enters the bushed nave of the bulky wheel. The body of the cart consists of two stout poles, the anterior halves of which serve as the shafts, while behind they are connected together by a square beam, from beneath which project two pair of wooden teeth holding the axle between them like a vice. On the top of all this lies little else than a light shallow sparred frame. The freight is either a cubical tea-chest covered with sacking, a cask, or some amorphous mass of ware. The distance that these caravans have to go is not so much evidenced by the leisurely pace at which the procession moves, nor even by the tired appearance of the horses, nor yet by the rude canopy of verdant birch-branches, skins, or coarse cloth stretched over hoops and erected on every seventh cart, beneath which the captain over seven lies fast asleep, as by the ugly black grease-bucket that hangs from the shaft, and by the two or three ambulance-carts bringing up the rear, on which are piled spare axles and duplicate wheels. The chief, armed with a couple of revolvers, may be seen riding on horseback up and down the length of the *cortége* to ascertain that the men are doing nothing worse than snoozing. From the back of each cart swings a bag of hay, so that when the caravan halts the horses can feed at pleasure with no trouble to the drivers. One often saw foals gambolling alongside of their mothers, enjoying a too brief freedom. A military caravan could be distinguished by a red flag flying from the leading cart, if by nothing else.

The drivers employed on these caravans are as wild and fierce as the *brodyagi* who infest the woods. One dark night a portmanteau of books, sent out by a philanthropist whose interest is in certain schools where the children of prisoners are educated, was cut off the back of our *kolyaska*. The discovery was only made at the next post-station, and as by a chance the *ispravnik* of the district happened to be in the village at that time, the circumstance was reported to him, although nothing was expected to come of it. Later on, after several weeks, my companion received a telegram to say that the books and portmanteau had been found, and were being forwarded. It seems that the robbers had not found the literature sufficiently interesting, and left the portmanteau by the wayside. Shortly after, in the grey morning, a caravan passed along, and the greedy drivers rushed forward on seeing the abandoned valise, thinking to have gained some great prize. Those who were farther back in the caravan caught up the cry and joined in the scramble, being anxious not to lose their share of the spoil. Meanwhile the ever-watchful highwaymen took in the whole situation and carefully lightened the last cart in the caravan of its merchandise, which they bore hastily away into the depths of the forest; and as the lazy disappointed drivers

AN OLD KARA FRIJUT.

simply stood about until their respective carts came up to them, it was some time before they learned what had taken place. They then found that they had lost their bearings, which made it useless for them to think of recovering the stolen goods. Thus were the biters bitten, and the caravan arrived at the next village in charge of sadder if not wiser men.

In time past a tax was laid upon this overland trade, to be devoted to keeping the road to Irkutsk in good repair. But in Trans-Baikalia the same standard of excellence is not maintained: indeed in the more out-of-the-way districts the road frequently disappears altogether. As late as the summer of 1896, one stretch—between Kansk and Nijni-Udinsk—was still considered dangerous to pass at night. Robbery was no unusual occurrence, although assaults of a more serious nature become less frequent. But you will notice more than one wooden cross, marking a spot where the post was attacked and plundered. One is inclined to believe that the navvies employed upon the railway—a heterogeneous lawless mass of humanity—are responsible for some of the more recent escapades. They live close to the road, so that all who pass along are practically at their mercy.

The lesser mishaps that occasionally befall one serve to lend piquancy to this delightful mode of travel. It was no uncommon thing for a young inexperienced *yamstchik* in charge of our quintet to misjudge his distance when driving somewhat on one side of the road with the laudable intention of avoiding the greatest number of ruts, with the result that the off-horse, considering that it would do just as well to run outside a telegraph-post, suddenly found itself constrained to describe a complete somersault. Subjected to this violent strain, the cross-reins would snap, when the animal was free to recover from its discomposure, wondering how it ever had succeeded so well in taking the place of the acrobat for once at a rural circus show. One had not to be put about because sheet-lightning in the middle of the night so disconcerted another team that they swerved off the road, and dragged the carriage vehemently down a small embankment (we were ascending a valley), although it refused to upset. Still nothing would move that *kolyaska*. It would not even yield to the entreaties of the *troika* harnessed to the hind axle, in the hope that it would surely return by the way it had descended. The only amusement one got out of the situation was in endeavouring to persuade the *yamstchik* and the armed guard on the box that they had both been fast asleep. When morning came—and it does so early about mid-time of the summer in these far lands—we saw how one wheel had been caught in a hole, and by means of the leverage supplied by a young branch-stript pine the vehicle was released from its embarrassment.

In descending any very steep declivity a shoe-drag was requisitioned, which was secured to the wheel by a long iron pin. On one occasion the rope to which the shoe-drag is attached snapped towards the bottom of a heavy slope, and the freed wheel flew round so violently with the clog affixed that the iron pin succeeded in tearing a great hole in the side of the carriage before its mad progress was checked. It was noteworthy that all these little incidents occurred east of Lake Baikal, where also, when attempting to gain the highroad after a detour to the silver mines of Nertchinsk, we were landed in the most awkward predicament of all as the sequel of many days of rain. We had set off at 4 A.M. from a certain post-station, but after making some 4 or 5 versts the horses stuck in the heavy

A FRESH START.

sodden ground, and refused to go farther. Accordingly the *yamstchik* left us in the rain to ride back to the village on one of his team for more horses. He sent out an older and more experienced driver in his place, and by the aid of an additional horse we reached the next post-station at 1 P.M. instead of at 7 A.M. After a hasty meal we started off again with five horses, but the difficult nature of the drive soon became apparent. The track lay up the side of a broad

River Ingoda, Eastern Siberia.

valley, but at times descended so perilously near the small stream which graced it that at certain points the overflow had found it advantageous to make use of the artificial course. In consequence, for a considerable distance, we not only drove up a gentle incline, but also against a somewhat strong current of water, which, however, never was more than a foot and a half in depth. Later on, we crossed the stream by a wooden bridge that was beginning to break up. Gradually the number of versts between us and the village mounted up, and what with driving through rivulets and jerking across open conduits whose overarching trunks had been carried away by the rising water, we were not allowed to feel the tedium of the journey. The spruce- and birch-clad valley after several versts opened into another of still greater size, scoured by a correspondingly more powerful stream, and the flood formed by the union of the two swept turbid and reckless down the main valley. The road traversed this river by a bridge, but so soon as the *yamstchik* saw the swollen tide, he expressed his conviction that we should find no bridge standing. The nature of the surroundings had made it necessary to lead the road across the tributary which we had accompanied so long before we gained the bridge over the united streams. The small corduroy still held its ground although the water was washing its under surface, and, as we dashed over, welled up between the planks. The *yamstchik's* worst fears were realised, for before we reached the second bridge that spanned the combined flow, we could see the hobbled horses and the carts of a caravan drawn up by the bank. The bridge had been carried away. The caravan-drivers who had complacently camped out in the soaking marshy ground by the river-side, content to wait till the waters subsided when it would be possible to begin the work of reconstruction, averred that the bridge over a third river ahead had likewise been floated away, and that a luckless *tarantass* had been caught between the two. They expected to wait three days if the rain held off. We preferred to return 26 versts to the village, where the *ataman* was interviewed, and promised to send men in the morning to see what could be done, if there was no more rain. Such are the uncertainties of Siberian travel, — post, prisoners, and travellers being treated alike by the impartial weather.

Two mornings later we set out to retrace for the third time the now familiar versts, for a man had come to the village reporting that two of the bridges had been repaired, and that the third would probably be ready by the time we reached it. We quickly gained the point where a temporary structure had been hastily thrown across the river, which did not seem to have abated much since we turned back from it two days before, and were nearing the second bridge when we met a troop of about thirty men on horseback, led by the *ataman*. They were the men of the village whom he had led out to the repair of the bridges that were within his domain. Most of the riders were barefooted, and each carried over a shoulder an axe or saw, while with the other hand he controlled his steed, from which two or three layers of coarse felt at the most separated him. Some had harnessed their horses to little two-wheeled runners on which trees had been dragged down to the water's edge. We drove on, but still the clouds maintained their leaden hue, and it looked as if further rain might fall any moment. The heavy road still followed the valley, on the sides of which certain regular brown patches showed where ground had been reclaimed by industrious labourers from the now infrequent larch and birch that gave the slopes the appearance with which one is familiar from Chinese pictures of their own scenery. And although one might have been able to count the individual trees upon the crests, those slopes that faced the south-east were bare under the influence of the prevailing wind. Progress was greatly retarded, because the streamlets that drained the right side of the valley had perforce to cross the road to carry their tribute to the main torrent. There was a time when they had been kept under control, but the long-continued rains had enabled them to burst through the underground channel that had been constructed to contain them, the beams of which could often be seen lying a little below the road, and since the playful water had seized the opportunity to widen the original conduit, we were more than once confronted by a miniature ravine three feet across and as many deep, making it the better policy to leave the road at that point, and try to go round the trench, even at the risk of sinking in the marshy ground. The third bridge, of which we have already spoken, spanned another tributary to the main stream, but had been completely broken up and swept away, giving place to a highly vibratory successor.

We were now within sight of the next village, or rather of its surrounding wattled hedge which rose out of water, and from which we were still separated by gullies like those we have described. The state of matters was such as to warrant the presence of the two or three men of the village who were waiting there on horseback outside the gate, prepared to give assistance. Across the first, which was comparatively shallow, the *kolyaska* was dragged with the help of a sixth horse, and the second was circumvented. Two of the men offered to ride ahead of us and show us the way, as most of the village and its pasture-land were under water, being unfortunately situated in the centre of the valley not so far above the normal level of the Unda. Hence, whenever the river rose to any considerable extent the result was widespread flooding. During the height of the recent storm half of the village had been under water; a bridge over a small tributary was gone, and the flood areas, which comprised many acres, were not easily forded in the *kolyaska*, owing to the varying depth of the water. In the middle of the village a stream, that drained the immense volume of water that had accumulated in the low grounds around, cut the road at right angles, having a breadth of at least fifteen feet, and a depth such that a man hanging on with extended arms to a long telegraph-pole thrown across it could not touch the bottom with his feet. The village was thus completely divided in two, and there had been a cessation of all serious communication for several days. The horses were taken out of the *kolyaska* and made to swim : a couple of poles were then laid over the torrent, the carriage-axles rested on them, when it was pushed and dragged across. It was a curious sight to see some of the men in their Kossak caps, linen shirt, and drawers, up to the waist in water, as they sought with much shouting and gesticulation to get under the carriage and push it with one arm, while they held on to a pole with the other. At the post-station we learned that it would be useless to attempt to reach the station beyond by the main road which lay down the valley; but finding that there was an alternative route over the hills, we decided to pursue it. The river was negotiated by means of a forlorn ferry-boat, which could only take the carriage on the first trip in addition to the rowers. It was pulled up stream by a rope from the shore for a considerable distance, and then set free, when by the conjoint efforts of a man with a long steering-oar, four others pulling at two small stout oars, and the current, the boat was moored to the other side about a quarter of a mile farther down the river. The rain had commenced again to fall, and the journey over the hills was slow; but at length we arrived, got fresh horses and men, and once again set out.

We had now changed our direction, and were ascending the left bank of another still larger river, of which we could only catch occasional glimpses through a thick fringe of

G

willows whose roots were too well watered. The surrounding country was bare, and the road skirted the ancient bank of the river that rose several tens of feet in height like a wall on our right, covered sometimes with coarse grass. But now the river was making a supreme effort to recover its former kingdom, and to follow the road entailed driving slowly through a sheet of water that more than once covered the axle-trees. About 10 P.M. we had made 28 versts, and were once again on the confines of a village. We drove through the gate, but the *yamstchik's* management of his team became increasingly careful, as we neared the great flood which, with its overflowed banks, lay between us and the as yet concealed post-station. At one point the current seemed to take a bend round a grassy promontory, out on to which we drove, only to discover that the swift black stream that swirled past in front of us simply represented part of the flood area with a breadth of at least 150 yards, with evidence of a shallow half-way across where the surface of the water was broken. Our place of vantage was then seen to be nothing more than a little rising ground in the lowlands by the river, and already in the possession of the post-waggon and its armed guard. They had waited there for several hours fearing to cross. When one regarded the immense volume of water as it rolled noiselessly by, dark, dull, stupendous, and, to all appearance, some twenty feet in depth, it seemed madness to attempt to cross. One could discern the unsteady lights of some human habitations about eight versts up the river, and we understood that there was a hamlet not more than seven versts away, but the stars seemed nearer.

It was now past midnight, and the moon, which had shone

for a while, disappeared behind some heavy clouds, which were spasmodically illuminated by flashes of sheet-lightning, while the mutterings of thunder in the distance betokened a renewal of the storm. Some of the men tried to light a fire on the damp grass, and the course of action was debated. By a majority it was resolved that we should at least make an attempt to ford the stream, which was probably by no means so dangerous as it looked. Accordingly our driver was despatched post-haste to the nearest point to seek assistance, and to request the presence of the *ataman* and others to direct us in our endeavour. He returned after an hour, and was soon followed by the *ataman* and some of his fellow-villagers on horseback. The clouds crept off the face of the moon, and the storm passed away to the south; but the sheet-lightning, playing at three points of the compass, served to show with what energy Jupiter Pluvius was still engaged not so very far away. The *ataman* suggested a certain line for us to take, and then the post, which in this remote region consisted of a single light *tarantass*, prepared to show the way. Lashing his horses, and shouting in the wild Siberian fashion, the *yamstchik* entered the deeps at a gallop, which was speedily checked to a slow walk, as the water rushed over the forewheels, and wellnigh covered the hind-wheels, while the horses battled with the current for a footing. At last he reached the place about 75 yards out, where the current did not run so fiercely, and paused a moment to let his team recover breath before they made their plunge into the farther broader flood, which, when they had entered, they were straightway lost to sight in the darkness.

It was now our turn. The *kolyaska* was taken back some distance from the edge, the quintet were flogged to the charging point, and frantically jerked the ponderous vehicle into the tide. The waters rose and swirled around the body of the carriage, and gurgled through the wheels until they were wellnigh overwhelmed, and it almost seemed as if we must shortly float. But they began to retreat, and the rim of the forewheels just showed above the inky surface, when suddenly—what is that furious lashing of the whip? The driver stands upright and hits out as hard as he can at the horses floundering in the water—so hard as to lose his balance and collapse upon the box. We have stuck: one of the team is down. In vain the *yamstchik* attempts to make it rise: so he steps down into the stream, which conceals his thighs, and going round to the horse—the outside left of the *troika*—brings it to its feet. Then he resumes his seat, and flings about his arms, his legs, his whip, yelling meanwhile at the pitch of his voice, but all to no purpose. The *ataman* then harnesses his extra horse, and there is a mighty troubling of the waters, but with as little result. The only thing that remains to be done is to abandon our vessel.

So two of these sturdy Siberian ponies were led up to the side of the carriage, and we mounted their wet backs. My friend went off at once, and the *ataman* rode in front of him to pick his path. I remained behind for a moment to arrange some bags; the five men also stayed to see what could be done for the halting conveyance; then I left them. What a curious predicament! Four figures splashing onwards 50 yards ahead. The dark bank just visible opposite in the light of the kindly moon. Above, a damp, raw atmosphere; below, a cold, black stream flowing so soft, so full, so strong; between, the damp body of a sturdy pony whose only trapping was a leathern bridle. How painfully slow were its steps, with a pause between each as if the creature were meditating where next to plant its foot, and could see through the thick waters where the best bottom lay. It took me 20 yards from the *kolyaska*, continually prodded with the heel of an unkind boot. Then it wanted to turn round and see how far off it had got from its fellows; evidently it did not like this sort of work. But we had now gained the shallow only to forge ahead into the deeper part beyond. Then we were startled by a cry and the sound of a splash, but the animal still moved on. It certainly was deeper now. The water crept above one's boots, and slowly ascended the scale of buttons on one's leggings. The pony become more anxious, and insisted on lengthening the breathing-spaces between each step. Still the water rose. It seemed every moment as if it must swim. But when the tide had reached the level of one's knees, and the creature's belly was well in the water, the flood began to retreat, and each succeeding pace raised one higher out of it. Soon we were beside our companion, who was eager to tell how the sounding *ataman* failed to reach the limit of a certain pool and disappeared therein with his horse, only to come up again a few yards below, while his follower was shown one line at least that it would be well to avoid.

Thereafter we crossed another intervening tongue of land, and came to the river proper, from the far side of which, in response to long-continued calls, the ferry-boat put off; but inasmuch as it was nothing more than a simple rowing-boat, the same precautions were necessary as before, and we went over in detachments. About that time also the pleasing sound of tinkling bells broke on us from the rear, and soon the men came up with the *kolyaska*, which, after being relieved of the weight of its four occupants, had been dislodged with the help of seven horses. Four versts still separated us from the post-station, into the court of which we drove at 3 A.M. cold and wet, and after an hour's halt were again *en route* for Nertchinsk. There is nothing unusual in these incidents; they may be the lot of any one who sets out on this trans-Siberian drive. The only pity is that the advancing railway lessens more and more the chance of such entertainment.

Several methods of ferrying the rivers are still in vogue. Of these mention has already been made of the horse-driven and the oar-propelled boat. The most common type is the

Pendulum ferry-boat on the Nertcha.

pendulum or "swing" ferry-boat, which takes advantage of the current in performing its passage. Again the required size of platform is only gained by lashing two hulks together. A rope, attached to the stern, is then led over the cross-bars that join each of a couple of pairs of upright poles, two of which are set up towards the bow and two near the stern, and thence carried over a series of free-swinging boats to the last of the line, which is anchored in mid-stream. The helm is put down and the current does the rest. Some of the smaller streams were spanned by a cable, along which, by the help of a wheel, the ferry-boat was worked by manual labour.

. . . .

It is, however, when one traverses these rivers in their length that the experience tends to become wearisome. Siberia has immense waterways at its command, but perhaps in no other country are they so little developed. The main route of other days into the country was by water from Tiumen to Tomsk, but the speedier railway is changing this relation, although the cheaper cost of river-travel will still enable it to command a certain amount of custom apart from mere traffic in merchandise. Reference has already been made to the Amur in this capacity, and the Angara has served as another type of the navigable river. But it is when gliding down the Ob or up the Irtish, hemmed in by grievous wastes, that one gains a true idea of Siberian river-travel. Of this more will be said later in its direct bearings on the convicts, for this particular route demands more than a passing reference, even if it be at the expense of partially repeating what has been so often told before.

In journeying, for example, from Tomsk to Tiumen, one first descends the river Tom. Its banks are by no means high though thickly wooded, yet even on this little stream one was impressed with the energy that characterises the laudable attempts directed to make and keep it navigable. Dredgers are almost constantly at work deepening the river-bed, while on a little island in mid-stream a hut could be detected, over which fluttered the flag of the Department of Ways and Communications, and a shallow skiff was moored to the last of a series of trim wooden steps that led up the steep bank, in evident convenience for some lonely watchman.

The Ob is one of those magnificent waterways that have done so much for Siberia. At any one point it gives one rather the impression of a great lake, owing to its exceeding breadth. When the wind blows from the north it is impossible to detect the strong current flowing quietly, steadily, voluminously to the sea beneath the great brown surface billows that look as if they were prepared to roll back to the foot of the Altai Mountains themselves. This is the battle of the wind and of the water, in which the former seems to conquer; but, nevertheless, the river silently obeys the law of its being, which things are an allegory. But when some fixed object, such as one of the myriad buoys or warning-posts, breaks the semblance of calm, then it is that one appreciates the marked velocity of the flow that carries everything on its broad bosom to Arctic realms. Look towards the shore, that is separated from you by yards of turbid stream,—a bank some 15 feet in height, built up of sandy strata gnawed away in the form of a rude giant staircase of colossal breadth descending to the water's edge, whose half-dozen steps are strewn with trees that have slid down from the higher level, and lie in great disorder just as they fell. Some of them rest with their roots in the water, others are in an earlier stage of ruin, their nether parts exposed and bare where the soil, like all that disappearing shore, has been licked off from around their feet. The top step is hidden by a hairy covering of long reedy grass, from which emerge the trees and shrubs. The banks rarely attain to any height, 12 or 15 feet sometimes screen the beyond, but at other times sandy flat expanses remain in view until they disappear into the *taiga* or a haze on the horizon. Across the water there may be a similar growth; more probably in the foreground the eye will be attracted by a fair expanse of yellow sand, and so the two constantly change from one side to the other with the direction of the stream. Occasionally, where the water is deep close up to the river-brink, one has before one the various strata of sandy deposit in good geological section. Sometimes the banks are cloaked over long distances with stately trees—aspen and other poplars, now and again relieved by willows; and even the low willow clothing wears out in time and is replaced by a fir-wood, green to

Fallen trees on the banks of the Ob.

appearance, but when you look into it, black as night. But more often between the trees and the sandy shore lie narrow strips, now of shrubby undergrowth, now of rich grass on which the cattle of the neighbouring village feed daintily. The islands, that seem to float silently past us, are likewise tree-girt, and thus distinctly proclaim their origin. The breadth of the river is borne in upon us as we gaze ahead and are baffled in trying to determine whether the next bend will be to right or left, for there meets the eye the similitude of an expansive lake skirted by a strip of yellow sand, whose breadth is as inconstant as the flinty particles composing it; and above it all the azure and the white clouds.

Very rarely we steam past some settlement spreading along the bank. Nets hung out to dry on poles advertise the staple industry. The boats are moored to the shore— long craft with considerable beam and far-projecting prows. The larger ones are propelled by half-a-dozen men seated at broad-bladed oars, which they pull with no regard to time, while the helmsman stands upright, and with a steering-oar attempts a little sculling on his own account. Sometimes we see individuals fishing with a line out of a smaller skiff, who, when they have caught a sufficiency, paddle homewards up-stream, keeping close to the edge so as to avoid the strength of the current. To take a heavy boat against the stream, horses are employed: they walk along the sand, or even, as in the case of a lumbering barge that was being urged against the current on the Angara at a point considerably below Irkutsk, the team of thirteen that dragged it with difficulty had each its rider, and was up to the knees in water. Sometimes the villages that lurked somewhere behind the halting-stations are visible from the steamer's deck, but it is impossible to see anything, *e.g.*, of Narim unless one scrambles up the bank, when the first erection that meets the eye is a booth at which the second-class passengers renew their straitened commissariat. Two Tunguses hurry along the shore, bending under the weight of as many large sturgeon. The noble ganoids are still in life, and vigorously flap their tails, to the discomfort of the porters. A miserable offer of 12 rubles for one of them is refused by the would-be vendors, who maintain that they know where they can at least get 14 rubles apiece.

Truly these waterways are splendid. Who first rode upon them? What must have been the *coup d'œil* when on the greater Ob of bygone centuries mammoths resorted in companies to drink, and wakened these quiet desolate banks with their wild trumpetings; when out of the thick undergrowth that clad the river's bank sneaked some poor savage in pursuit of a young member of the herd, greedily desirous to win the luscious marrow of his bones. And since these times the Ob has still run on: run past the slower procession of life that thronged its sides or sought protection in its flood, —run past them all to bury its sorrows and its joys in the profound abysses of the Polar Sea. Its sorrows, for is there not the lengthy period when its activity is greatly checked by the cruel frost's strong fetter? its joys, when, the brief summer through, it rolls for ever north on its long inland voyage.

The sunsets on the Ob are gorgeous, especially if the steamer happens to be traversing a south-westerly bend towards evening. The wind has fallen, and the glassy surface of the stream is only broken by a gentle ripple. Two flocks of wild duck are paddling hastily ahead, casting behind them timid glances; four seagulls wheel about the mast. Otherwise there is a strange absence of animal life—out of the water. The only sound comes from the advancing steamer as it cleaves the water. A wooded promontory seems to jut out into the river; it is only the inside of a sharp curve, but for a moment we go due west. Each bank is differently wooded—birch to the left, fir on the right. In the west hang no clouds, but in the zenith a few flecks dot the expanse. Gradually the birches are tinged with yellow, and the dark conifers look darker by reason of the strong light that shines behind them. On either side of the sun's couch a glorious blend of pink and gold tints the sky. Overhead each fleecy speck is bathed in a delicate purple. The brilliant orb sinks slowly behind the fir-trees, and then his rays glint through their topmost branches to strike the upper reaches of the opposing birches. But gradually they fail to penetrate as the sun disappears, and when we round the promontory he is gone; the screaming wild duck follow him, and we are alone. Alone on that great silent mass of

Sunset on the Ob.

water that yet moves ever quietly onward in fulfilment of its destiny! Alone, surrounded by forests that have never as yet resounded to the foot of man! Alone in the depths of Asia! Follow the Ob to the Polar Sea. Ah, there is desolation! And even at that moment we are skirting banks clad with lithe birches that stood out on the promontory, a windy wall; for their branches have grown in the direction of the prevailing breeze, like subjects bowing before their lord. And the gold and the pink where the sun has died give place to the pink alone, and the pink gives place to a delicate blue, and the delicate blue loses itself in the twilight, and then the night covers all.

At one point we stop to take in fresh fuel. At the outset of the journey great piles of logs $2\frac{1}{2}$ feet long monopolised most of the main-deck, but were gradually flung down below to feed the insatiable furnaces. At 12.15 A.M. we are awakened by the energetic whistling of the steamer —a harmony, nay, an exact fifth, for she always blows her fog-horn and her whistle together. The engines have slowed down, and we draw close in to the side at a spot where the fir-banks reach the quite unusual height of perhaps 40 feet. A huge log-fire reveals four dusky figures crawling along the bank, with lamps. A second blaze a little way off is demanded by the precipitous nature of the surroundings, over which progress is slow and difficult. There is no moon, and the sturdy spruce strain upwards into the darkness. A few more shadowy figures make their appearance, and catch the mooring-ropes that are flung to them. Two or three stealthily edge towards the fire, evidently bearing some light burden upon their heads; the lurid glare sets in relief the outlines of women who have come down with laden birch-bark creels and baskets of food for sale. Black bread, milk, eggs, sterlet for a few kopeks, *nelma* or *omul*, they offer you; but the late hour is not conducive to good trade. On the top of the embankment are some half-dozen monumental piles of sawn wood. It was usual for the soldiers from the convict barge that we had in tow to load the vessel with the necessary wood at these stations. This operation had to be repeated every twelve hours on an average.

As we drift towards the west there are more frequent signs of population. Both banks fall in altitude, much of the timber has been cut down, and the land put under cultivation. The Ob also increases immensely in breadth. It is pretty to see the little streams bringing in their tribute. We work along the shore, and perhaps notice it gradually projecting into the river at one point till it ends in a spit of yellow sand; and when we get in line with it, we see it shields the complacent tributary, moving slowly, it almost seems, because the willows gently brush it back.

When we pass into the Irtish, the scenery and environment are very markedly different—a prophecy of what the Ob itself will be one day. The banks of the Irtish present

Village on the banks of the Irtish.

greater variety of interest than do those of the larger stream. Although higher, they show evidence of a comparatively thick population. Unpainted skiffs are drawn up on the banks, bottom upwards, and nets hang out to dry; but the contented cattle lying on the warm sand, and the stacks of hay dotting the green background, convey a more correct idea of the agricultural people in whose midst we are. We have come again amongst the settlers, the number of whose small communities is truly remarkable; while in the too fresh appearance of many of the cottages, and the first rush of carefulness that marks off the newly acquired plot with a little hedge, we learn that two months ago this open land was untenanted. Above Tobolsk there is a great increase in population: at any point one may see peasants standing on the bank; at any bend a village may come into view.

The Irtish winds much more than the Ob, and the greater difficulty of navigation demands a pilot. His task has been lightened considerably by the Department of Ways and Communication. At comparatively short distances numbered grey cabins with red roofs adorn one bank, each protected by a tall white-and-black painted flag-post, from which flutters the white, blue, and red pennant with the crossed axe and pickaxe of the Department. In connection with the stations are red wooden signals (lamplit by night) recording the depth of the water and other needful items of information, which, together with the host of warning-poles, and of red and of white buoys (the former on the right, and the latter on the left bank), reduce the possibility of danger to a minimum.

Animal life is not any more in evidence than on the Ob. At one point two or three flocks of cranes get up and fill the air with their hoarse cries, then slowly wing themselves away to a safe distance. We also saw wild duck and gulls, and from one swampy spot some curlews rose to give vent to their mournful wail. Where the water washed the bank closely with any depth a geological section results when the river falls, showing from the deck of the steamer about 6 feet of lenticular strata of brown peaty soil, on which were growing some hardy spruce, and it in turn rested on a clayey basis of lighter colour in which also the layers were very distinct.

What timber fringed the banks of the Irtish has been almost all felled, and when we take in wood, we no longer, as it were, help ourselves at deserted piles, over each of which floats the flag of the steamboat company that owns them. For any industry is made an excuse to erect log-houses, where the wood-cutters live; and while the lading progresses, women row over from the other side in their

Taking in wood.

peculiar boats with provisions for sale. The cutting down of the forests in Russia has been attended with lamentable results. Her great waterways as such are being lost to the use of humanity. The Volga is shrinking: the steamboats of thirty years ago can no longer travel on its bosom. They have to be built of less draught every year, and the riverbed is being choked up with sandbanks. A short distance below Nijni Novgorod there is a shallow extending across the Volga well called the Calf's Ford. But this contingency will be guarded against in Siberia.

The river season is short. Already on the 3rd September, by our time, one experienced the first snow of the succeeding winter; the sere leaves were falling fast off the infrequent trees, and one felt the first nip of a frost that would soon have the whole country in its grasp. Such voyages may be tedious, but as long as there are romantic souls on the earth, they will not fail to have their lovers.

CHAPTER IV.

MONARCH OR MONK? A LEGEND OF TOMSK.

TOMSK — DESCRIPTION OF THE TOWN — "ALEXANDER'S HOUSE" — THE LIFE OF THEODORE KUZMITCH—HIS DEATH—THE LAST YEARS OF ALEXANDER I.—DID HE ABDICATE?

TOMSK town, which with its 45,000 souls still ranks us second in all Siberia, lies in a province of the same name, the most populous after Tobolsk. It may, in truth, be called a gold-born township, for before 1830 it was little more than a Siberian village. But, in addition to the discovery of gold in the vicinity about that date, it owes much of its importance to its position on the great highroad that unites the East and West. After eight weary days on a river-boat from Tiumen, or half as many in a *tarantass* from Krasnoyarsk, men gather hope when suddenly Tomsk breaks upon their view. Part of the town is built on the edge of a high plateau, which, extending from the foot of the Altai Mountains in the south, somewhat abruptly descends about this latitude to the lowlands of the Ob, that are in turn continuous with the treacherous *tundra* of the north. Part also is situated on the plain below, wedged in between the right bank of the river Tom, a tributary of the Ob, and the bold bluff above. So, in approaching the town from the east, the traveller is unaware of its existence until he wellnigh reaches the broken brink of the high level; and it is this half, too, with its statelier buildings, that first attracts the notice of the river-voyager.

The road from the south affords the same pleasant surprise, for it is only when one stands on the left bank of the Tom,

On the outskirts.

awaiting the paddle ferry-boat of three-horse power, that one becomes aware of the presence of human habitations. After gaining the other side, the traveller passes between two brick pillars, each surmounted by the imperial eagle. These mark the entrance to the town, as also the beginning of a long broad street (if the rough and deeply rutted thoroughfare can be dignified with such a name) that traverses the lower quarter with a continual though gradual ascent. Here the appearance of the buildings still resembles that of a Siberian village, for they consist of two rows of decrepit shanties, each with its little yard enclosed by more or less of a high wooden paling. Sometimes these squalid tenements lack the power of even standing squarely on their foundations by the roadside,—probably because they have none. But as you penetrate farther, by degrees all this is left behind, till at one sharp steep bend you pass into the upper terrace, and soon find yourself in the central square, in the middle of which stands the massive white Troitsa Cathedral, with its golden bulbous dome attended by four cupolas reflecting a pale-blue tint. Opposite its main entrance is the long white Government building, at one corner of which is the artistic little residence of the governor. Tomsk is a strangely unequal town in every sense of the word, for not only is it built on many different levels, but habitations noble and mean contrive to set off one another even in the more aristocratic parts. Towards the north side the irregularity in level necessarily becomes more noticeable. The highest knoll has been secured in the interests of the town: from it rises the watch-tower that surmounts the fire-station. Pacing round the summit of the tower a fireman keeps ceaseless watch, and warns the inhabitants of the time of day by sounding out the hours on a harsh-toned bell. Here also one used to find a hotel, where the lodger who took a room had to content himself with an iron bedstead, mattress, table, and chair. But better days have dawned, and a new establishment opened recently will satisfy the desponding traveller who imagines that he has left all comfort west of the Urals.

Tomsk has a certain charm. It is not the dull sleepy place that one could well imagine it to be. Its noblest edifices command attention: it is the centre of a pretty considerable local trade—*e.g.*, as it is the starting-point of the great post-road across Siberia, thousands of *tarantasses* and other vehicles are built there yearly; and it has "sights" of a very varied order. Be the traveller a physician, he will not regret a visit to the hospital. Be he interested in penology, Tomsk boasts of three prisons. If educational matters attract him, he will find some thirty schools, illustrating a great diversity of principles. These, with the magnificent University opened in 1888, bid fair to make Tomsk the intellectual centre of Siberia.

The University lies on the outskirts of the town. The stately structure stands off the road in a garden, through which run avenues and footpaths. Beside it is the Arboretum, where most of the labour is performed by women. The Observatory peers above the multitude of shrubs and trees that throng the gardens; from it one gets a charming view of the surrounding country. The University consists as yet of but a single faculty [1]—medicine—and of its 400 students only some 30 per cent are Siberians. The others come from the outlying districts of European Russia, and even, it is said, from the Caucasus. But its great treasure is the Library, which is second only to that of St Petersburg. Its nucleus consists of the private collection of Count Stroganoff, which contains amongst other rarities a very early illustrated edition of Luther's Bible, bearing the date 1565, a first edition of 'Daphnis and Chloe,' and a valuable assortment of painted designs of exquisite workmanship from the private collection of Louis XVI., which show evidence of having come originally

[1] A faculty of law will shortly be added.

from the Vatican at Rome. There is also a very fair Archæological Museum, with a startling array of antiquities that he must first explain away who would deny that Siberia too has had her Stone, her Bronze, and her Iron Age. Moreover, it was only in March 1896 that Professor Kastchenko discovered near the town some mammoth bones that had been split open. As he also found close at hand fragments of charred wood, there almost seems to be justification for his assertion that the cleavage was not due to natural causes, but was the work of man desirous to obtain the marrow. Thus he interestingly suggests the probable comtemporaneity of *Homo sapiens* with *Elephas primigenius* in these northerly latitudes.

If the visitor has yet failed to discover anything that arrests his attention, he can at least drive about a town where the *isvostchiks* take fourpence for a course, even if it be over what are nothing more than badly kept country roads. Perhaps he will notice how, in the construction of a house, women bring up the carts laden with bricks, and transfer them thence on broad four-handled trays to the men, who do the building proper. Or maybe, if it is towards evening, he will pass a gang of convicts returning to the local prison after a day's work in the town, chatting pleasantly with the two or three warders, who, armed merely with revolvers, have been in charge of them. But woe to the traveller if he venture out to walk by night, for the uncertain gleam from the electric lamps does little to reveal the insecure and dangerous wooden pavement, whose planks have been surreptitiously removed at many points to serve an infinity of purposes, from use as firewood to repairing crippled roofs.

The environment of Tomsk will not allure the stranger much. The landing-stage on the river, where he might reasonably hope to find some entertainment, is at a distance of three versts from the town, and the road thither (which is on a par with everything of that description in the district) strikes across an arid plain. There also the new railway-station is built, on a piece of ground granted by a majority of the town councillors, to the great inconvenience of themselves and their fellow-citizens.

It will only be a chance if he now learns that he has not seen everything. For Tomsk has still one other choice possession, and her populace regard it with reverent eyes. Indeed they do not care to include it among the "sights" of their town: they love it, treasure it, almost conceal it. If, however, he asks some pensive *droshky*-driver who has drawn up by the side of the road (for there are no stands, and the *isvostchiks* take up a position where they choose) to bear him to "Alexander's House," the prospect of a modest fare of 20 kopeks tends to shake the once firm resolution of the *isvostchik* that he at least will conduct no stranger to gaze with unhallowed eyes on Tomsk's most holy memory, and, although somewhat reluctantly, he finally yields the point. Quickly our driver sought out the Monasterskaya, and stopped at the courtyard entrance of what was an imposing house. We got out and entered the yard, which was a scene of great activity. Some men were carrying boxes and bales from the house to carts in which stood sturdy draught-horses, while others were lading them. Numerous storehouses and small sheds were built irregularly round the yard, and the house of the merchant Khromov still seemed to be the centre of some form of business. The court extended to the back of the house, where the outhouses partook more of the nature of stables and cart-sheds. When once the rear of the main building has been reached, the visitor observes on its other side a square plot of ground corresponding to the courtyard. This probably formed a pleasure-garden in days gone by, but is now like unto the garden of the sluggard. At least, from what one can see through the tall black paling that to-day surrounds this sacred spot, one would imagine that no tending hand had touched it for many years. The grass grows rankly on what was once a lawn. The paths are buried under a wild waste of weeds. Some dark dejected spruces serve to increase the gloom.

A woman soon appeared from a backdoor of the house, and, opening a padlocked gate in the paling, allowed us to enter the enclosure. She led the way to a corner of the square, where in the shade of a brooding conifer stood what seemed to be a very open wooden hut. Closer inspection disclosed, however, that what had appeared to be "Alexander's House" was not so in reality, but was merely a protecting shed: the real thing lay inside. The outward covering had not struck one as being of any size; but this quaint domicile beneath, this *maisonette*, how insignificant, how humble!

Our guide entered, devoutly crossing herself. The door was apparently left open without fear,—no one could enter but by that padlocked gate, and the hut was well protected by its ample case. One stooped in crossing the threshold, which lay on the left of the front exposure as you face the house, and thereafter became aware of a short passage that ended to all appearance in a recess. But off the right there opened the single chamber of this house,—the home of him whose memory is still revered.

A window not 2 feet square admits through its dull glass what rays of light can penetrate the thick branches of the surrounding trees and bend under the eaves of the protecting edifice. In the corner immediately to the left of the door is the whitewashed brick stove, along a wing of which is placed a plank-bed with pillow to match. This is so arranged that the head is next the wall, and is of such a breadth that it takes up almost all the spare room between the stove proper and the door. From the free end of the stove to the opposite wall extends a shelf, now crowded with relics of the former

The home of Theodore Kuzmitch.

resident. On it you may see some sacred literature, the cowl and garments of an anchorite, cooking utensils of the simplest quality—china cups, a metal teapot curiously enough, and a spoon. The wall above the bench is hidden by numerous portraits of the great monarch Alexander I., whom one imagines to have been, perhaps, the special hero of the late occupant of this room, or, as is more likely, the reigning monarch of his time. But these pictures differ from those in any ordinary Russian house in this, that they represent the Emperor at different periods of his life. The apparent design of this hero-worshipper has been to collect as complete a series as possible of the object of his adoration. One sketch supposed to represent the monarch in death is particularly striking, and you wonder why there is placed alongside of it the picture of an older man also in his last long sleep; and as you gaze at the two, you almost fancy that you see a resemblance. But this is absurd.

The wall opposite the door is now a mass of *ikons* and sacred pictures, but these are later accretions. An altar stands against the wall, and serves as the depository for another group of *ikons*, amongst which are dispersed candlesticks with dimly burning tapers, while a lamp faintly but steadily illumines the regular *ikon* in one of the far corners of the room. In the opposite corner by the window a censer hangs, and the musty odour of incense pervades the cheerless chamber. On the fourth wall, between the window and the door, are disposed prints and lithographs of a white-haired and bearded old man, dressed in a loose single garment to which the modern dressing-gown best corresponds. He holds one hand across his narrow chest, and has shoved the other carelessly into the hempen belt that gathers his mantle about him. Beneath one of the portraits is the inscription, "The Bondservant of God, the old man Theodore Kuzmitch, who passed a hermit life in Tomsk, and died in 1864 in the cell of Khromov."

Such is the little house that the Tomsk people consider to be one of their chiefest possessions. For the history of the mysterious being for whose sake they venerate it we are most indebted to his patron the merchant Khromov, who built the cell for him, and to whom alone was at first revealed the secret of his life. In the following account, which is largely drawn from an abstract of Khromov's memoirs, some of the leading features in this extraordinary story are briefly stated.

Somewhere in the "thirties" an old man appeared in the town of Tomsk. He had come from European Russia with a prisoner band, having been sentenced to exile in Siberia for vagrancy by the court of a small town in the government of Perm. After a short stay in the Forwarding Prison at Tomsk, he was conducted to the village of Zertzal, in the government of Tomsk, as his place of residence. On settlement he gave very little satisfaction to all eager inquiries about his past, merely stating that he had received twenty strokes with the *plet* for vagrancy, and giving as name the commonplace appellation of Theodore Kuzmitch. In outward appearance he was of high stature, while his years might have been put down at sixty. Add to this that he had a noble carriage, could with all truthfulness be styled good-looking, and ever spoke in a quiet sedate manner, so that from the first his peasant neighbours felt bound to treat him with marked respect. His general bearing and manner of conversation proclaimed him to be an educated man, and notwithstanding the simplicity of his life and speech, it was evident that he was not a man of common origin.

Amongst his fellow-villagers was a convict who had reached the stage of a "free-command," and was employed in Government works there. Old Theodore took an interest in him, and, desiring company, shared his hut with the fierce creature. The following year the peasantry roused themselves and built a log cabin for him, in which he lived for over eleven years a life of self-effacement, with a bare subsistence on bread and water. He would, however, make occasional excursions to the neighbouring villages, where it was his peculiar pleasure to gather the children round him and teach them their letters. Latterly, on the invitation of a peasant named Latishev, he left Zertzal and took up residence in Krasnorjetchinsk, the village of his host, who erected a special hut for him which he occupied in winter, while in summer he passed his time in the woods beside the woodcutters. His private property merely included the clothes on his back and a few sacred books.

It was in the year 1858 that, at the invitation of the merchant Khromov, Kuzmitch passed a winter on his farm, about 4 versts out of Tomsk. Ultimately Khromov built for him in a corner of his garden the little domain described above, where his guest spent the greater part of the last years of his life in prayer and fasting.

The kind-hearted merchant had first made the acquaintance of Kuzmitch in 1852. His curiosity had been aroused by the tales which a friend recounted to him about the aged hermit, and having occasion to pass through the village of Krasnorjetchinsk, he resolved to seek him out. This was in the summer-time, and Kuzmitch was as usual with the woodfellers, sharing a modest little home with his peasant host. Their dwelling was situated at a distance of 2 versts from the village that formed the centre of operations for those who were at work, and it lay on the bank of a rivulet. Khromov relates how he arrived at the cell, made the sign of the cross, and entered, as the door stood open. He saluted the white-haired inmate, who, in true Russian style, demanded of him whence he had come and whither he was bound. "I come from Tomsk, and go to Yeniseisk on matters connected with gold-mining," answered the merchant. To his surprise his interrogator would not let the subject drop, but talked long on the gold industry, finally exclaiming, "Vainly you are occupied with the gold industry, for without it God will sustain you." Khromov was fascinated by his new acquaintance, and used to pay him a short visit each time he passed that way. But on whatever themes they discoursed—and they were varied — the old man always returned to this maxim, "Do not endeavour to discover the mines; thou hast enough, and Another will provide."

In 1859, while resident on Khromov's country estate, Kuzmitch took seriously ill, and his host, thinking that it was high time he learned something about his mysterious guest, asked him on several occasions if he would not disclose his identity. But the reply, if continually the same, was at least decided: "No; that cannot be revealed—never."

His illness was of a somewhat serious nature, and it was with great difficulty that those who were anxious about him could persuade him to take anything beyond his accustomed bread and water. Khromov remarks how during this time he observed that the knees of the anchorite were covered with excrescences, the result of persistence in a kneeling posture during prayer, and it was difficult to know to what extent he suffered, as he kept so very much to himself. He exercised great care in the selection of his visitors, and when later he was restored to some measure of health, he never left his cell except to enter a church. If he ever referred to his vagrant life or journey to Siberia, it was only to speak in the kindest terms of his fellow-prisoners, as also to eulogise the treatment that he had received at the hands of the convoy soldiers, and in short from all who had had anything to do with him. It seems that he now removed for a change to a Kossak village not far off, and lived in the house of one of the inhabitants. He had, however, a renewal of his old trouble, and not being perfectly happy in his new quarters, was quite ready, even in his weak state of health, to accept an invitation from Khromov to stay with him in Tomsk. Knowing how matters stood, the worthy merchant went himself to bring his friend to town : this was in 1863. Kuzmitch, fearing that there might be some well-intentioned effort made to keep him in the Kossak village, resolved not to disclose his plan of leaving till the last moment, when he engaged in quiet conversation with his host, and explained to him very shortly the reasons for his sudden departure. This device was successful, and during the time spent in arranging him and Khromov comfortably in the latter's *tarantass*, the whole village came out to see him off. In return Kuzmitch merely said, " I thank you all for everything you have done for me."

The journey was taken slowly, and it was only after a couple of days that the party eventually arrived at their destination. Khromov, who was much affected by the low state of his friend's health, desired to pass the first night with him in the little wooden house which he had prepared for him. He relates that the old man spent much of the night in prayer, and that he could repeatedly catch the words, " I thank Thee." He was roused at 5 A.M. by the patient, who said that he felt better, adding that the cause of the improvement was a vision that he had seen in the night-watches. His look seemed to be keener and his conversation brighter, and Khromov hoped that perhaps he might still live. On the morning of the 20th January, as Khromov was leaving for his business, he asked that the old man would bless him.

"Nay, rather," said he, " bless me." In the course of the day the merchant ran over several times from his office, but did not speak much with Kuzmitch, who was lying on his hard bed, with his face to the stove. In the afternoon Khromov had occasion to go a short distance out of town on some business affair, but was soon hastily summoned by his nephew, who reported that the aged sufferer had suddenly become worse, and might at any moment pass away. The merchant returned home at once, and on arrival found the little cell crowded with anxious friends who had come to make inquiries, having heard of the serious turn matters had taken. Kuzmitch was tossing restlessly about, now lying on one side, now on the other, but saying nothing. Khromov's wife sat by him, powerless to give relief. He suffered, like an infant, in silence, and his only action was to continually make the sign of the cross.

About 9 P.M. the visitors departed, and Khromov was left alone with the old man. He asked to be raised in his bed. He sat up for a little, but evidently had not strength for the exertion, for he fell back, and requested to be laid on his left side. He lay for a little while in this posture, and then suddenly turned on his back. The watcher noticed a distinct change in his eyes, and sent for wax-candles, for the end was not far off. Kuzmitch once again asked his benefactor to lay him on his right side, and for a moment he seemed to find satisfaction in weakly clasping the merchant's hand. Then came a short sharp struggle with the last enemy, a single long-drawn sigh, and Khromov was left alone. " Quietly and peacefully, without a moan, died the servant of God ; his right hand grasped a crucifix, and his left hand lay upon it. We wept for our father, the man of prayer and our instructor, and then proceeded to prepare his body for interment." So runs the unvarnished narrative.

We learn also that they dressed the body in a "new white shirt," but did not employ that upper garment already described as having a resemblance to a dressing-gown, and for this reason. While Theodore was still alive, Madame Khromov once asked him in the simplicity of her heart, with reference to his usual attire, "Father, in the event of death, shalt thou be clothed in that black dressing-gown?" "Nay," he replied; "I am no monk." And Khromov carried out his wish the more readily, as he well knew the surpassing humility of his strange guest. "Friend," he had said to him once, "I am not great." These incidents have their interest, in that they are two of the few instances on which Kuzmitch ever referred to himself.

His body was carefully deposited in a chaste coffin of cedar-wood, and, by his wish, his grave is in the monastery at Tomsk. There was a large assemblage gathered on the 23rd January to witness the last rites and to do honour to this well-loved saint. The Archimandrite addressed a few words to the crowd, in which he briefly alluded to the suffering life of their late friend, as also to his travels, for this side of the old man's life had exercised a strong fascination over the populace.

It seems, then, that with one important exception Theodore Kuzmitch, as he chose to call himself, spoke to no one on the subject of his origin, nor ever dropped hints as to his identity, except occasionally of a negative kind. It was his secret, and it almost seemed as if he would carry it with him to the grave. On one occasion Madame Khromov, somewhat exasperated at his reticence on this topic, said, "Father dear, disclose to me at least the name of thy guardian angel." "That God knows," was his quiet reply, and more than this he would confide to no one.

It was only natural that round the story of the life of such an unusual personage should cluster a tangled growth of fanciful and far-fetched tales. He was popularly credited with a marvellous power of foresight, which was probably nothing more, as is often the case, than deep insight into character. Thus they say in all simplicity that on one occasion a priest named Israel, who was formerly attached to the Cathedral of Archangel, desired to see the old man while yet he was with Latishev at Krasnorjetchinsk. He reached their humble home towards evening, and without any ceremony stepped into Kuzmitch's room, crossed himself, and proceeded to salute him. The startled occupant, still sitting on a bench, briefly made answer, "Good day, Father Israel," and this "when as yet he had not heard of him or his arrival, or named his name." A similar story is told of him, on the occasion of a visit which he received from a priest who belonged to Krasnoyarsk. They are probably the same incident, with merely a difference in the name. The best instances of Kuzmitch's remarkable perspicacity are, however, related in connection with private interviews that he had with people who went to consult him when in difficulty. This makes it the more probable that he was gifted with a very remarkable power of observation and insight into character rather than with any supernatural power such as the average Russian is so ready to believe in. There was in particular one woman, a Government official, resident for some time in Krasnorjetchinsk, who used to call on him frequently to ask his blessing on any new projects she was about to undertake. She recounts how he often seemed to foresee her wants, and sometimes gave her advice in epigrammatic sayings.

Another somewhat extreme episode is to the effect that

Khromov, intending to visit Kuzmitch on one particular occasion when passing through Krasnorjetchinsk on his way to the mines, suggested to his wife, who was to accompany him, that she should take a linen shirt of the finest quality as a gift for the old man. But she considered that it would be better to supply him with a garment of some thicker material, and so took a coarser woollen article. To her surprise, when making the presentation, she was reminded by the aged recipient that her husband's wish had been that she should provide for him a shirt of fine linen, and that therefore she ought to have accomplished his desire. "But," he added, " for me, who am now a vagrant, what you have given is more than meet."

Again, in the year 1867, Khromov happened to call on a brother merchant in Moscow, and in the course of conversation began to talk about this strange individual. The man whom he was visiting said that when he was in business in Krasnoyarsk, he had called on Kuzmitch, who confronted him with these extraordinary words, "Why didst thou take that copper money? it was not for thee." "And," confessed the Siberian trader, "I did verily on one occasion lay hands on money that was not mine, but you may be sure that no one knew about it!"

One of the many visitors to the cell in Khromov's garden was a highly respected lady member of the community in Tomsk. According to her own account, she once omitted to make the sign of the cross on entering Kuzmitch's cell, when he addressed her thus: "And tell me, lady, which Tzar honourest thou the more, the worldly or the heavenly?" Taken much aback, she replied, "Dear father, the heavenly." Upon this he answered, "How is it that thou didst not do honour to the heavenly Tzar? thou camest and didst not pray." And much more he spoke to her in a similar strain. Another time she took her young daughter to see him, and the aged hermit turning to the mother said, "See, beloved, this little bird will ultimately grow to feed and shelter thee." Later the girl was sent to the Irkutsk Institute to be educated, which she only left to be married to a naval officer serving in the Amur province. "And," says the chronicler, "in 1871 there arrived in Tomsk this young damsel and her husband, and she took her mother back to live with her, and so was fulfilled the prophecy of the old man Theodore Kuzmitch."

Two other sayings of his may be recorded. He showed intimate knowledge of all matters connected with the State, and frequently discussed political questions. He was once heard to remark, "But the beloved imperial service is not without its needs"; and once again, more significantly, " The house of Romanov is firmly rooted, and deep are its roots."

. . . .

Who was this mysterious saint, this reader of men's thoughts, this prophet, this unknown personage without beginning of days? There are some people who know or think that they know everything, and the Tomsk populace will tell you without any hesitation that he was none other than Alexander I. This is the creed of all Siberia as to that strange individual. And so the people call his cell "Alexander's House," have covered its walls with portraits of the Emperor (and now you do not wonder that you see a resemblance between him and Theodore Kuzmitch), and venerate the relics of the departed great in the manner that only Russians can. Khromov himself is mainly responsible for this belief, for he has declared that shortly before death the self-named Theodore Kuzmitch gave him papers showing conclusively that he was none other than his Emperor: these papers Khromov took back to St Petersburg with him. It has been the lot of almost every Russian emperor to have it said of him that he did not die according to official bulletin; but for those who love this sort of mystery a better case can hardly be made out than in the instance of Alexander I.

Born in the year 1777, a son of Paul by his marriage with Maria of Wurtemburg, he soon showed himself to be possessed of a mind of his own. He received a liberal education at the hands of his grandmother, the Empress Catherine, with the assistance of foreign tutors. In the year 1793 he married Elizabeth of Baden, and was called to succeed his father on the throne in 1801. At first everything augured well. The charitable young ruler commenced his reign by a series of generous reforms, that were especially welcome after the somewhat austere rule of his father. The country was again opened up to foreigners, and permission to travel abroad was granted in turn to Russians. The strict press censorship was relaxed, and the secret police service was in part allowed to fall into abeyance. But there were even further-reaching schemes. The question of the emancipation of the serfs was mooted, and, if not a *fait accompli* until 1861, it now first assumed the air of probability, and much was done to alleviate their lot. Very lenient also was his attitude towards Sectarians and Dissenters. "Reason and experience," says one of his edicts, "have for a long while proved that the spiritual errors of the people, which official sermons only cause to take deeper root, cannot be cured and dispelled except by forgiveness, good examples, and tolerance. Does it become a Government to employ violence and cruelty to bring back these wandering sheep to the fold of the Church?"[1] Surrounding himself with a body of young Ministers, Alexander pushed his reforms into every department of the State. Political and educational institutions were remodelled, and the Council of the Empire was formed, which, including the chief dignitaries of the State, became the legislative power in the country.

But even more in foreign affairs was it felt that with Alexander's accession there had begun a new *régime*. In July 1801 he put an end to hostilities with England, and being desirous to remain at least outwardly on good terms with France, commenced negotiations respecting the indemnification of Bavaria, Wurtemburg, and Baden in Germany, and Naples in Italy. Napoleon showed very little sincerity in the matter, and Alexander joined the Coalition of 1805; but at the battle of Austerlitz the combined Austrian and Russian forces were routed by the First Consul. The following year Alexander, who, feeling that Napoleon must be crushed, still inclined to war, allied himself with Prussia, only to be again defeated at Eylau and Friedland. The Treaty of Tilsit (1807) was the outcome, on which occasion Alexander and Napoleon talked together for two hours on a raft. Its articles decreed the fall of Prussia, a few states being left to Frederic William III. out of Napoleon's deference to Alexander's wish. The Tzar soon after declared war on England, and thus reversed his previous policy, in order to fall into line with that of France. This change in external politics involved a change in his home advisers. He also attacked Sweden, the ally of England, and it was at this time that Finland came into the possession of Russia (1809). While letting Napoleon bear the brunt of a contest with Austria, Alexander entered into conflict with Tur-

[1] Rambaud's History of Russia, tr. by L. B. Lang, ii. 312.

key, and this war continued until the Peace of Bucharest (1812).

Not for long was it possible that France and Russia should thus remain in league. Many causes led to an open rupture. Mutual mistrust and jealousy, together with the more personal incident of the abandonment of Napoleon's projected marriage with the sister of Alexander, had mainly served to bring this about. The "Patriotic War" followed, with the burning of Moscow, and the destruction of the Grand Army (1813). Thereafter Alexander made an offensive and defensive alliance with Frederic William of Prussia, and the struggle with the conqueror was renewed. During a short armistice the allies had time to repair their once more shattered forces (Lützen, 1813): it was the lull before the final tempest, which soon broke ominously on Bonaparte. Spain had now been lost to him, the Prince of Sweden had joined the Coalition, Austria had again become restive. This time fortune favoured the Coalition, and the occupation of Paris and downfall of Napoleon quickly succeeded one another. Round Alexander centred the consequent diplomatic and political arrangements. By the Congress of Vienna he rested content with only a portion of Poland, and in the end carried out more loyally than the other two co-partitioners (Prussia and Austria) the terms of that treaty which bore on the ill-fated land. In 1815 men saw the restoration of Poland under Alexander as king, who presented the country with a new constitution.

Through his influence Russia had become the leading Power on the Continent. This was the supreme moment of his authority: soon after a great change came over the liberal-minded Tzar. The Congresses of Aix-la-Chapelle (1818) and Troppau (1820) had served to show the influence of the man as a factor in European politics; but on the other hand such demonstrations as attended the reaction in Germany in favour of constitutional government were little tasteful to this champion of divine right. "He grew gloomy and suspicious. His last illusions had flown, his last liberal ideas were dissipated. After the Congresses of Aix-la-Chapelle and Troppau he was no longer the same man. It was at Troppau that Metternich announced to him, with calculated exaggeration, the mutiny of the Semenovski, his favourite regiment of Guards. From that time he considered himself the dupe of his generous ideas, and the victim of universal ingratitude. He had wished to liberate Germany, and German opinion had turned against him. . . . He had sought the sympathy of vanquished France, and at Aix-la-Chapelle a French plot had been discovered against him. He had longed to restore Poland, and Poland only desired to free herself completely."[1] The result was that the Emperor, who had moved too fast for his slow-stepping country, faced round, and completely reversed his youthful home-policy of toleration. The revolt in Greece unconsciously served to bring him into complete opposition with the feeling of his people. They were strongly in sympathy with the weaker party in this infamous struggle, whereas Alexander contented himself with addressing a few harmless notes to the Porte, as he considered the rising to be an insurrection. In 1824 there was a terrible inundation at St Petersburg, which the Russian people openly affirmed to be a judgment on the unavenged massacre of the Greek population in Constantinople (1821). But, far more than this, the death of his daughter whom he adored, and the rumours of a Russo-Polish conspiracy against the house of Romanov, wholly unnerved the once

[1] *Op. cit.*, ii. 320.

brilliant man. He was in advance of his day, and his noblest resolutions to promote the good of his and other countries had been coldly and suspiciously regarded, and he became like unto those around him. In September 1825 he set out on a journey to the Crimea for the sake of his health, but died at Taganrog on December 1. And the horrified Russian people likewise referred to the wrath of God "the premature and mysterious death of Alexander." So far received history.

To return to Khromov, who died only a few years ago. Relying on the papers that he received from Theodore Kuzmitch, he held to the end that Alexander I. of Russia, like Charles V. of Germany and Christina of Sweden, abdicated the throne through disappointment and chagrin, desirous to be quit of the reins of government and at peace from the strife of tongues. Alexander "died" in 1825, aged forty-eight. Theodore Kuzmitch appeared in Tomsk somewhere in the "thirties," after having led a vagrant life for several years, and died in 1864, at which date Alexander would have been eighty-seven, if Khromov is correct. In support of his theory there is also to be adduced the resemblance in the portraits between Alexander and this old vagabond, as they adorn the walls of his humble dwelling in Khromov's garden. Coming home across the Urals, we had as travelling companion for a portion of the journey an old Kossak officer who had not heard much about Kuzmitch. He listened quietly to my fellow-traveller's narration of the story, and then added that he was a boy in St Petersburg at the time when the remains of the deceased Emperor were brought up from the south, and that he remembered distinctly how it was quite openly remarked that the body that had thus been transported home was not that of Alexander. "And also," he said, "it was a cause of comment at the time that people were not allowed to pass by and look on the face of their late Emperor, as he lay in state, according to custom." I also asked one of the professors in Tomsk University for his opinion on the whole matter, thinking that he at least would be above all popular fancies. He rather surprised me by saying, "Well, if the old man was not Alexander, he was at any rate some one very highly connected at Court." Such, then, is this little episode, it may be in Russian history, it certainly is in the history of Tomsk.

It is needless to remark that the best Russian historians do not credit the theory that was to Khromov more than fact, while others relegate it to the number of those questions that can never now be solved. This at least is beyond all doubt, that it will be many years before the belief is eradicated from the mind of the Tomsk populace, that for a season they had their Emperor dwelling amongst them in all humility, and knew him not.

CHAPTER V.

ON THE MARCH.

DEPARTURE OF A CONVICT GANG FROM THE TOMSK FORWARDING PRISON — THE PERESÍLNI PRISON AT MOSCOW — OVERCROWDING — THE RUSSIAN MUJIK AT HOME — LODGING-HOUSES IN ST PETERSBURG — TIUMEN FORWARDING PRISON — A CONVICT BARGE — LIFE ON THE RIVER — ARRIVAL AT TOMSK.

A convict.

IT is a bright morning towards the end of June. As our horses climb the rising ground to the north-east of Tomsk where lies the Peresílni or Forwarding Prison, a heavy haze enshrouds the lower quarter of the town. Soon we have left the last houses behind; but in front of us we can now see the grim palisade, typical of most Siberian prisons. It is commonly, as here, some 15 feet in height, while the individual stakes composing it preserve their natural appearance, and are pointed or rounded according to the whim of the constructor. Above it, as seen from a distance, peer the dull red roofs of the low barracks that comprise the prison proper; but as we approach nearer they gradually drop within, till there only remain visible the church tower, and the goodly edifice of brick—the *natchalnik's* house—that intersects the palisade at the centre of what is thus constituted the front exposure. Soldiers in white linen tunics, cloth caps covered with a similar material, and dark-green pantaloons tucked into tall boots, are standing about with bayonets fixed. A dozen loafers have gathered at the spot, and chatter to one another, or critically examine the *telyegas* that are employed for the transport of political prisoners, the sick and aged, and the belongings of a convict gang. The hum of suppressed excitement is audible; even the stolid soldiers are not unaffected by it. A large iron-bound gate discloses itself in the stockade at that point where it becomes continuous with the wall of the governor's house; in one of the wings is a wicket, guarded by a sentry. As we drive up, a sound of voices, accompanied by the rattling of chains, proceeds from the other side of the wall. But all at once the tumult ceases, and a stentorian voice raises itself above the faint murmurs.

"Gotovo?" (Ready?), "Otkroi" (Open). A fumbling of keys ensues; the lumbering bolt turns noisily within the lock, and the wings of the heavy wooden gate swing open upon the first of the convict band. They step out briskly in Indian file to the harsh music of their iron fetters. Dressed in the summer garb of unbleached linen, over which some choose to wear their grey frieze *khalat*, while others have it slung round their backs, they march forward a few paces and then lounge about till the whole of the party has passed out. You notice that each man bears upon his shoulder a sack or bundle, of dimensions apparently varying with the amount of his personal property. In his hand he carries a pan and tea-kettle, or suspends them from his waist-belt. The soldiers spring to "Attention" and surround the gang at intervals, facing them. The prisoners busy themselves adjusting their iron anklets or their culinary utensils. The idlers walk round and round the group, now talking a few words, now lending a helping hand—nothing more, and that only from a morbid curiosity. At length the convicts deposit their burdens on the *telyegas*, and the appearance of a dozen men, mostly young, in blouses of different shades and breeches of varied pattern, following slowly in the wake of a special waggon laden with small trunks and boxes, shows that the procession is almost at an end: these were the politicals.[1] The gates close again on the last of them.

Political prisoners, together with the women and all children under fifteen years of age, have the right to be conveyed by *telyega*. This arrangement also holds for any of the ordinary criminals who may fall ill on the march. Politicals may even go by themselves in *tarantass* if they have sufficient means; but they must pay the expenses of their convoy not only *en route*, but also back to the point whence it came. It does not often happen that they can afford this luxury: once only did I see advantage taken of it.

The party numbered about 350, of whom fourteen were political. The captain of the convoy, a bronzed-looking individual with a grey beard, was the last to appear. Under him were some twenty soldiers, the number sent being usually in the proportion of one to about every twenty prisoners. Quickly he gave his orders. Some three or four soldiers marched off at ease, then the convicts followed in an extenu-

[1] The term political is used throughout in place of the longer equivalent political prisoner.

ated body flanked on either side by an occasional soldier, then came another handful of guards at the rear. The women and children who were voluntarily accompanying certain of the prisoners formed the next body: they walked, or were ensconced in the *telyegas*, while one or two soldiers marched beside them. Shortly after the others had moved off the political prisoners set out, tramping, of their own accord, behind their special cart. They had more soldiers to look after them in proportion to their numbers. Such was the start on the 2000-mile march which lay before the majority of the band to the silver mines of Nertchinsk.

"When will the party reach Irkutsk, say?" we ask the commandant. "In three months." Three months later, as I was visiting the little local prison at Nijni-Udinsk, which is 484 versts west of Irkutsk, the *natchalnik*, who was personally conducting me over it, was suddenly accosted by one of his soldiers, who intimated that an expected gang had just arrived. We got round into the open square in time to see the gates unbarred, and the same party that I saw set out from Tomsk tramped into the prison-yard. Some of the convicts sank down on the ground exhausted. The political prisoners, at once distinguishable by their ordinary clothes and by the haversack slung across one shoulder, withdrew into a corner of the yard and lay down, or stood about, talking to one another. And as the gate in the enclosing palisade still remained open to admit the *telyegas*, a cordon of soldiers posted themselves, and stood at "Attention" watching them. The women had not been conducted into this yard, but had been led off elsewhere. But one had contrived to linger behind and gazed longingly in the direction of a stalwart form that would not, perhaps could not, respond to that mute appeal. He hid himself among his fellows, but she sat by the gate and watched, mounted on the two small green boxes that she had herself lifted off the *telyega*. How long she would have waited there I do not know; but two soldiers who were off duty saw her, spoke to her kindly, took up her baggage, and after one final parting glance she followed them reluctantly.

Tomsk is, however, as almost every one knows, an advanced point on the convict route across Siberia: from this town the march proper begins. To see where this now famous experience commences we must go back to certain of the larger Russian cities, by preference Moscow, and visit the Peresilni Prison there. As it has been described somewhat minutely by previous investigators, it seems superfluous to do more than simply outline its leading features. Situated in one of the humbler suburbs of the town, it presents a somewhat imposing appearance. It is a three-storeyed solid brick building, clean and well lighted, with large airy corridors. During the daytime little restraint is exercised upon the prisoners, so that one of them was able to come down to the main entrance to get a key from a warder there. On this spot the darker rays of Russian criminality, many of which have their origin in some of the most remote parts of the European portion of the empire, are brought to a focus. This prison is also put to the secondary use of serving as a house of detention for all passportless individuals who may have been arrested within the precincts of the great city, having wandered thither from the surrounding country. Their identity and native village are then determined, and they remain in the prison until such time as a party shall be made up which goes in that direction, when they are joined to it, and conducted home again.

Prisoners bound directly for Sakhalin leave in the spring

(March and April) by boat from Odessa, *viâ* the Suez Canal, Hongkong, and Nagasaki. Such a transport vessel as the Yaroslav, which belongs to the so-called "Volunteer Fleet," is built to carry 800 souls; and while the men are despatched at one time, female convicts, together with the women and children voluntarily accompanying male convicts, are sent at another time. The trip occupies two months as a rule, and after October all navigation to the north of Vladivostok is closed owing to the ice.[1] In spring also commences the great movement of convicts by land. Although undoubtedly in Siberia progress is made with their transportation across the country in winter, yet the journey between Moscow and the Siberian frontier is only undertaken during the summer. The consequence is, that although as at the moment when one visited the Moscow Peresilni Prison—in September—there were only some 300 or 400 people in a place that was built to accommodate at least 1000, with the procession of the winter months the building gradually becomes filled up, and there is a tendency to overcrowding, so that by the spring, shortly before the first batch has been despatched to Nijni, the conditions may become alarming from the Western point of view.

Upon the overcrowding in Russian and Siberian prisons much has been written, some writers denying it, while others

[1] The following statistics relate to 1894, and may be taken as typical. The Yaroslav left Odessa on March 28 with a contingent of 802 male convicts, and discharged them at Alexandrovsky-Post, Sakhalin, on May 18: one man died on the voyage. On August 27 she again left Odessa with a similar complement, and reached her destination on October 22: on this occasion there were three deaths. The steamship Moscow left a few days later with 142 female convicts and 23 of their children ; she also carried 131 women and 248 children, who were voluntarily accompanying the male convicts. These figures represent the total influx of penal population into Sakhalin for that year.

have given thrilling accounts of this sad feature of the prison life. It is not a question, however, on which to judge hastily. I may say that I have seen overcrowding: Tiumen Prison seems to be in an almost chronic state of congestion, while the limited size of the *étapes* simply means overcrowding every time a gang of more than a certain number is sent along the road. The overcrowding occurs where we would naturally expect it, and where it can hardly be avoided under present circumstances. Thus Tiumen is not unfrequently overcrowded, because only at intervals of a week or ten days do convict-barges leave for Tomsk, and within a given period they may carry away fewer people than pour into the prison. Tomsk is not so crowded, because parties set out regularly every week on foot, sometimes oftener. Tomsk Forwarding Prison has, unfortunately, acquired an unenviable reputation. But from what I saw, the prison at Tiumen was much the less desirable place of the two, and yet the people of that town consider it a well-conducted institution compared with others farther to the south.

Again, the peculiar habits of the Russian must be taken into account. It is not enough to say that these go for nothing—that there are certain hygienic laws that hold for all mankind, as, *e.g.*, that every man must have so many cubic feet of air. Such propositions are not laws till men become accustomed to them.

Come and see the low-class Russian as he lives at home in the gloomier haunts of St Petersburg. It is a little after midnight. Perhaps some late visitor walks at a smart pace homewards, some student rolls in the direction of his lonely lodging. Otherwise, save for an occasional *isvostchik* who has drawn up by the edge of the pavement, and half reclines, half sits on his narrow perch with his head on his breast, wrapped in profound slumber, and the drowsy *dvorniks* seated by the courtyard entrances or lying on a bench hard by, the electric-lighted streets are desolate. Our *cortége* of three *droshkies* glides quickly along the partly wood-paved thoroughfare; but as we near the lower quarter of the town the neat hexagonal sections of pine give way to coarser cobbles, over which our vehicles rattle with sharp jarring notes. Tall factories loom above us, but these we also pass, and descend into smaller streets or *pereüloks* flanked by unsubstantial, uninviting buildings. At last our leader halts at the gate in a high paling that hinders access to the courtyard of one of these houses. The detective who accompanies our party springs out, whispers a few words to the surprised *dvornik*, and we pass in. We cross the yard, come to a low building containing a few rooms, enter it and walk along a dark passage; the detective leads, and finds his way by means of an uncertain candle. We reach a room, and the stove that heats both it and a neighbouring apartment roars with the straw that has just been piled into it. We open the door and a warm unsavoury odour rushes out. It is a chamber perhaps 22 feet in length by 16 in breadth. A narrow passage extends to the opposing wall, between a couple of platforms which are raised some 30 inches above the floor and occupy the rest of the room. On and underneath these lie crowds of sleeping men: their deep low breathing is very audible, while some snorers combine to produce a greater effect. One of the sleepers, disturbed by the invasion, rises on his elbow, indulges in a dreamy stare, then turns over and is soon again beyond the things of sense. The licence of the lodging-house proprietor permits him to accommodate twenty-five people in this room: there are exactly forty-nine. And not only are the lodgers seemingly unconscious of the closeness due to overcrowding, but they must needs have the stove lit in addition. For all this they pay 5 kopeks a-night, and some relish the accommodation so much that they have engaged the right to sleep there for two years in advance. In the morning they can get tea and bread for a trifle more.

We went to see a Government lodging-house by way of contrast. The building was scrupulously clean, and the rooms of good size and well ventilated. The *nari* or sleeping platforms ran down the centre, and the space allotted to each individual was plainly defined by the thin wooden partition that traced out the middle line of the erection, thus separating the heads of any two opposing sleepers, and at the same time sending off like ribs at right angles to itself every 3 feet or so, other partitions that served to separate each person from his immediate neighbour on either side. Moreover, a slight surface slope, culminating in a pronounced upward bend as the axial screen was reached, contrived to make the plank-beds the most comfortable things of their kind that one could well imagine. The tariff was 9 kopeks for the night with a good meal in the morning,—in every way a better bargain than the other from the Western point of view. But the institution was poorly patronised, and there was not the same look of contentment on the men's faces in these more sanitary apartments.

What we saw of a third large tenement, also a Night Shelter capable of holding considerably over 1000 souls, showed it to be simply a repetition of the first case on a grander scale. The charge was 5 kopeks, and the lodgers could enter for the night at 7 P.M., but were required to leave at 8 the following morning. Here, indeed, was overcrowding: one saw rooms that would have been full with

200 men crammed with half as many more. Sleepers lay about everywhere—on a large central platform that occupied a considerable space, beneath it, on the supplementary shelves that skirted two of the walls, under them, even in the passages. They were often miserably clad, and slept in their clothes; others had partially disrobed or were stark naked. So thickly were they strewn that one had to pick every step : beyond a certain distance progress was impossible. And this is not distasteful to the Russian peasant; the Government lodging-houses, as well conducted as any in more Western lands, and cheaper than the ordinary lodging-house, are practically deserted in favour of the latter.[1] These are the men you find in the overcrowded Siberian prisons; but the Petersburg Night Shelter surpassed anything I saw in the land of *tundra* and *taiga*.

The railway journey from Moscow to Nijni-Novgorod is the work of a night. Here the prisoners are embarked upon barges that are towed down the Volga and up the Kama as far as Perm. From this town they resume travel by train, and, crossing the Urals, descend on Tiumen. This last stretch of a day and night presents no hardship : the ordinary third-class car lighted by barred windows is a luxury compared with the horse-waggons in which the emigrants who pass along the Trans-Siberian Railway have to spend a week.

Tiumen is the first town in Siberia proper that greets the traveller when following the northern route. Its most interesting feature is the Forwarding Prison, of which no one has yet said a good word. It stands on an open piece of

[1] Further study of the slum life of St Petersburg, by Mr J. F. Willard, seems to indicate that this marked preference for the less desirable type of lodging-house finds its chief ground in the facts that no vodka is allowed on the Government premises, while, on the other hand, the interests of the State religion are not forgotten.

ground on the outskirts of the town: close by runs the railway, so that there is no difficulty in conducting the convicts from the waggons to their new quarters. The appearance is that of a rectangular three-storeyed building of whitewashed brick, rising out of a surrounding courtyard, which in turn is bounded by a high wall, erected in keeping with the prison as regards material and colour. Immediately to the right of the main entrance leading into the yard is a small edifice built on the wall, and used as a guardroom. Following the wall in its enclosing circuit, we find that on the next side, to the right of the main building, it supports the residence of the second-in-command, and farther on the gaily painted church. In the portion of the yard behind the prison is a large detached wooden barrack used only in summer as Peresilni quarters, for it has no heating apparatus: it might hold 150 persons. Through a postern in the wall immediately behind the prison we pass into a new enclosure surrounded by the ordinary wooden palisade: it contains two recent log buildings, in one of which is set up machinery for grinding corn. Continuing our survey of the outhouses surrounding the main prison, we find on the third side a continuous line of single-storeyed log barracks, and before we come round to the front entrance again, we pass a two-storeyed building lying between it and the last of these outer Peresilni barracks, being in close connection with the latter, although not on the same wall.

On the ground-floor of the main building are situated the *kontora* or office, a small *karaŭlnaya* or guardroom, and the clothes-store. Also, in a series of stuffy, poorly lighted rooms lying to the back, are the kitchen and bakery. Through the steam escaping from boiling caldrons we could see spectre-like figures, some of them stripped to the waist,

gliding about over the rough brick flooring. And as the
men and their existence, so was the labour of their hands.
The bread here was poor and the *kvass* bitter compared
with what we found in other prisons. Not far removed
from this were the silent cells of correction. More will be
said later about punishment as it figures in the Siberian
prison system. Suffice it for the present that in this particular instance a gradational series of cells, perhaps half-a-dozen in all, opened off a corridor. There was the plain
whitewashed cell, with plank-bed, and window out of reach.
There was the smaller, bare, windowless cell with double
doors—a hole. In one of the latter a refractory individual
had been confined for seven or eight days, and when the doors
were opened he blinked like an owl, and commenced a
violent tirade on the *natchalnik*. "Why is he there?"
"Because he disobeyed me"; and I confess my sympathies
were all on the side of the official. The fare for those who
have merited such dismal isolation is bread and water, and
this system is found to prove effectual in the great majority
of cases.

On the second flat was a great number of small rooms,
some of which were crowded: one of them, which would
have looked full with fifteen men, contained twenty-nine.
The interiors of the rooms had a general appearance of
cleanliness, and some of the walls had been recently whitewashed. In one of these *kameras* was a motley group of
half-a-dozen dangerous-looking politicals condemned to hard
labour. With the exception of an uncouth Jew, clad in a
sombre frock-coat, who was deeply engrossed attending to a
decrepit samovar, they belonged to that class of mischief-making Poles who live on the Austrian frontier and revel in
intrigue. One of them had passed several years in prison at

Warsaw, and was now on his way, reduced almost to a skeleton, with shaven head and in chains, to try his fortune in the more select Siberian prisons.

This prison, which was originally built to lodge a good 600 souls, can now, along with the out-buildings, accommodate over 800. On the day of our visit the board at the gate reported that there were 752 prisoners inside the walls—*i.e.*, considerably under the limit. But so natural has this overcrowding become, that while some of the rooms were empty, others contained an undue number. Now for this there can be no other reason except that overcrowding within certain limits is not the same thing to the Eastern *mujik* as it is to the Western traveller.

We then proceeded to visit the hospital, which is located on the top storey. The female wards were empty at that moment, and presented a clean tidy appearance. Iron bedsteads with a black tablet attached to the head on which is inscribed in Russian the nature of the occupant's affliction, a coarse straw-packed mattress, sheet, blanket, and a pillow, were the usual furnishings. The food supplied to the male invalids at the midday meal was of a very fair order, one man consuming some chicken tea and chicken with evident relish. But the general impression was that the prison was old and in a poor state.

Coming out into the court again, we went round the outbuildings in turn. The two-storeyed house already described as situated on the wall to the left of the entrance was converted below into a blacksmith's shop, while two rooms on the flat above, which opened off one another, were occupied by a few individuals working at bootmaking and carpentry in a desultory fashion. The labour took rather the form of doing repairs, as it is the glory of Tiumen, as of all Peresilni prisons, that the man who enters it shall do nothing more than exist; indeed it is hardly worth his while to settle down to anything. Then we inspected the adjacent ampler *kameras*—three or four in number—that constitute a large part of the prison accommodation. Round three sides of the wall of each of them ran the usual *nari*, consisting of planks sloping up to meet the wall, from which their outer ends are distant 6 or 7 feet and raised about a couple of feet above the ground. Along the edge of this gigantic shelf stood a double row of men. The central free space —so limited — was out of all proportion to the size of the room and the number of men in it. In one of these rooms amongst the crowd of 150 men stood half-a-dozen politicals, noticeable at once by their finer type of face and private clothing. One man in particular, a tall strapping fellow, with high boots and prim black overcoat with fur collar, seemed sadly out of his element amongst the other coarser specimens of humanity. This was, of course, a contravention of rules, as there is usually provision for the separate housing of politicals *en route*. These men were of the order of Administrative politicals—of whom later. It may also be provisionally stated here that one great category of Siberian exiles includes those who, after having suffered a period of imprisonment, not exceeding four years, in Russia, present themselves for readmission to the village commune, but are refused this privilege, and in consequence have to go to Siberia as settlers; such persons as are banished by sentence of a court; and the everlasting *brodyaga* or passportless vagrant. Sixty per cent of the souls in Tiumen Peresilni on that day were drawn from this earth-cumbering army.

In answer to a question the *natchalnik* said that the actual daily cost of keeping a prisoner in food at Tiumen was 3 to 4 kopeks—that is, three farthings—a sum, however, which goes immensely further in Siberia than in this country. He also stated that over 20,000 people passed through his prison annually. As we walked round, an interesting performance was taking place in one corner of the square, close to the large Peresilni wards. Twenty or thirty prisoners were standing in a group cracking jokes at the expense of one of their number, who, seated on a chair, was resignedly submitting himself to the prison barber. This perfunctory individual speedily shaved one side of the man's head with a horse-clipper. Those who are going out as hard-labour convicts (*katorjniki*) have the right side of their heads shaved, while those whose destiny is simply that of exiled settlers (*poselentzi*) are shorn on the left. And after each man had undergone the operation he retired slowly to his log barrack, feeling the back of his head with his hand and shaking it to displace loose hairs, while his chains made a merry jingle and the bystanders jeered.

As the head can always be covered with a cap, and it is possible to break the fetters with a smart blow, these indignities are obviously no deterrents to escape, and indeed form no actual punishment. All that they do is to brand a man as a criminal so long as he is within the prison walls, and this is unnecessary: once he has escaped, they become functionless. And that this is probably an approximation to the truth is borne out by the fact that in certain prisons the men are neither left in chains nor are their heads shaved. On the march it might be useful to distinguish the convict from the exiled settler, and one might think that a fettered convict would have a poor chance of running away; but after all it is the prisons and the guards who are mainly

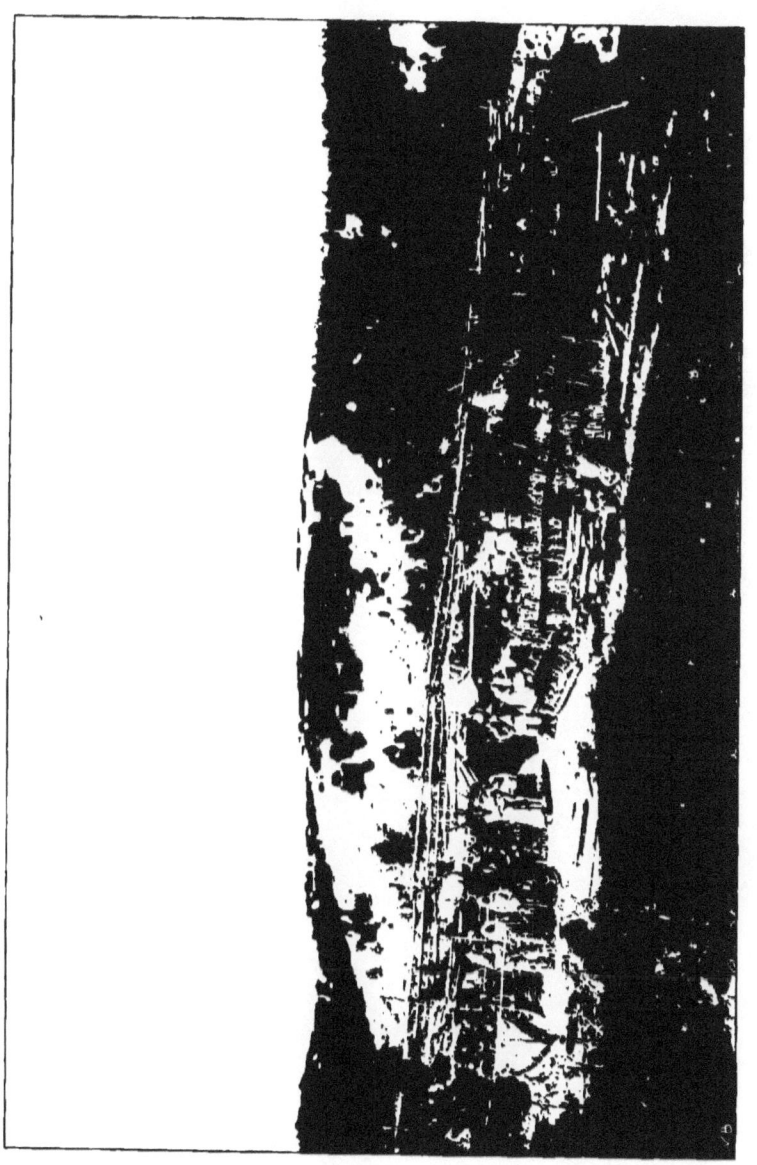

A SETTLEMENT OF VOLUNTARY FOLLOWERS, EASTERN SIBERIA.

instrumental in preventing this, and even they are only partially successful.

Vis-à-vis to the Peresilni Prison, on the other side of an ill-defined road, are the women's prison, and apartments to accommodate the *dobrovolni* or voluntaries (mainly women and children) who accompany relatives in the gang. But what was most pleasant to behold was the candid acknowledgment of the antiquated condition of the prison as evinced in the construction of a series of new buildings in close proximity to the present women's prison. When transportation of convicts by rail comes into vogue, Tiumen will naturally decline in importance, and will become simply the local prison of the district — *i.e.*, its "forwarding" aspect will disappear. With this in view, the first new building in process of erection at that time was a hospital which might excite the envy of any small town, far less a prison, fitted out as it was with the very latest ventilative and hygienic appliances; but the wards were of no great size. A new laundry, also on a generous scale, had just been erected, together with several storerooms. Wood was the material used in the construction of all these buildings, as during the winter it keeps in heat much better than brick or stone.

During the height of the season a convict-barge leaves Tiumen for Tomsk on an average every week. It may be as well to describe briefly the general appearance of one of these slave-dhows, of which there are three, as it presented itself to us during the tedious eight days' sail from Tomsk to Tiumen. Two steamship companies are under contract to tow them between these towns, and the price of a single barge may be set down at 15,000 rubles (£1500). In length it was about 250 feet, with 30 feet of beam — *i.e.*, the dimensions were similar to those of the ordinary merchant barge. The sides of the vessel were painted black above and red below the water-line, and were broken only by a line of oblong port-holes. The main deck was free at either end for a space of about 30 feet, but the rest was occupied with two deck-houses separated by a lengthy menagerie-like cage. Communication between bow and stern was secured by a narrow passage running on either side between bul-

Convict-barge on the Ob.

warks and deck-houses; or one could mount the deck-houses by means of a ladder, traverse the upper deck over cage and cabin, and descend by a similar convenience at the other end. Day after day the floating prison was dragged in the wake of our paddle-steamer, presenting to view her sombre prow, above which peeped a capstan-head, while behind loomed the dun deck-houses. The bare expanse of upper deck surmounting them was relieved only by a few black ventilators standing upright like great grim sentinels, a lonely mast, the galley chimneys, and a low wheel-house back of them all. There was commonly no sign of life aboard her save the incessant movements of the drab-coated sentries on their short beats up and down the aforesaid passages. As we were voyaging in the opposite direction to that in which the vast majority of prisoners go (although no barge ever returns from Tomsk to Tiumen without a few vagrants or returning exiles on board), it was only in passing a Tomsk-bound boat that we caught a glimpse of the gloomy reality.

Anything was gladly welcomed that promised to provide some *divertissement*, however small, upon this wearisome journey. As soon as another steamer was sighted there was a general rush of all the passengers to secure a good place from which to watch her going by. Our captain stepped on to a paddle-box and waved a flag on the side where he knew there would be the greatest depth of water for the other ship to pass. Gradually they approached: at the moment of opposition our skipper made inquiry with his speaking-trumpet as to the depth of water farther up the river. But the excitement was greatest as we passed the convict-barge. The poor fellows crowded to their side of the cage, and the old hulk heeled over. It was a dreary day, and as certain hurrying inky clouds threatened to relieve themselves of their load of moisture, the prisoners had wrapped themselves up warmly in their grey *khalats* that seemed to match the outside world so well, and gazed with longing eyes on the boat that was carrying us back to the land that some of them had so lately left for ever. The barge, however, was not suffered to wear a very dismal aspect, for there had evidently been some laundry-work attempted in primitive fashion, and she was brightly decked out with drying blouses, print gowns, and other articles of clothing of various gaudy hues. The windows of the aft deck-house were evidently barred: it formed the hospital, as we found later.

At a subsequent point opportunity was afforded to make a fuller investigation. These prison-barges are built to accommodate up to 800 people, and each makes half-a-dozen journeys or so in the season (May to the end of September or the beginning of October). The military staff comprises eight-and-twenty men, including a *natchalnik* and doctor. One hundred and eight soldiers are told off for this work of convoy. They are divided into three companies of twenty-eight, who live on the continually moving barges, while twenty-four are left in reserve at Tiumen in case of an emergency. The deck-houses commence, as already stated, at about 30 feet from either end, and are roughly 35 feet in length. In each case a median corridor bisects them, opening at one end into a cage, and at the other to the exterior, close by the ladder giving access to the upper deck, at the fore or aft end, as the case may be. Thus, then, we have a third method of getting from one end of the vessel to the other—viz., through deck-houses and cages.

Visiting the fore deck-house first, we entered, on one side of the corridor, the single cabin in which the six-and-twenty soldiers have to stow themselves away. Inside there was barely sufficient space for two men to pass one another, while all round was a most economical system of narrow bunks. This is only one of several facts which show that the lot of the guard is not so very much better than that of his charge, with the exception of the immense difference between them as warder and ward. And as the former are on the whole a steady uncomplaining force, one should listen with less sympathy to the murmurings of the prisoners. Across the corridor were the apartments of the *natchalnik* and his wife and family; together with a few smaller cabins, one of which was occupied by the doctor, another used as *kontora*, and the remainder reserved for special politicals. The fore-cage is supposed to contain some 250 human beings what time they are allowed to come up on deck to breathe fresh air. Eight stout vertical iron posts connected the main

In the cage.

and upper decks, and between these a thick wire-netting, with hexagonal meshes of about 1½ inch in diameter, was stretched. In bad weather with driving rain a tarpaulin is carried round the inside of this wire fence, so that the prisoners can come up on deck for exercise and air without being drenched. The breadth of the cage was perhaps

24 feet, which would leave about 3 feet for each of the sidepassages already mentioned. The caboose separated the forecage from the hinder one, which is almost twice its size. The netting was led round three sides, so that the caboose was shut out, and food is handed through holes in the caging. The kitchen itself, which might be 16 feet in length, had not, however, a breadth equal to that of the cage: the space thus saved formed the head of the companion that led to the sleeping quarters below.

The hinder cage was some 70 feet in length, and also had its staircase down to the Inferno: it was for men, as the other was for women. Now we have reached the hinder deck-house, consisting on one side of two rooms with barred windows: they served as hospital and dispensary. There was no entrance, however, to any cabins across the corridor from the inside; but on going round to the outside one saw that the caging extended here right along, with a sliding-door in it by which access was gained. This was usually reserved for the *intelligenti*. I entered, and then descended some steps in one corner that led to the dormitory. This cage was occupied at the moment by half-a-dozen passportless men who were being conducted back to Russia: a soldier paced up and down outside, armed with revolver and cutlass. There was nothing to attract notice about this quarter of the barge, except that the men who were inhabiting it were evidently not inclined to any special cleanliness of habit. The oblong port-holes were provided with a sliding window-sash, and there was a primitive arrangement of wooden bunks which were not any worse than those in the soldiers' cabin. Overcrowding of course would make life intolerable in such a vessel, but I am not prepared to profess knowledge of any such abuse. I asked, as usual, to be taken to the ordinary prisoners' sleeping quarters. To my astonishment the *natchalnik* refused point-blank. I explained to him that never before had I been refused anything at any point in our journey, and showed him my letters again ; my companion of the moment, an *attaché* of the German Embassy in St Petersburg, threatened him, but he was obdurate. I very much suspect that the place was in bad order, but also believe that 5 rubles could have got us in. The politicals' " saloon " was dull and dreary enough, but what it must be to spend the night in these dark holds is best left to the imagination.

At one station where we halted for a few hours, great stores of dried fish were taken on board and piled on the upper deck ; these with black bread form the staple articles of food for the convicts during their eight days of close confinement. From Tomsk to Tiumen by water is a journey of about 2200 versts (1467 miles). It is obvious that as the distance to be travelled on the river Irtish is much less than what you cover on the Ob into which the former falls, there will also be some difference in the length of time taken, according as you go in the one or in the other direction. Thus while the large steamers can run between Tomsk and Tiumen —*i.e.*, down the Ob and up the Irtish—in six to seven days, the return voyage from Tiumen to Tomsk may extend over eight. In spite of the careful and almost minute way in which the rivers Ob, Irtish, Tobol, and Tura have been attended to hydrographically, it requires great caution to ascend the latter two, especially if towards the end of the season there has not been rain for some length of time. Of this we became painfully cognisant, as after leaving Tobolsk behind us, and ascending the Tobol for some considerable way, we had finally to change our ship for one of lighter draught. Even with this smaller vessel, to keep in the line of deepest water was an undertaking fraught with great anxiety to the wary old pilot; and often when at some sudden bend in the course of the stream he felt that the three men at the wheel were not sufficiently energetic in their endeavours to get the nose of the vessel far enough round in time, he would fly to the rescue, and all four would throw it round as fast as they were able, while the stern of the boat would be scraping the river's bank. So we ascended slowly, while the man at the bow with his sounding-pole cried out every quarter of a minute the varying depth of water in mid-stream. At last one evening we reached a point where a dredger, moored in the middle of the channel, and illuminating the scene by means of an arc-light, was deepening the river's bed. After the solitary steamers that once in four-and-twenty hours or so had served to remind us that we were not the only representatives of the human race, it almost seemed too much of a good thing to remark how both banks were sheltering six or seven boats, even if a couple of them appeared to occupy too prominent a position —right in the line of our intended course. We soon learned that more than half of them were aground. A few minutes later, during a noble endeavour on the part of our fearless pilot to steer us past the seductive spot, a harsh grating sound, followed by complete cessation of motion and the fierce churning of the water by paddle-wheels that were now incapable of doing anything save driving us farther on to the river's silted bed, proclaimed that we too had followed the example of those with whom we had only a moment before been sympathising. We began to feel the seriousness of the predicament. But when the only steamer free to move gallantly left its moorings amidst a general trumpeting and brave sounding of its fog-horn, to come to the rescue of our passenger-boat, and ended by also running aground in a ridiculously simple manner, the whole situation partook of the nature of a joke. There was nothing for it but to empty our vessel of its freight, so far as that was possible. The convict-barge behind us was still afloat, but it was manifest that even if we did get off, it would be impossible to take it along any farther with us. So by means of planks we all made our way to land.

The scene was one that will not easily be forgotten. The point at which our voyage had come to this abrupt termination was about 75 versts (50 miles) below Tiumen. To-day there was only an *arshin* (28 inches) of water, and yet they said that fifty hours before the soundings proclaimed a depth of nearly half-a-dozen feet! It was a cold evening in the beginning of September: that morning the ship's deck had been thinly covered with the first snow of the season. And already the twilight, all too short, had vanished, leaving us shrouded in thick darkness. We crept ashore, and clambered up the slimy bank, thankful for the well-worn path, now cut almost vertically into the soil, by which the river-watchman strives to reach his lonely cabin built into the river's bank, displaying of itself merely the door and window set in a fractional wooden wall. The sound of the droning dredge, the helpless shrieks of the steamers, and the high-pitched shouts of men as they endeavoured to dislodge their ships, were borne across the water. The penetrating electric rays threw grim shadows behind the spruces that seemed to keep the opposing bank warm. As for us, we appeared to be in quite a different latitude ; for long coarse grass, damp with the evening dew, hid our soaking feet, and patches of willows rose out of the night ahead. Far to our right all was hidden in murky fog, the product of the chill and cloudy night that enveloped us; only one or two stars had the courage to shine through the oppressive gloom. Our orders were to proceed up-stream for half a mile, and there await developments. So in the dark we wandered aimlessly, now skirting the river's bank, now picking our steps through the willows as well as we might by the uncertain momentary flare of matches, now plunging into some boggy spot, now tearing our way through the tall grass that grew so easily on the sodden soil by the river. After a time we halted and listened to the shouts and steamer-calls, accompanied by the lashing of the water by relentless paddle-wheels that sounded pleasantly in the distance, for they were our assurance and our hope. Two young students bound for Kazan University busied themselves preparing a fire, and when its lurid glare had lit up everything for yards around, we crouched shivering about the crackling branches and avoided as best we might the flying sparks. And after we had waited and discussed a thousand times how we should spend the night, and how we should best come to our destination by hiring horses from some visionary village, the thunderous beat of the paddle-wheels seemed to approach nearer, by-and-by the lights of our steamer heaved in sight, and a cheery voice sang out the query, "Where are you?" We responded immediately, and then the captain bade us step on a few feet farther to where the water was somewhat deeper close in to the side, and we sprang up with a sense of relief, and hurried to the appointed spot. The thoughtful ones seized a flaming branch out of the fire to illuminate their path, but it was heavy walking through that swampy ground. We had wandered some little way inland latterly in our attempt to discover

THE EMBARKATION.

where haply we might tread on firmer ground, but at last a single idea took quick possession of the whole party at the same moment, and we made a straight line for the bank. Six ugly faces surmounting the sombre garb that every Siberian knows so well suddenly broke out of the willows, but there was a loose cordon round them, consisting of a score of brown-clad beings with bayonet and rifle across their shoulders—and the timid ones felt that they were safe. They were the prisoners from the barge, who also had disembarked and now waited till we had passed. A track was torn through the willows that thickly screened the river from our view; a narrow gangway, spar-crossed to prevent one slipping, was brought from the ship and placed at an awkward angle against the steep bank, while a sailor stood at its head and held a candle-lamp. A bonfire was lit on the shore, and in its glare we descended the perilous staircase. In the rear came the soldiers and their charges. Two guards stood at the bottom, and then the jail-birds slid down merrily, for the muddy boots of those who had preceded them had obliterated all trace of spars, and converted the slender bridge into a greased pole, or rather a chute. Some carried their bundles under one arm and a tea-can under the other, thus experiencing difficulty in the maintenance of equilibrium, for it was no laughing matter to descend that staircase. The soldiers in their brown overcoats and caps, with cutlasses encased in sheaths of brass and black leather, revolvers by their side, and Berdan rifles which made creditable balancing-poles, distributed themselves amongst the delinquents. Down they came out of the darkness at the top, into the light of the glowing fire below, from which the cold night-wind drove tongues of flame in ever-shifting directions. So we got off again, but occasionally a gentler grating sound reminded us that at any moment we might be called upon to repeat this little night excursion. This incident serves to show what diversions may enliven even the lot of the hapless prisoner as he is borne on these long rivers in confinement.

The convict-barges which ply on the Volga and Kama between Nijni-Novgorod and Perm are constructed on very similar principles, but seem capable of conveying a greater number of persons, as the only specimen one saw had a double tier of deck-houses. But the idea of the menagerie was still perfectly obvious. The convicts had just disembarked at Perm on the morning that we got there, and were lying about on the wharf, while the military maintained a casual watch over them.

There were days, however, when the convicts had to walk across the Urals: in fact, in the olden time they had to make the whole journey from Moscow on foot except where it was possible to employ water. Thereafter they were driven by post-horses from Perm to Tiumen, as the outlay thus involved was found to be less even than that required to provide the convicts with food during that weary march. And to-day they travel third class by the workmen's train.

On arrival at the landing-stage in the vicinity of Tomsk (being as it is some 3 or 4 versts distant across an arid plain) the prisoners disembark and are conducted to a yard, where they pass individually before the governor of the Forwarding Prison; and as each man is called up, his crime, destination, and duration of sentence are read out, and he is identified by the photograph that is appended to every paper. By this simple device, as also by that related on p. 152, the old trick of "exchanging names and identities," as practised by the *katorjniki* and the *poselentzi*, has been rendered futile. Then each one is examined by a soldier to see if he has] been provided with the regulation clothing by the province in which he was condemned. Such a procedure occupies considerable time, as the barges seldom convey less than their full complement.

CHAPTER VI.

ON THE MARCH—*concluded.*

DESCRIPTION OF THE FORWARDING PRISON AT TOMSK — ATTITUDE OF THE SOLDIERS TOWARDS THE PRISONERS — CONVICT DRESS — TRANSFERENCE BY ÉTAPE — ÉTAPES AND POLU-ÉTAPES — ALLOWANCES ON THE MARCH—THE *BRODYAGA*—ÉTAPES AT MARIINSK AND NEAR KANSK—LIFE ON THE MARCH — ÉTAPES IN EASTERN SIBERIA—POLITICALS *EN ROUTE*—CRITICISM—CHANGES EFFECTED BY THE TRANS-SIBERIAN RAILWAY.

A convict.

WE return now to the Forwarding Prison at Tomsk, which, although built in a commanding position, produces no marked impression from the exterior, owing to the low character of the buildings which comprise it. Exception should, however, be made in favour of the large whitewashed brick house that, as already mentioned, now fronts the institution, and consists mainly of the governor's private residence: one soon learns that this, too, like the palisade, is typical. After the party already described had fairly left, we went over the prison, which at that time lodged a comparatively small number of inmates—611 being the score chalked up on the board at the gate. Tomsk rejoices in three prisons, the other two being the Gubernski, a provincial prison for somewhat heavily sentenced individuals, while the Arestantski is reserved for local offenders with milder sentences. These, however, do not fall to be described here.

The space enclosed by the outer wooden palisade was divided into about nine squares unequal in dimensions, each of which was partitioned off from its neighbours by walls similar to those which surrounded the whole. In several of these squares one found prison barracks, to the number of two or three—low wooden structures with red roofs and walls. In the centre of the principal square rose the pretty little church, surrounded in part by young birch-trees. It holds 300 persons, and divine service is conducted every Sunday and on all the important calendar days. There was no trace of any sort of paving in the courts, only the bare soil; but narrow raised pathways of planks led in each instance from the entrance-gate in the wall to the doors of the buildings that stood in the square.

One form of barrack consisted of four *kameras* into which a T-shaped corridor gave admittance, with a central lavatory facing the door—*i.e.*, at the end of the main corridor: two *kameras* opened off each wing. A large lamp built high up into the wall, protected by grating on the inside, and only accessible from the corridor, dimly lighted each room. The *nari* were arranged down the centre of the room, while a shelf above the heads of the sleepers was covered with their bundles and bags. As we went through the building, the poor fellows would hurry to the square spyhole in the padlocked door, guarded by two crossed iron bars, to see what was going on. Any little incident that broke the monotony of their prison existence was acceptable. The *kamera* was heated by a large stove built into one corner. Most of the barracks were only double-chambered, with a diminutive dividing corridor. I was impressed with the cleanliness of this prison, in contrast with that at Tiumen. This is of no great consequence, as it was one of three instances in which I know special preparations had been made for visitors: still it was interesting to see what could be done on occasions. When one entered a *kamera*, in response to the gaoler's premonitory shout of "Smirno" (Silence) the men instantly disposed themselves around the wall, dressed in their dark-grey frieze coats, and replied heartily to the Russian greeting "Zdravstuite" (Good morning). At the head of the row—*i.e.*, nearest to the door—the *starosta* or elder took up his position: he is their representative in all dealings with the authorities. One of their number, elected by themselves, he is responsible for the general behaviour of the room, and in return receives some slight amelioration of his lot. There was of course no overcrowding at this moment, and a young Russian engineer who had come with us, agreeably surprised by what he considered to be the satisfactory state of everything, remarked to one of the convicts standing by, "It is very good here." "Yes," replied the breaker of the law—"yes, it certainly is good, only we wish that it were not quite so good, and that we were free." "If only they would let me out on Sundays to see my friends, I would stay here all my life," observed a prison *habitué* to a friend of mine who was visiting one of the Moscow jails.

Many of the prisoners were engaged in ordinary duties. Some were drawing water out of a deep well at the bottom of which floated large blocks of greenish ice. Others were carrying hot water from the immense boiler that supplies the convicts with the wherewithal to prepare the much-loved tea. A few were at work in the bakery, and a couple were busy in the dispensary. The different faces were a fascinating study. There were men who looked as if they had never had a chance; others were perpetually smiling (some men can laugh their way through life); and while the countenances of a few were pale, haggard, and drawn, the appearance of the majority was villanous, even to the hair of their head. Very rarely you saw a sympathetic, thoughtful, far less an attractive face.

The prison fare was that supposed to be common to a great majority of these institutions, consisting mainly of one substantial meal in the middle of the day, at which the inmates get as much soup as they can consume—commonly *shtchi* made of cabbage with little pieces of meat in it—and 2½ lb. of black bread. A bowl and a spoon, together with the mug out of which they drink their *kvass*, are thus the only articles that require to be washed up after this simple dinner. There is an evening meal about six, at which the principal dish is *kasha* (gruel). The convicts also drink tea twice in the day, but have to supply themselves with the fragrant leaf. For the sale of it and other commodities, such as tobacco and *vodka*, there is a little store in the prison, which the men value. I propose to take up the question of the prisoner's fare more fully at a subsequent point, for it is interesting to note how it varies in different quarters with the economical tact of the prison *natchalniks*.

The hospital occupied two separate squares. In one of the buildings was a large dispensary, and a room for the examination of patients. Although the food was superior to that which obtained in the prison proper, yet the other arrangements were not correspondingly good. Wards for infectious and non-infectious diseases were found under the same roof, with merely a log wall to divide them. The male wards were comfortably full, but there were only three female patients. Indeed the number of female convicts in the prison at that time was not more than half-a-dozen, and they had a large *kamera* to themselves. While we were in it, one of them came forward, fell down at the feet of the *natchalnik*, and begged that her daughter, who was with the *dobrovolni* in a separate building, might be allowed to be with her: her prayer was granted. In another square were the baths and laundry, in which some women were employed washing linen under the surveillance of soldiers. Political prisoners have, of course, their own apartments.

I was struck here, as I had been all along, with the gentle, friendly attitude of the soldiers towards the convicts as a whole. They are members of a service that stands on its own footing, but which is only open to those who have served their time in the army. The pay ranges from 15 to 25 rubles per month, according to rank. Drawn from the same humble class of society as that to which their charges originally belonged, it is not, however, to be supposed that they are totally unaffected by their environment. Still, they are popular with the Siberian people.

It may be well to describe the convict dress somewhat more particularly at this point. There are two distinct costumes—the outcome of the climate. The summer outfit is as follows: Next to the skin the men wear a shirt and trousers of unbleached linen. In place of stockings the Russian peasant winds rolls of linen, about a yard in length and 8 inches broad, around his leg much after the fashion of a bandage. The convict has to wear chains, which are, however, more an emblem of degradation than anything else.

THE CONVICT DRESS.

Two anklets are riveted on the man's legs, but beneath them he wears either a piece of leather—sometimes a regular laced legging—or thick felt (and below that his stocking substitute), so that chafing is impossible. The length of chain from one rivet to the other is about four feet, and the convict commonly passes his leathern waist-belt or hempen girdle through a middle link somewhat larger than the rest, and thus supports the weight of the chain. But as he walks along he is constantly annoyed by the continual striking of the links against his knees and thighs. Their weight is inconsiderable, varying between 5 and 7 Russian pounds (the Russian pound being slightly under the English pound)—*i.e.*, less than the weight of the Berdan rifle that the soldiers carry. The *khalat* or overcoat (with or without a belt), which very closely resembles a dressing-gown, is made of a frieze (soldier's cloth). The common shade is a grey, though this is not constant throughout Siberia, as it varies from brown almost to white. The cap is of similar cloth, but is not uniform in shape. The summer boots (*koti*) are light, and may often be more accurately described as closely fitting shoes. As such they are preferred, because the boots proper do not admit of being laced or drawn together at the top except by a piece of string outside, and so perpetually fill with dust and fragments of stone on the march, much to the discomfort of the walker. The clothes are made in three sizes—small, medium, and large. A distinct garb has been lately introduced for those persons who have been arrested on a charge and are awaiting their trial or the completion of their process. Formerly they had to wear the ordinary prisoner's dress, which was felt to be somewhat of an indignity. In winter, in addition to linen under-garments very similar to what constitute the summer dress, the convicts wear a suit of the same frieze as that used for the *khalat*, in place of which each prisoner is provided with a *shuba* (sheepskin) and a warm cap with ear-flaps. The linen leg-wrappers are relinquished in favour of more suitable appropriate coverings. The winter boots (*brodni*), though rough, are the high boots so dear to the heart of the Russian peasant—shapeless, it is true, and often of only partially cured leather, but an excellent protection against the snow. Woollen mits, with leathern ones above them, complete the equipment. The habiliments of the women, *mutatis mutandis*, are practically the same, except that their summer gowns are of some plain print, while their head-dress consists of a white handkerchief bound in a simple manner round the head and tied under the chin. Women are now never put in chains except on very rare occasions: I did not see a single instance of it. Corporal punishment also has been abolished for several years in their case, mainly owing to the philanthropic efforts of Madame Narishkine.

Tomsk, then, is the starting-point on the now famous Trans-Siberian march. The system adopted is known as transference by *étape*, the latter being the name for the small places of confinement in which the convicts pass a night or two in the villages *en route*. In Western Siberia the *étape* was commonly in the village, generally at the extreme end of the double row of wooden cottages that form that interesting community, more rarely in the centre; but in Eastern Siberia these temporary halting-places are usually situated right outside the village on some clear space of ground. It is natural that one should have a somewhat vivid remembrance of the first *étape* that one saw. It was in a village far off the main road: a great fire had recently devastated the community, and the *étape* was one of the few enclosures that remained untouched. One of the buildings that formed part of it faced the road, and through the bars of its open windows inquiring faces peered. The *étape* at a village farther on afforded a more convenient object of study. It took the form of a square plot of ground shut in by a 15-feet wall of barked and pointed stakes—just such a palisade as surrounded the Forwarding Prison at Tomsk. As in the latter case also, it did not run round the entire square, for at the two corners that stood on the road were planted the buildings that lodged the prisoners. Each of these buildings had thus two walls contiguous with the stockade. An iron-barred gate in the palisade between the buildings opened into the yard. The *étape* was empty at that moment, but two heaps, one of half-charred logs and the other of chips and shavings, betokened the expected presence of a party in the near future. I should imagine that the square was some 60 feet across, but the *étape*, being off the great highroad, was smaller in every particular than the usual type. We entered the left-hand corner house, which was constructed of thick beams of wood caulked with moss. A short passage, on each side of which was a single small room, led into the inmost chamber. Of the two former, that on the left, which was lighted by a single window looking out on to the muddy village track, was the *karaúlnaya*, or soldiers' quarters. The room opposite, which was, however, more of the nature of a recess, simply contained stands for fifteen muskets. The third apartment was as long as the building itself, and was illumined by three closely barred windows, two of which, like that in the *karaúlnaya*, fronted the outside world, while the other opened on to the court. The interior was bare, the walls being not even whitewashed, but the general impression was that of cleanliness. Along the far wall from window to window ran the *nari*, 6 feet in breadth and 3 feet above the floor. The stove, in this case an iron one, stood well out from one of the walls, and took up a large amount of space in what was only a moderately sized room. The second building was similar, the only difference being that the keeper and his family occupied what corresponded to the *karaülnaya* in the first. Also one noticed here what was very seldom seen in other *étapes*, its purpose being fulfilled by other expedients—viz., a wooden bar running along outside the walls of the two houses at a distance of 3 feet from them, intended apparently to prevent any one from coming close up under the windows.

There are two distinct classes of *étape*, corresponding to regulations connected with the march. They are known as *étapes* or full *étapes*, and *polu-étapes* or half-*étapes*. The former, as will be seen, are much larger and more serious establishments, with a resident captain in charge, who has under him between forty and fifty soldiers and two or three subordinate officers, whose duty it is to convoy parties to the next *étape*. That is to say, the usual practice formerly was for the necessary number of soldiers to convoy a party past a *polu-étape* to the full *étape* immediately beyond that, where they handed over their charges to the *natchalnik* there resident, who in turn supplied the necessary soldiers for the two following stages. This arrangement still holds in part, but is being replaced by the infinitely preferable one demonstrated in the diagram by which the exchange of prisoners takes place at the *polu-étapes*. Thus the number of nights during which the soldiers are away from their *étape* station is reduced to a minimum, and it will be seen that the circulation from any *polu-étape* past the *étape* to the next *polu-étape* beyond, and back again to the starting-point, just occupies a week. The number of people convoyed from east to west (largely composed of returning exiles) is only one-twentieth of those escorted in the other direction.[1] The proportion of one guard to twenty exiles, politicals excepted, is generally maintained. The prisoners march two days out of three—*i.e.*, they rest two nights and a day at the full *étapes*, and pass the night only at the *polu-étapes*.

ITINERARY OF THE ÉTAPES No. 1.

Circulation of the detachments of prisoners from the town of Tomsk to the town of Atchinsk, and farther through Eastern Siberia to Irkutsk, and back again, they being escorted weekly and incessantly—*i.e.*, each convoy-command escorting a detachment to the nearest night-resting (*polu*) *étape*, at which the exchange of prisoners between the commands takes place.

TOMSK PROVINCE. Names of the *étapes* and night-resting (*polu*) *étapes*.	Distance in versts.	DAYS OF CIRCULATION OF CONVOY.		Between which convoys and at which points must take place the exchange of prisoners.
		On the outward journey.	On the return	
Tomsk (*étape*)		..	Tuesday	
Semilujnaya (*polu-étape*)	31	Monday	Sunday	The Tomsk and Khaldeyeva convoys exchange prisoners, commencing May 7.
Khaldeyeva (*étape*)	14½	Tuesday Wednesday	Saturday Friday	
Turguntayeva (*polu-étape*)	23	Thursday	Wednesday	The Khaldeyeva and Ishimskaya convoys exchange prisoners, commencing May 10.
Ishimskaya (*étape*)	22½	Friday Saturday	Tuesday Monday	
Kolyuonskaya (*polu-étape*)	21	Sunday	Saturday	The Ishimskaya and Potchitansky convoys exchange prisoners, commencing May 13.
Potchitansky (*étape*)	22½	Monday Tuesday	Friday Thursday	

The above is a reproduction of the first part of an actual

[1] Thus while from February 1895 to the same month of the following year 11,000 persons passed through Krasnoyarsk going eastward, only 667 were convoyed westwards past that town. The soldiers' work is therefore very light so long as their faces are towards the setting sun; indeed they often return to their *étapes* empty-handed.

travelling-paper drawn up for a gang marching from Tomsk to Irkutsk. From these figures it will be seen that the average length of the daily march on this part of the journey is 22½ versts; the average over the last six stages is 30 versts, and this is the truer figure.

The daily allowance granted to each exile on the march is nominally 10 kopeks, and to *intelligenti* 15 kopeks. As, however, 1½ kopek is deducted in return for hot water supplied to them at the *étapes*, the actual dole is only 8½ kopeks in the case of the former. The method usually adopted by prisoners of all categories to militate against the consequences of this slender grant is that of clubbing together in little groups, and so by means of a common purse and the feeling of comradeship that impels the more fortunate amongst them to share their ampler means with their less prosperous companions, they get along better. It comes hard on the man who from any cause, such as shyness or unpopularity, is prevented from joining one of these circles, for where the prices of food are high he often has to be content with very little.

It is, however, the category of exile comprising the *brody-agi* or vagrants which commonly proves itself to be the real cause of tribulation to any gang. This is partly due to their numbers,[1] partly to their marvellous *esprit de corps*, and partly to the fact that they consider themselves to be the highest class of prisoner. Their contempt for the hard-labour convicts proper, who always march a little ahead of the rest of the gang, knows no bounds: to them they give the nickname of "grasshoppers." But if they discover that any one of these is traversing the *trakt* (as the great Siberian highroad is called) for the second time, they treat him with a cer-

[1] Of prisoners under supervision in the Amur and Trans-Baikalian provinces they form 20 per cent.

tain measure of respect. Their watchword is freedom, and he is prince among them whose tale of bold escapes is greatest. So in the *étapes* we often saw men who on their own confession were passing through for the fifth or sixth time, while on one occasion a vagrant was called out from the gang whom the *natchalnik* of the *étape* recognised as now receiving its frugal shelter for the nineteenth time.

With a grim sense of humour they adapt their names to circumstances, and Ivan the Sufferer who trudges along so resignedly through the winter snows will appear the autumn following at some prison gate as Ivan Don't-Remember, and Peter the Patient who toiled so manfully during the darksome days in a penal settlement will deliver himself up elsewhere after the next harvest has been gathered in as Peter Know-Nothing. But the period between these two dates represents an existence brief but ideal,—vagrancy: for consider their mode of life.

So long as the outer world is under the sway of the Great Ice-King,—when the lone majesty of winter's night is disturbed only by the fir-trees groaning beneath their snowy burden, or the startling report of some frost-split stone, or the warning howl of a famished wolf, and when the day seems lost in the night,—so long the *brodyaga* is well content to live and work inside the prison walls, or even march towards some far destination that he never intends to reach. At least he is sufficiently clothed and passably fed: with card-playing and good company after the hours of labour, the days do not drag heavily. But there comes a time when the ice mantle begins to disappear, and the snow weeps off the prison roof to the black earth beneath, and the trees come out of bondage, casting away their chilly fetters, and the song-birds rejoice in the spring. And one day the now wearying *brodyaga* hears the cuckoo call to his mate,[1] and from that moment an irresistible impulse seizes him, a wild discontent transforms the man, and not long after at the evening roll-call there is no response to the Sufferer's name. He has countless methods of gaining the bosom of his beloved *taiga*, where he lives through the speeding summer, and subsists on berries and mushrooms, roots and water. At night he sleeps in the shade of the aristocratic cedars, or amuses himself by waylaying harmless travellers, even using violence if he cannot otherwise obtain profit for his pains. The peasants also leave small stores of food for them in their summer quarters, whither they repair annually during a brief season for the harvest and for cattle-breeding purposes; otherwise, when they return some months later, the probabilities are that they will find the farmstead burnt to the ground, if in the interval some hungry vagrant has visited it with disappointment.

The *brodyaga*, it may be, turns westward in the hope of regaining the land of his birth, and retraces his steps along the great highway, from which he can easily slink into the forest on either side should he wish to avoid his fellowmen. At night, in spite of the dogs baying at his heels, he may steal into a village to beg for a morsel of bread, or remove the scrap of meat left by some tender-hearted cottager upon the outside window-sill.[2] Examine some of the gates set up where the post-road is intersected by the fence round the pasture-land of a village. You will notice mysterious signs rudely graven upon it. One evening a starving *brodyaga* scoured the village in vain search of food, and while

---

[1] From this circumstance originates the Siberian name for vagrants as a whole—"General Kukushka's army."

[2] A heavy penalty is attached to the crime of housing a *brodyaga*.

BRODYAGA BRANDED B.

the idiot porter slept, he carved his disappointment on the wood, so that some other fellow-vagrant reading might take heed. But few ever reach their home. The passportless vagrant finds no place where he can rest the sole of his foot, and when the first of the night frosts in September heralds the approaching death of the year, and it is no longer possible to lie out on a mossy couch, he sees before him one of two prospects—a tragic end in the woods, or self-surrender at some penal station, where, after receiving a few strokes with the *plet*, he will again be taken into the community. And it is now that he finds it convenient to forget his past, even to his name, and describes himself as Don't-Remember. Suppose, for example, that it is some hard-labour convict with a heavy sentence who has been thus fortunate with his summer holiday. When he gives himself up he will be judged anew, and a milder sentence for vagrancy will be passed upon him, and thus it is possible that he may reduce the term of his enforced exile very considerably. The number of these vagrants, although decreasing, is still so large that the Don't-Remembers are now being sent to Sakhalin, where it is suggested to them that they can remain until such time as it dawns upon them who they are and whence they came.

On the march they used to be the domineering factor in every gang, principally because they always constituted the majority. They would form an *artel* or union, each member of which was bound to help the other, while the individual who was elected elder or *starosta* of the *artel* had enormous power. They were able to ensure that some of their number should be chosen as cooks for the gang: thus they contrived to obtain for themselves the best of what was going, and the luckless "grasshoppers" got what was left over. Each of the *telyegas* provided for the transit of women, children, and the sick, is supposed to hold four persons. Whatever places remained over were commonly assigned to the aged and feeble; but this was a matter left in the hands of the *starosta*, and he could put them up for auction and sell them to the highest bidder. This was one of his main sources of income. If the *brodyagi* felt inclined to lighten the purse of any more fortunate member of the gang who did not belong to their *artel*, they could always achieve this by force. A long-standing practice was for a *brodyaga* to plan escape with an unsuspecting convict whom he knew to be possessed of a certain amount of money. Once they were safe in the *taiga*, the *brodyaga* would then despatch his accomplice, and live on his money during the summer.

The custom usually followed in the old days, when a gang had come within sight of the *étape* where the night was to be spent, was to draw it up in a double line and call the roll. Thereafter the convicts sometimes made a rush for the open gate of the yard, and the crowd of 300 or 400 struggled and fought for the best places in the *kameras*, which thus fell to the hardest fist and the most brutal tongue. Directly a garment or cloth was laid down on a spot, an inviolable rule safeguarded the selected coign from all intruders. The *starosta* was often admitted into the *étape* even before the muster-roll was called, and it was a simple matter for him to appropriate the choicest places for his vagrant confederates. An extraordinary code of unwritten laws ruled the vagabond community with penalties that did not stop at capital punishment, and the older men relate how there used often to be murders in the dreaded Tomsk Peresilni Prison, and how all that the authorities could do was to carry out the bodies in the morning, as the members of the *artel* well knew that a similar fate awaited any informant, however far he might contrive to remove himself from the rest of his *artel*. For the sum of the *artels* composed the body of the vast *brodyaga* community, and one of its members might pay in Eastern Siberia the penalty of a misdeed perpetrated against the community or some member of it in the West. But times have changed much since then. The officials have now come to learn the various dodges and subtleties of the vagrants, and the *artels* have been successfully broken up and rendered null by new regulations. And the old *brodyagi* lament that the good days of the past are gone, and the "grasshoppers" can now raise their heads.

"Early to bed and early to rise" is the convict's rule on the march. And so one often found that the "grasshoppers" and vagrants had already lain down to rest by seven o'clock. But many of them prefer to sit up and play at cards by the light of flickering candles fixed high above their reach. And those sleep who can, but the timid wakeful ones shudder as they hear the coarse excited yells of the card-players or the stifled groans and sudden cries of those whose crimes pursue them even in their dreams.

Mariinsk is the first town of any importance through which the convict band passes after leaving Tomsk. It possesses an unimportant local prison; but it is the *étape* that demands our attention. This is situated half-way between the village and the new railway station. It was naturally a full *étape*, and the caretaker's house, with the soldiers' quarters, stood in the middle of the encircling stockade, while the gate, with its attendant black-and-white zigzag-striped sentry-box, was somewhat to one side. Two log-built houses faced one another in the quadrangular yard: each consisted of two apartments of unequal size. The larger rooms were heated by cylindrical stoves, and the sleeping-platforms, sloping up to meet one another in the middle line, extended down the centre. In the smaller chambers they were disposed along two sides of the room. The date of the last whitewashing was remote, and the lighting seemed insufficient.

The *étapes* are not built on any regular plan. Thus in the case of a specimen which I visited near Kansk, the surrounding wall of high pointed stakes, that one had come to consider an essential part of every *étape*, was replaced by a lower and more simple boundary of broad planks lying in the horizontal, with their ends reposing securely in stout intermediate pillars. Sentry-boxes at each corner might almost have been considered as testimonies to the fact that the authorities evidently thought escape was easier from such a domain. Here also, as a further variation, the *karaülnaya* opened to the outside only, so that the soldiers who were required within the court had to enter it by the gate. All the buildings were arranged on one side of the yard. Twenty-four men had been locked up in a single room, and as there was not sufficient space for them all on the *nari*, some had laid out their palliasses on the floor. These lesser comforts the majority of them possessed. Indeed, although they are not provided with anything of this description by the Government, and convicts are supposed to have the luxury of sleeping accommodation only on plain deal boards, still one very rarely saw a man without some species of bedding convenience. In this, as in many other matters, the laws are very humanely enforced, and general laxity rather than strict discipline struck me with surprise as the predominant note of the Siberian system. The prisoners here had obtained a very fair supply of food from the village women who come to sell: the numerous rolls and ringlets of bread that lay about testified to this. The room, though small, was well lighted by four windows, and, as we have seen, overcrowding up to certain limits is a thing to which the Russian people are quite accustomed. The men seemed to be very hearty, although somewhat surprised to be visited at that late hour by a stranger. As usual, one could distinguish two or three Tatars by a peculiar tendency to keep their heads hung down.

At another *étape* one saw the possibility of originality in the management of the system. In itself the *étape* was much like the ordinary run of these buildings—not particularly clean, and with an aggregate of five rooms for the convenience of the unwilling travellers. The larger rooms, which on the *natchalnik's* admission were intended to accommodate sixty persons, lodged considerably over that number: they had sufficient heating apparatus in two large stoves, but the four windows were small. The *natchalnik* had attempted something in the way of organisation. Finding that the prices of provisions had risen considerably, owing to the fresh demand resulting from the presence of railway labourers who were for the moment engaged in great numbers near that village, he had bought up twenty cows, made his own bread, cultivated his own cabbage, and bought tea in large quantities. This he had done out of his own pocket as a speculation. The money that he received for the upkeep of his staff of soldiers and for supplying the prisoners' allowance (which is distributed to them at each full *étape*) he retained, and furnished them with food instead. If, however, the exiles felt uncertain about the arrangement, he let them have their allowance, and sold bread to them at the rate of 3 kopeks the pound, whereas it cost 5 in the village. He said that at first the prisoners, being shy of such an innovation, generally asked for their money; but when by report and by experience they and others came to learn how the scheme really worked to their advantage, they adopted it and went away well satisfied. What the *natchalnik* strongly insisted on was that 8½ kopeks were not a sufficiently adequate allowance under present conditions.

Convicts on the march for the first time prefer the life, after what they have experienced in the prisons of European Russia. Existence is freer, and they have a little money to dispose of practically as they wish: at the first glance these two circumstances seem very inviting, and outweigh everything else in their minds. But those who are wise from past experience hurry over the march as quickly as they may, because the sum-total of its miseries greatly exceeds those attending the comparatively easy life in the convict settlements. The *natchalnik* of an *étape* is not bound to do anything towards the maintenance of his charges. The village women who come to sell at the *étapes* dispose of their merchandise at a ransom.

During the summer of 1896 there were many complaints regarding the impossibility of the convicts obtaining the necessary food on their 8½ kopeks a-day. At another *étape* the *natchalnik*, who had only come three months before, was in a state of despair as to how he was to feed his soldiers, far less his prisoners, for the prices of food had gone up greatly owing to the additional demand, occasioned as before by the advent of navvies. A large party of convicts had just arrived at this *étape*. The majority were busy surveying their new quarters, the first wild rush for places in the *kameras* having subsided. Some were lying about in the yard on their *khalats* or on their miserable mattresses, adjusting their chains; others, who had flung their greatcoats over the somewhat low palisade, were disposing themselves in a quiet corner preparatory to stretching themselves out at full length in the sun. Each had his little bundle. Many of the gang were in the rooms arranging for the evening. Already some were reclining on the *nari* or lolling beneath them; a few were smoking. One of the *kameras* was 20 feet broad by 50 in length; the rafter roof was some 10 feet above us, and daylight was admitted by four windows. All the ventilation was conducted by four narrow slit-like holes in the wall leading out to the exterior. The atmosphere was stifling, according to our ideas; but even among the wealthy merchant classes of Moscow the principles of ventilation are now only slowly being learned.

The officer in command of the *étape* drew up a list of three grounds of complaint, which he expressed in a demand for the following three things: (1) A larger daily grant than 8½ kopeks for the prisoners; (2) an extra shirt for each man (the allowance is three shirts to each man); (3) 15 rubles to whitewash his *étape*. Their only interest is to show the lines along which a Russian officer felt that improvement was needed.

One other *étape* on the road to Irkutsk may be shortly described. It was in a very tumble-down condition, and the wooden entrance-gate was represented now by only a third of its former self—"not very like the door of a prison," as the captain remarked; but he added, "I have very little money, and so what can I do?" There was also a small hospital in connection with this *étape*, which was much cleaner and tidier than the *étape* proper. There were only two wards, one for women and another for men: an iron bedstead with pillow, blanket, and mattress completed the rough-and-ready arrangements.

Sometimes we met parties on the road. On one occasion it was simply a party of women, most of them elderly, driving in carts. Four soldiers were in charge, and everybody was taking matters very leisurely. One guard walked in front, another in the rear, while the remaining pair supported the flanks.

East of Lake Baikal one noticed some slight differences in the general character of the étapes compared with those

An étape, Eastern Siberia.

farther to the west. Almost without exception they were now situated on a bare patch of ground distinctly outside the village at its eastern end, so that the convicts traversed its whole length on arrival. Thus they have an opportunity of exciting the compassion and generosity of the villagers.

This they contrive to do by uniting to the best of their ability in a weird discordant chant, the burden of which is a cry for mercy intensified by realistic word-pictures of the desolation of their existence. The *étapes* had always a smart appearance from the outside, and were more cleanly within than those in the west; while if the smaller *polu-étapes* sometimes looked lonely and anæmic, the same could hardly be said of the full *étapes*, which were enlivened by the presence of gymnastic apparatus on a large scale for the benefit of the soldiers. Piles of sawn birch, the black-and-white-striped sentry-boxes at each corner, and a similarly coloured post that held the Imperial eagle aloft, were common to *étape* and *polu-étape* alike. Both classes had dark-red roofs, chimneys of whitened brick, and the lines of the windows were picked out in white on the natural dirty yellow of the seasoned logs. Often a slight deception was practised which gave the semblance of a sure foundation to the *étapes*: about 3 feet from the ground the trusty logs were discontinued, and planks with their broad side in the vertical were substituted. In Siberia it is no uncommon thing to find the log-houses poised on stone foundations; but the foundation is laid *last*. A square log box, as it were, without a lid, is erected, and rests about 2½ feet above the ground on four corner supports. The doors and windows are then sawn out, and the stone foundation is built in below. So the *étapes* were built, save that their foundations are still of wood.

One other *étape* in the vicinity of the Nertchinsk silver mines deserves mention, not on its own account—for it had no palisade, and the door was sustained more by its padlock than the hinges[1]—but on account of the captain who was in

[1] It is only fair to state, however, that a new *étape* was being built to take its place.

charge. Truly the lot of the soldiers and officers is often as hard comparatively as that of any of the convicts. Formerly our friend had been a captain in one of the crack Chasseur Guard regiments, and when the time came for his compulsory retirement he was forced to accept this forsaken post, after the gay life of an officer of the guard. The one other person in the village approaching his station in life was a nervous little individual, who only seemed happy when in his uniform with a hand on the hilt of his sword: he was in command at the post office. The neat habits that the guard officer had acquired remained with him even in this benighted spot, for his few possessions were laid out on a table with extreme care and good taste. Except for the fact that he was a free man, how was he any better off than the politicals who passed through his hands? The gentle courtesy of manner that should have been expended on the subject of a single photograph that occupied the centre of the table, inscribed with the one word "Manya," remained with him still, as also a calm unmurmuring resignation. "Weland [the great smith of the Eddas] and the kings of the Goths suffered and bore their weird, and so may I. The All-wise Lord of the World worketh many changes."

He said that the lowest number of soldiers that he was allowed to send on to a neighbouring *étape* was four theoretically, and that he must send this number even with two or three prisoners—one being in command while the other two go on guard, with a third to relieve. He had only one thing of which to complain, and it did not affect himself. If any of his soldiers should fall seriously ill, he would have to send the sick man either to Srjetensk (150 versts) or to Gorni-Zerentui (90 versts) to a hospital. "I have only castor-oil and a little quinine."

As already stated, political prisoners who are able to pay their way can travel by post. I saw only one instance of this. We were rejoining the main road after having paid a visit to Alexandrovsky Central: about six in the evening we had reached a new station. The villagers came and stood about, gazing admiringly at my friend's *kolyaska*, and making remarks thereon to one another. Suddenly the sound of approaching bells caused them all to look up, and they quickly separated to make way for a *telyega* that was being dragged along by a couple of Siberian ponies. In front sat the driver, and beside him a soldier, quite a small man compared with the long rifle with fixed bayonet that lay over his shoulder. He was attired in the ordinary garb of the convoy guard—white linen tunic, dark-green trousers, cap, jacket, boots, and leathern belt, to which was attached a very conspicuous cartridge-pouch. Behind him, reclining on the baggage which strewed the bottom of this cradle-like conveyance, were two men who excited one's curiosity immediately. One was enveloped in the grey *khalat* that seems to be always given a size too large to each prisoner, but with a hat of his own selection; while the other affected a tall cap of astrakhan, a black blouse, and dark trousers. It was amusing to watch the way in which they ordered their military warder about, and made him unload the cart, as it was necessary to change both vehicle and team. Thereafter they disappeared inside the post-house to discuss a cup of tea, while their attendant mounted guard at the door and adopted a very careless attitude, joking with the bystanders about his charges.

Farther on the road that day we passed a tiny procession, consisting of some twenty *telyegas:* the number of convicts was small, mainly women. There were, however, half-a-dozen men in chains dispersed throughout the *cortége*. On one cart were seated an old woman and a soldier who was chatting busily with her; his rifle-butt rested on his knee, and the muzzle pointed towards the heavens. Another waggon held a man in chains, his wife, and two or three small children; but the *natchalnik* of the convoy had paid no special attention to him—his children were a sufficient guard. A third cartload of young women was willingly escorted by a couple of soldiers, who were evidently enlivening proceedings for them with their coarse witticisms. In this extraordinary gang no prisoner was walking. There seemed to be a large proportion of soldiers for the size of the party, so that one assumed that the *telyegas* were transporting men of criminal distinction. A few waggons weighted with sacks and bags brought up the rear.

In attempting criticism of the march as a whole, one naturally seizes on three points: (1) The food allowance; (2) the condition of the *étapes;* (3) the hospital accommodation. With regard to the first of these, one remarks that while in ordinary circumstances 8½ kopeks would be quite sufficient, the fluctuations in market prices make it imperative that there should be no hard-and-fast allowance throughout Siberia at all seasons of the year. Nor is this the case; for it has always been customary to grant a higher allowance in Eastern Siberia, where the prices are dearer than in the west. Difficulty seems rather to manifest itself in the adjustment of the necessary rise to the periods of distress. The consequent state of affairs has been extravagantly depicted by a Russian writer, who sarcastically adds that when once, during a year of famine, orders were given from headquarters that the daily grant should be increased in a certain quarter, owing to official delays the rise did not come into effect till the year after, when there was a super-abundance. Be that as it may, this I know for certain, that when my companion telegraphed to St Petersburg how matters stood in the districts already described, the ordinary grant was immediately raised from 10 to 13 kopeks. It has also been suggested that all the food should be bought beforehand by the local authorities at prices strictly fixed by the Crown: this would obviate the annoyances associated with the individual dole. Further, if those members of each gang whom it elects as cooks could be sent on ahead to the *étape*-destination for the night, it would be possible to have a good meal ready awaiting the arrival of the prisoners.

The condition of the *étapes* has excited comments from all observers. Those in the east are in vastly better order than their western equivalents, some of which are said to date from the "thirties." But to stigmatise them all as enormous gloomy structures, "ancient, skeletonised, and draughty," is unfair; many are in excellent condition. A large sum is spent every year on the reconstruction and repairing of *étapes* — admittedly not enough: at the same time, the Government naturally does not feel justified in making any great outlay in this particular direction, considering that the railway will shortly do away with the need for the greater number of these buildings. Still, one cannot help remembering that transportation by *étape* antedates all dreams of railway enterprise.

On the subject of the hospitals I intend to say more in a later chapter. Any man who falls ill on the march is left at the nearest town; but as in Eastern Siberia it may be more than a hundred miles distant, he may suffer a great deal before he reaches one. This affects soldiers and prisoners alike. Moreover, the tiny lazarets that are occasionally found at the *étapes* do not as a whole look specially inviting. On the other hand, the devices to which the prisoners resort in order to obtain admission to a hospital of any class is a testimonial of a very high order.

But the death-knell of this grim march has been sounded: hereafter the humaner railway will relieve it of its horrors. The autumn of 1896 was to witness the last long river-voyage to Tomsk in the menagerie-like barges. Perhaps that crowded floating prison, dragged in the wake of a hardly less miserable steamer, that greeted us in mid-stream of the Ob on that quiet autumn evening, was then making its final journey. Perhaps the desolate low banks of that cold unresponsive river then listened for the last time to the convicts' plaintive melodies, and heard strains tender and subdued give place in wilder chorus to the reckless *motif*—

> "Cease, brother, youngster,
> Thou surely art not a girl;
> Sing, sing, care will fly away."

A provisional arrangement was to come into force in 1897, whereby the convicts would still be conveyed by boat from Tiumen, but only up the Irtish to Omsk, at which point they would join the railway.[1] At Kainsk one got a glimpse of what this new departure will mean. The brick building that is to serve as station had evidently not been long completed, and the platform was still in process of construction. In the lee of a log office crouched a group of convicts, surrounded by some fifteen guards. At a sign

[1] I have since learned that this project was not accomplished, and that during the summer of 1897 the transportation was effected in the ordinary way. Only from the spring of 1898 onwards they will be conducted straight from Russia by the Trans-Siberian Railway to their destinations, and the closing of the *étapes* has already commenced.

LOADING A CONVICT WAGGON.

from the sergeant they rose to their feet, and commenced singly to clamber up into the waggon—the last of a short train—that stood on the side-line beside them. It is hard for one who has not seen the circumstances of the march to estimate the far-reaching benefit to humanity that the Trans-Siberian Railway will render in this respect. For those exiles whose destination is the silver mines of Nertchinsk, the weary march will each year become more of a vanishing quantity. Moreover I should not be surprised if, when the railway is completed as far as the town of Nertchinsk, the need even for it in the capacity of convict-transporter will have entirely disappeared, for one gets the impression that we are seeing the last phases of a system that is passing away.

On the horizon.

CHAPTER VII.

ALEXANDROVSKY CENTRÁL.

PAST OPINION REGARDING SIBERIA — EVOLUTION OF THE PRISON — STATISTICS — THE SIBERIAN EXILE SYSTEM — DISTRIBUTION OF EX-CONVICTS AND EXILE SETTLERS — ALEXANDROVSKY CENTRÁL — THE NATCHALNIK — THE ORPHANS' HOME — THE CHURCH — THE PRISON BUILDINGS — UNUSUAL PRECAUTIONS — THE OUTHOUSES — CAPITAL PUNISHMENT — THE PLET — BRANDING — INDOOR LABOUR — THE PER-ESÍLNI PRISON — THE HOSPITAL — LOCAL PRISON AT IRKUTSK — CONTRASTED WITH ALEXANDROVSKY CENTRÁL — OF ANIMAL FOOD — THE DARKER POSSIBILITIES OPEN TO A "FREE-COMMAND."

> " Thence come we to the horror and the hell,
> The large great kingdoms, and the dreadful reign
> Of Pluto in his throne where he did dwell,
> The wide waste places, and the hugy plain,
> The wailings, shrieks, and sundry sorts of pain,
> The sighs, the sobs, the deep and deadly groan ;
> Earth, air, and all, resounding plaint and moan."
> —*The Mirror for Magistrates*, 1559.

THESE lines from a poem by Sackville, Lord Buckhurst, in which he describes his descent to Avernus, may be held to represent more or less the idea of Siberia still entertained by the average Briton. And if one were asked what causes had mainly conduced to the production of this state of opinion about that country and its peculiar association the exile system, one would reply, Three chiefly — descriptions of the country by travellers who have traversed it in winter; isolated paragraphs in the newspapers; and the work of Mr George Kennan, combined with the literary and other efforts of political refugees. Of English-speaking men who have devoted attention to these matters on the spot, and are the popular accredited exponents more particularly of the exile system, three stand conspicuously in the foreground—Dr Lansdell, Mr George Kennan, and Mr De Windt. Into the question of the respective merits of this distinguished trio it is not my intention to enter: suffice it to say that at least in grasp and penetration the American exceeded his rivals. At the same time, Mr Kennan's account, dealing strictly with the state of affairs in a past decade, cannot in the nature of things be supposed to be an accurate picture of the conditions which subsist to-day.

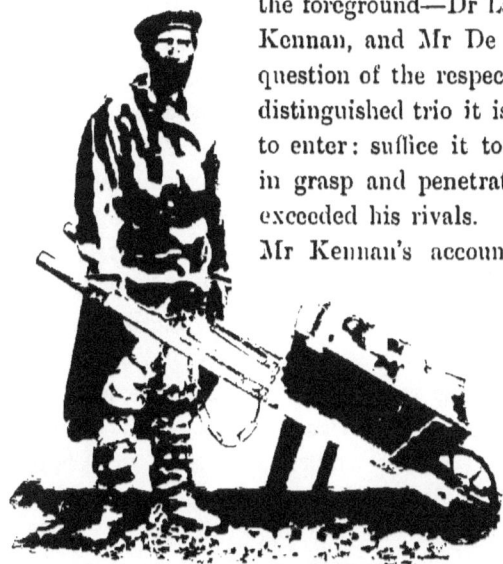

Convict chained to wheelbarrow.

In ten years much can be done; and while the leeway that Russia has to make up is still considerable, the land of the Tzar is probably progressing more rapidly than any other European State. Mr Kennan and Mr De Windt represent two extremes of opinion: the truth, as ever, lies between.

It is perhaps possible to trace two stages in the evolution of all that we connote by the word "prison." The first stage is that in which the place of incarceration may be typically regarded as a dark hole into which the unfortunate misdoer is thrust, and where, if law has not yet attained to any sublime form of practice, the pursuer at whose instance the imprisonment has taken place, or even the executors of the law itself, may contrive to make the offender's existence more miserable by torture and maltreatment. While Russia was in this stage—and some pessimists hold that she is in it still—flogging, branding, amputation of limbs, and impalement were no uncommon inflictions. These, however, are coarse methods of procedure, but there was a certain exquisite refinement of cruelty in the law by which the harmless snuff-taker had the septum of his nostrils torn out before he was banished to Siberia. It was during this time—and herein lies the chief interest of the stage for us—that the system of exile to Siberia arose, but whether in the first intention as an easy method of getting rid of all such mutilated and therefore useless members of society, or as a laudable device by which to reduce the number of death sentences, it would be difficult to say. So we read that men first set out on that terrible Siberian march after the proclamation of an ukaz in 1648 by Alexei Mikhailovitch.[1] What we are apt to forget is that every country has passed through this stage.

The second definite point in the evolution of the prison is that in which it is represented externally by an edifice erected in accordance with known hygienic principles, and where the inmate is set to work at some useful task. The prisoner's punishment is an education : the main end aimed

---

[1] Up till 1822 the annual number of exiles varied between three and four thousand. The following year a law appeared establishing the deportation of vagrants, who, up till that time, had been employed in building fortifications. In 1824 the number of exiles consequently rose to over twelve thousand.

at is that he shall have a chance given him to come out a better man than he entered. We are in this stage: Russia is passing into it, if indeed she is not well within it. And one sometimes wonders if there is not a third stage, in which the community will in some way suffer with the defaulting individual for having let it be possible, by its failure to secure a morally wholesome environment and education for all its members, that he should descend to crime. In a 'Notice sur l'Histoire des Prisons et de la Réforme Pénitentiaire en Russie,' Mr Salomon, the present estimable Director-in-Chief of Russian Prisons, makes the remark that corporal punishment (replaced by loss of civil rights in the case of privileged individuals) was the basis of the old Russian penal system. Deportation had simply the character of a supplementary punishment. The code of 1845 exactly reversed this state of matters. Thereafter deportation and the deprivation of liberty, aggravated by compulsory labour more or less severe, were looked on as the principal punishment, to which the other might be added in certain cases. Moreover, punishment was now meted out on a regular scale.

According to official documents, the large army that yearly crosses the confines of Siberia comprises eight separate divisions [1]:—

		Per cent.
I. Exile convicts . . .	935	9·92
II. Exile settlers . . .	2,300	24·40
III. Exile vagrants . . .	1,111	11·79
Carry forward . .	4,346	46·11

---

[1] The figures here quoted are drawn from the Prison Report for 1894. Figures for a later year are in my possession; but in view of the changes that are being introduced, it is better to take numbers that are not too recent and yet of not too remote a date, so as to get a fair idea of this aspect of the question in an average year.

		Per cent.
Brought forward	4,346	46·11
IV. Exiled by court *na jityo*[1]	178	1·89
V. Exiled to Siberia, having been refused re-admission to commune after sentence and punishment	1,979	20·99
VI. Banished to Siberia by order of the commune	2,674	28·37
VII. Banished by administrative order	249	2·64
	9,426	100·00
VIII. Voluntary companions	6,772	
Total	16,198	

Of these, I., II., and III., being banished for life, are deprived of all civil rights. The others, who need not necessarily be criminals, retain some of their civil rights, and may hope to return to Russia. In Siberia, exclusive of Sakhalin, the daily average of exile convicts at hard labour was 5300 in round numbers. If we add 7000 for Sakhalin it gives a total of 12,300, of whom 94 per cent were confined in Eastern Siberia and only 6 per cent in the West. The exile convict class forms 16 per cent of the total number of Russian prisoners. To complete the above, it need only be added that women formed only 5 per cent of the categories I.-VII., while in VIII. they formed 64 per cent. Again, while 52 per cent were exiled by administrative process and the commune—*i.e.*, without trial,—48 per cent left for Siberia, having been banished by court.

In order to explain the extraordinary size to which class VIII. attains, it is necessary briefly to examine the system.

The convicts are divided into three great categories, according to the length of their sentence:—

[1] *Na jityo* = lit. to stay, not necessarily for life.

(*A*) Those condemned to penal servitude for life or for a period of from twelve to twenty years.

(*B*) Those condemned for periods varying from eight to twelve years.

(*C*) Those condemned for periods varying from four to eight years.

The penal life of each convict is again subdivided into three stages, the first of which is regarded as a period of trial or probation, during which he carries his chains, and is subjected to the full rigour of prison discipline. For those who are included under (*A*) this first stage is graduated in length, as follows :—

(*a*) Those sentenced for life remain in it eight years.

(*b*) Those whose sentences range from fifteen to twenty years remain in it four years.

(*c*) Those whose sentences range from twelve to fifteen years remain in it two years.

Again, for those under (*B*) this period of probation lasts one year and a half; while for those included under (*C*) it lasts one and a half or even but a single year, according as their sentence is from six to eight or from four to six years. And since twelve or even eighteen months may be—have been—occupied on the march, especially if the destination be remote, and delays owing to sickness and indefinite orders be incurred, it follows that, in the case of those with the lighter sentences, the convict may often appear at the gate of his penal home ready to pass into the second stage, in which his chains are removed. This may be described as the Reformatory stage,[1] and the length of it for (*A*), (*B*),

---

[1] Strictly speaking, the second or Reformatory stage includes also what is here described as a third stage—*i.e.*, the Russians recognise two stages only : three have been introduced in the text for the sake of clearness.

and (*C*) is three years, two years, and one year respectively. But although the limits of this second stage are thus strictly defined, they are not always observed, and according to the man's behaviour during the first period and the good pleasure of the *natchalnik*, it may not exceed ten days in the case of a man in class (*C*), while it also may be extended to two years. Thereafter the individual passes into the third stage of a "free-command," when he lives outside the prison walls, either in certain barracks or in his own house, and is free to marry if opportunity arises, but must of course come to do his hard labour every day. At this-stage also his private money, which is taken away from him at the first, is returned. Looking forward to that third stage of relative freedom, the large companies of lovers, relatives, and friends lighten the steps of the banished by their sympathetic presence.

The after-history is brief. The life-sentenced convict, if his conduct has been good, may after twenty years of hard labour pass into division II. Convicts who have been condemned to labour for a shorter fixed period pass into freedom from labour as settlers, and become subject to the regulations established for exiles entering straight into settlement. Those who compose division II. may after ten years of settlement be registered as peasants: in this way they pass from the control of the Exile Administration, and receive a formal police sanction for free movement and residence in the country districts.

The distribution of ex-convicts and exile settlers throughout Siberia is conducted on a regular plan. Certain thinly-populated districts are selected, and the *poselentzi* are added to the number of old inhabitants of the peasant class. In no village must their number exceed one-third of that of the original population. Able-bodied exiles only

"FREE COMMANDS."

are forced upon the communities in this way, and to each a grant of 15 *desiatines* of land is made. The political exiles of this class are usually to be found in the towns. Again, attempts have been made to distribute the exiles in localities according to their religious beliefs: thus Lutherans have been settled in one district, Jews in another, Mohammedans and Dissenters in yet others. Two characteristic restrictions attend the distribution of the Jews: (*a*) they may not be settled within 100 versts of the Chinese frontier (this to obviate smuggling); (*b*) they may not be settled near centres of the gold industry. Siberian criminals are commonly sent to Sakhalin. For the first three years settlers enjoy exemption from taxes; thereafter for seven years they pay half of the assessment, being burdened with the whole at the end of that period,—ten years from the day of settlement. Those who are disabled in any way or who are older than fifty-seven are freed from payment of taxes; those absolutely unfit for work are taken into the poorhouses. It is also possible for a colonist to reduce this ten years' term of settlement previous to enrolment as a peasant to six years by good conduct. He now has the right of movement in Siberia, is unaffected by the laws relating to exiles, and may settle permanently within the country where he chooses. It would seem, however, that the practice of this system is attended with considerable difficulty, and the proportion of exile settlers who move off from the place assigned to them, preferring to lead the life of *brodyagi*, is very considerable. Leave of absence is supposed to be given only to those who have definitely settled, but many take it without asking.

Lastly, there are a happy few (*e.g.*, administrative politicals) whose sentence of exile has been comparatively short, and to whom there comes a day when they may begin to retrace their steps, and say good-bye for ever to the land of their sojourn. Again, one sees that the number of criminals in Siberia under sentence for life must be relatively small at the present moment, when one recollects the number of manifestoes that have been issued within recent years (the last being at the Coronation), by which all sentences are appreciably reduced in a corresponding ratio. This suggests that the lot even of a Siberian exile is not without its element of hope.

. . . .

Seventy versts to the north-west of Irkutsk lies the famous prison Alexandrovsky Central, which the traveller can easily reach in seven and a half hours from that town. At first he will follow the road to Yakutsk, and its miserable condition, so long as it runs within the municipal bounds, will readily help him to believe what he may have heard the citizens say in jest—that Irkutsk is a penniless city, with not even money enough to pave its streets. At a certain point he will come to a clearly marked line, where the disgraceful track that is the shame of Irkutsk resigns its travelling commission in favour of the macadamised highway that is the glory of the neighbouring village interested to maintain it in good order. The road climbs slowly up a series of wood-clad ranges of no great height, winding circuitously for about fifteen versts, so that in time a point of vantage is attained whence we look out on the city away beneath us. Three post-stations break the journey into as many stages. One of the villages contains a factory. In another a shrewd *ataman*, after exploiting his fellow-villagers to the extent of several thousand rubles, built at a cost of 400 a little shrine to commemorate the

THE VILLAGE OF ALEXANDROVSKY. 203

preservation of Nicholas II. from the hands of the Japanese assassin, and the unsuspecting peasants worship the memory of the pious donor. After a time we begin to descend by the same sandy road among thick woods, in which spruce, birch, and larch predominate, and eventually Alexandrovsky appears in view.

The village is situated in a pretty valley: it is of considerable size, and at the far end, as you approach from Irkutsk, stands the prison. As we pass down between

Alexandrovsky Central.

the double row of cosy cottages, we occasionally notice a rough pole erected over a courtyard gate, and supporting a wisp of straw as pennant. This marks the presence of infectious disease in the home. We meet a group of half-a-dozen convicts trudging along under the eye of a couple of warders armed merely with revolvers. Towards the end of the main road we see men in convict dress standing about outside their cabins: they are "free-commands." We next come on a party of three or four, who with spades and brooms are cleaning up the road for the day, while others pass them dragging a water-barrel: no guard overlooks their labour. A few are standing about idle, and respectfully remove their caps. It is, comparatively, a scene of leisure and repose. The "free-commands" go about their business, and no one takes any notice of them.

We drive up to the neat little house that has been built to accommodate inspectors paid and unpaid. The outlook is broad and varied, and one sees the hospital and Peresilni barracks across the valley, while the magnificent church, the work of convict hands, is a short distance farther along the road. At the door of our abode we were greeted by the *natchalnik*, who was in many ways the most remarkable man that I met in Siberia. A magnificent forehead rested above a kindly face, while his iron-grey hair, although brushed back most carefully, refused to be restrained, and occasionally fell over his ears and streamed across his face, when he would shake it back with a smile. It was one of those tender yet eager expressions that you do not expect in such a place. His medium height still carried well the dark-blue uniform with gilt embroidery that is the *natchalnik's* pride: a sword and a single order completed his outfit. A large room on the left of the entrance passage was our dining-room, but at its far end a raised platform, on which a double-bass and 'cello were lying, hinted at a strange tale,— the prisoners sometimes have private theatricals!

Two men emerging from an inner door suddenly made their appearance. One, fair in complexion, looked very trim in a delicate pink *rubashka* girded by a sash of darker shade, both of which were set off by black velveteen trousers that in turn lost themselves in shining jackboots. He was nervously ready to translate the slightest sign from the *natchalnik* into some thoughtful action. That other man beside him, equally anxious to do his master's bidding, and emulating his fellow-servant so far as he might with his dark-red, white-spotted blouse, would also predispose you favourably towards him to a similar extent if you did not notice the stamped linen trousers and the coarse boots,—Ivan is a " free-command." But all honour to the " free-command ": he served us as smartly as any waiter in a Moscow restaurant. The cook also was a convict of the same stage, and in monthly receipt of eight brown ruble-notes for the hard labour of preparing food for occasional visitors. If he desires to remain on in this position after his sentence is finished—*i.e.*, during the period that he must serve as an exile settler before he can be enrolled as a peasant— he may send in an application to that effect, which in ordinary circumstances would not be refused.

The same evening we went to see one or two accessory institutions connected with the prison. Having left the church and the *natchalnik's* house behind us, we turned sharply to the right, into a lesser valley, at the foot of which the waters of a little stream had been dammed up to form an artificial pond of considerable breadth. A small pier, erected for bathers, projected out upon the unruffled surface, and looked like some great centipede that feared to quit the land. A soldier was fishing off it, and beside him were seated three convicts, chatting with him as pleasantly as if he and they were the best of friends. We passed a smithy where half-a-dozen men were still at work,— simply the occupation of their better days. Continuing on our course, we next saw barracks for the " free-commands." A little farther and we came to the Orphans' Home, the object of our quest. The name is a misnomer, for of the seven girls and thirteen boys whose home it is, the majority, though motherless, had come out with miscreant fathers who were now sojourning in the prison. A large school-room formed the principal feature, where not only the inmates but many of the village children receive instruction from the lips of a wise and pleasant woman. This particular institution was founded by the *natchalnik*, and is largely supported out of the surplus that accrues from his economical administration of the prison. Happy and bright were the criminals' children, of whom the eldest had not yet seen the darker side of thirteen, while the youngest was a baby.

After this we retraced our steps considerably, even to the outskirts of the village at its eastern boundary, and then ascended the opposing slope till we came to some exceedingly old prison buildings. In one were gathered to meet us about thirty families, in all 130 women and children. They were the wives and children of the poorest prisoners, and the *natchalnik* had utilised the buildings to give them a roof over their heads. In addition to this he provides them with fire and light, while each family is allowed to appropriate and to cultivate a certain portion of the kitchen-garden which lies to the rear. Otherwise, these people would have had to live in the village and find work there: as a matter of fact, some of them had gained employment in that way. Twice a-week the wives are allowed to go and visit their husbands in prison. One poor Dungan woman and her child fell down begging for a little help; she had not a single kopek in the world. A Moldavian gipsy woman with her three daughters, whose husband was going to be sent on to the silver-mines of Nertchinsk, prayed that she might be allowed to remain where she was, as life was harder, she had heard, at the great penal settlement.

The next day was devoted to an inspection of the prison in all its different branches and activities. Alexandrovsky Central, originally built as a distillery, will hold 1000 men; but with the "free-commands" who live outside the prison

The church at Alexandrovsky Central.

walls, there are half as many again upon the roll. It is unusual to find a convict there whose sentence extends over half-a-dozen years.

As you drive down towards the western end of the village, where are the prison buildings, you observe that they are largely hidden by the beautiful church which stands out boldly, lying, as usual, east and west. A pair of artistically painted *ikons* adorn the eastern outer wall. As already stated, the church is entirely the work of convict hands. The terra-cotta bricks, with their white pointing, harmonise delicately with the tasteful bluish-grey that clothes the roof and cupolas, while the outlines of the windows are also accentuated by being picked out in white. The outside effect, therefore, cheery and gay (as are all Russian outside effects), is essentially agreeable to the eye. Ten yards from its main entrance on the west, and immediately opposite to it, is a gate opening out of the prison-yard. Thus there is no difficulty in the transit of prisoners to the building, which acts also as the village church. As a rule, however, the prison sanctuary is within the grounds. In this case there was a gallery, which is unusual in Russian churches. It, of course, only furnished standing room, in the shape of three broad steps ascending towards the back, thus making it possible for all to see. The gallery extended continuously round the building, except on the east side. Access was given to it by staircases rising from the two sides of the nave close to the transept. The nave itself, which was unusually short, was railed off from the rest of the church by a high iron grating with a gate in it. I have thus minutely described the church, because in its arrangement it served to show how much a capable and thoughtful man may do to improve the station of which he is in charge. The customary method is to shut off the nave, and place the prisoners there behind iron bars—the menagerie idea once again. "All men are equal before God," said the *natchalnik*, and so he arranged the church with this serviceable gallery into which the convicts are conducted, so that in His house, at least, they may feel that they are as other men. The officials and villagers stand in the transepts and body of the church, with the prisoners above, and yet may rest secure, as an iron partition is interposed between them and the nave. The whole building is a monument to carefully directed convict labour, and even some of the finer *ikons* in the interior were painted by sentenced hands.

In the prison buildings, men of heterodox creeds were put together for the sake of companionship. The Mohammedans were in one room. In another a copy of the Law in Hebrew, hung over the front of a small altar, advertised the congregation of the men of Israel there as surely as other characteristics that are, after all, more easily recognised.

The prison, then, stands immediately behind, *i.e.* to the west of, the church. The surrounding wall, rectangular and of white-pointed bricks, with a coping of green zinc, encloses a very liberal allowance of courtyard. Outside at each corner a wooden platform, almost equal in height to the wall, extends along two sides of it for about 20 feet. Mounted on this a soldier constantly paces up and down, being thus able to command the courtyard and the road at the same time. The prison itself is a large two-storeyed brick building, also with a green zinc roof, through which the brick chimneys seem to have broken their way: the eaves and cornice are coloured white.

The interior is a study. One can see the whole Siberian prison system of accommodation at a glance, in its evolution from the old-time *nari* to almost the latest form of folding-up camp-bed. The wellnigh spotless condition of the wooden flooring suggests that there has been some special cleaning for the visit of my companion, and when questioned the *natchalnik* does not deny the insinuation, although he very sensibly adds that if it were commonly in a filthy state, one washing, however thorough, would be entirely insufficient to produce the effect that has attracted our notice. Alexandrovsky is undoubtedly a very old building, and to this there was frequent testimony. At points on the corridor walls where the whitewash had disappeared and the plaster given way, one got back again to the warm brick.

Inside the courtyard.

Even the courtyard wall showed signs of great age in some parts, and, at the south-west corner, where it bordered on the little stream that flows through the main valley to join the Angara, it had sunk with the soil, and in consequence displayed several wide fissures. Moreover, the wooden staircases inside were well worn, one of them having too close a resemblance to a yellow venetian blind.

We first visited one of the refurnished *kameras*. Round three walls of the room was disposed the new type of bed, which takes the form of large grey panels, each perhaps 6½ feet by 3 in size, and numbered from 1 to 25: they are attached by hinges at one end to the wall, against which they can thus be folded up when not required. The outer end is supported in the horizontal by a wooden stool of moderate size which the prisoner uses in the daytime. The beds, however, when folded up, do not lie flush with the wall, but with a wooden framework, which, as its sides project outwards for some 6 inches and are connected by three shelves, presents the appearance of a cupboard. The bottom shelf, which is continuous with the camp - bed (indeed it is to it strictly that the beds are hinged), supports a block of wood, triangular in section, which, fitting so as to present a sloping surface to the exterior, serves as a pillow. On the shelf above will be found the prisoner's bedding, and on the highest one are stowed his private effects The beds are usually grouped in threes, in order to save space. When a trio has been swung up, an iron bar, fixed at one side, is led across the top ends of the beds, and secured at the other side by means of a padlock during the day. When the conduct of the prisoners is beyond reproach, the beds are not locked up in the morning: or rather the kind old *natchalnik* began by trusting the men, and granted them the opportunity of resting on them during the daytime, while letting them distinctly understand that this was conditional. Moreover, there is this additional benefit to be derived from the good man's bounty, that during the daytime their personal belongings are accessible to them. The middle of the ward is occupied by a long table: in one corner is the stove, and two large windows let in a flood of light. Strips of coarse matting are laid down on either side of the table, and you step on to a mat of woven birch-branches in entering the room: there is even the refinement of four wooden spittoons. A feeling of comradeship assists the men in keeping their room tidy, for, as the *natchalnik* laughingly remarked, "If a man does not make use of a spittoon when he should, then the others cause him to feel pain." In short, it is not worth a man's while either to be unclean or untidy or to misconduct himself in any way, for when all know that the good behaviour of the company is the condition of such privileges, the others immediately fall on any one of their number who threatens to imperil their high prerogatives, and force him to be amenable to reason.

The great majority of the *kameras* were survivals from the old *régime*. In them the wooden sleeping-platforms were constructed on the usual model, but, being ancient, many of the boards composing them did not meet together, and so great quantities of dust and filth had congregated between them, and could not easily be removed. In one or two other particulars they also differed from those furnished in the newer style, for they were without central tables, and the personal property of the men hung on the walls from nails, or lay on skirting shelves that varied in size and range. Although the disparity in the amount of private possessions in the case of different individuals was very evident, yet every one had a tin can of some sort, while many possessed a rough kind of bedding. From the middle of the ceiling a lamp was suspended,—another instance of the *natchalnik's* trust. One type of room, which was perhaps 15 feet high, 24 feet broad, and 36 feet long, was lighted by two large windows. There were other larger *kameras* with four windows; the number of

THE READING-ROOM AT ALEXANDROVSKY CENTRAL.

prisoners inhabiting them was proportionally greater, but in those of the ordinary size the regulation number of twenty-five was never exceeded. I stayed behind in one, asking the more intelligent-looking of the men if they got sufficient food and clothing—in short, if they had anything of which to complain. One vigorous fellow replied that he could not say a word against the food and clothing, of which they got "enough." "Our complaints are all of one class, directed against our sentences: we think we have been too hardly dealt with, we think that we were in the right, we always feel sure there has been some mistake about us." Of course one can always say—and often with truth—that the men are frightened to complain. Still, I hope to be able to show that in this instance the answerer spoke in verity and without fear: further, it surely is possible to detect when a man says what he feels, and when his response is dictated by secret terror. But when he mentioned justice, he touched a point where there is something to be said on his behalf.

One of the ordinary *kameras* had been fitted out as reading-room and library. The librarian was a striking man, fettered by a painfully romantic past, and now imbued with a keen sense of the importance of his position. The prisoners are allowed to come and read when they wish out of labour hours, and every Sunday a lecture is given on some historical or geographical subject.

In spite of its antiquity, one could only say that the building was admirably managed in every respect. All matters sanitary were unimpeachable. The kitchen, which was in one of the outhouses, presented some features of interest. The buildings themselves were in a somewhat dilapidated condition, in consequence of which they were to be reconstructed in 1897, but the internal arrangements were excellent. In one long hall there was an array of brightly burnished copper caldrons for making soup: lentil brose and *shtchi* predominated, according to the bill of fare for each day of the week, which hung from a pillar. The men dine at 11 A.M. Here also, unlike most other prisons, they get tea served out to them gratis morning and evening: this is only possible where a definite attempt is made to conduct the establishment on strictly economical lines. To this cause may also be ascribed the possibility of supplying each man daily with 3 lb. of bread instead of the normal 2½ lb. The fast days, Wednesday and Friday, in addition to the four great fasts,[1] are of course observed. The allowance of meat on ordinary days is 40 *zolotniks*, and during the fasts the men receive a proportionately larger amount of soup. The food allowance of each prison seems to depend not only on its income but on the efforts of the local committee: still, there is a mean, about which they all fluctuate.

Again, one has often heard the remark made that in certain prisons the men do not receive their full allowance of food because the officials appropriate portions of the money grant,—this of course in support of the epigram in which some one has described Russia as the country where "the Emperor makes the laws and the officials make the profits." It is a charge which the average individual has little chance either to verify or to disprove. At Alexandrovsky Centrál no one could entertain the idea for a moment, although the precautions adopted forcibly suggest that the practice is not unknown elsewhere. One man is chosen by the prisoners from their number, and his sole duty is to see that each

---

[1] These are—(1) Lent; (2) Fast of St Peter, from after Whit Monday to June 29th; (3) Fast of the Virgin Mary, from August 1st to August 14th; (4) Fast of St Philip, from November 15th to December 24th.

day every person gets his proper share. His position is permanent, and one guesses rightly that his allowance exceeds that of the others. But to safeguard the system, the prisoners elect daily two more of their number to act as his controllers, and it is their special function to see that he does not fail in the performance of his task, and to report so in person to the *natchalnik*. Thus three men, of whom two are changed every day, are responsible for this department; and it is on them that the wrath of their comrades would fall if anything went amiss. This scheme also was evolved by the *natchalnik*. We asked if complaints about the food were common, and one of the controllers remarked that with the occasional exception of men of a mathematical turn of mind, who surmised that they had received half a *zolotnik* less than their 3 lb. of bread, such a thing was unknown. Even against this contingency extraordinary precautions are taken. The great brown loaves, like ruddy curling-stones, are carefully divided up, and if the last slice falls short of the regulation amount, the balance is attached to it by means of a peg of wood. So watchful are they that there should be no waste, that one has often noticed a portion to consist of half-a-dozen pieces run together on a wooden skewer. Whatever is left over—for some find that 3 lb. exceed their requirement—is collected and made into *kvass*, which the prisoners receive in addition to their usual allowance of that beverage.

Everything seemed to be thoroughly done here. The soiled linen is washed and disinfected in turpentine and ammonia weekly. Employment in the laundry seemed to be the most serious form of hard labour practised in the institution. The heat in the boiler-rooms was overpowering, and the men were glad to work in a minimum of clothing. From the wash-house it was but a step to the baths, which, although also showing signs of wear, were scrupulously clean. Once every week the prisoners troop in with glee to the bath-chambers and disport themselves, battering one another's backs with wet branches of leafy birch, or lying on the steps of the pyramidal scaffolding built over the brick stove, where the warmth becomes more intense the higher you ascend.

After this we visited a long narrow building—the place of solitude and punishment. It consisted of a corridor skirted on one side by a wall, while a series of cells opened off the other. Each of these was lighted by a window well out of reach, and had its own little outfit of plain furniture. Two only were occupied. In one was an elderly man, with short grey hair, fidgety, and evidently disconcerted by the presence of visitors: he was there by his own request. It seems that in some way he had offended his fellow-prisoners, —perhaps had broken the rules of the *artel* to which he belonged, and feared lynch law in consequence. The other man in solitary confinement illustrated what cannot be said to be common in Russia—miscarriage of justice. The Russian penal code makes no provision for capital punishment except in the instance of regicide. At the same time, every Governor-general has the power to transfer a case from the common court in order to have it tried by court-martial, if the authorities feel that the extreme penalty is called for. But a strong public feeling that considers the infliction of capital punishment to be a retrogressive step compared with the highly developed system that has been explained above, prevents such advantage being taken of this option as might easily be imagined. Russians are curiously unanimous upon the point: men who differ much on almost every other question under the sun, will be found to be equally strong in their denunciation of capital punishment. Still, the results of the practical working of the alternative scheme as evinced in the Siberian system leave almost as much to be said against it as in favour of it. But to resume: a serious murder was committed long ago in a certain district of Siberia, and the perpetrator was caught and sentenced. While being transported in chains under charge of two guards, from one prison to another, he succeeded in murdering the two soldiers, and effected his escape. Some time after, a man was arrested on suspicion of being the now famous murderer. He was tried at Irkutsk by court-martial, found guilty, and sentenced to death for the murder of the two soldiers. The sentence was carried into execution; but thereafter doubts began to be entertained as to whether he really was the culprit. Latterly it was found that a mistake had been made, and now after about eight years the real perpetrator had been taken, and faced us in his cell. Heavily ironed, with low forehead and auburn hair and beard, he smiled as the old *natchalnik* stepped up to him in his peculiar little way, faced in the same direction, and then arched his head so as to bring his ear under the miscreant's lips. He wanted to know what was going to happen him. The Procurator who accompanied us was able to put his mind at rest: he would not suffer now—" Ça serait trop."

At Alexandrovsky it is still possible to see a *palatch*; but to what a pithless condition his function has descended can be gathered from the fact that he was in one of the *kameras* along with other prisoners. "You will find him in room 15," said the chief warder. At Sakhalin, Nertchinsk, and Tobolsk, where employment is still found for professors of this art, they are kept apart from the prisoners, whose feelings towards them can readily be imagined: they do no other hard labour, and are well fed. When vacant, the position is thrown open to offers from the prisoners, but is filled with difficulty. It seems that if in a local

Palatch *with* plet.

prison in Siberia discipline or punishment for a crime has to be enforced with the *rozgi*—a species of birch-rod—then one of the prisoners is elected by lot to perform the service. The *plet* is not given in Russia, and if a man about to go into exile is in addition condemned in Russia to punishment with that instrument, he suffers at Tobolsk, shortly after he has entered Siberia. The *palatch* at Alexandrovsky had more than once asked to be relieved from his unenviable office, as it was a sinecure. The *rozgi* had not been given there for three years, far less the *plet*. The latter is a modification of the famous *knut*,[1] which was abolished in 1845, and although people still often speak of the *plet* as the *knut*, the former term is alone used in law. The implement has a short stout handle, and the thick lash, after tapering for some distance, divides into three tails. It is never given for a first offence, but in such instances as that of a recovered *brodyaga* or of a murderer who repeats his crime as a "free-command," it comes into requisition. In the case of the *brodyaga*, forty to sixty strokes may be given. The culprit is laid on a board, but the executioners commonly contrive to make the heavy tails fall beyond the man's body.

Although the practice of branding has been known in Russia since the fourteenth century, it is somewhat difficult to give the exact date of its introduction into the penal code. From 1691 onwards, however, all offenders sent into exile in place of suffering capital punishment were subjected by law to this disfigurement. The form of the mark was very various. In the seventeenth century stamps were in use with the word *Vor* (thief), with the initial letter V only, and with the letter B (for *buntovshtchik*—*i.e.*, rioter) upon them. In 1698 it was enacted that all Siberian exiles convicted of disorderly conduct and idleness should be branded with the

[1] "Chastisement by the *knut* is an atrocious form of punishment of Tatar origin. Suffice it to say that in giving twenty strokes one hour was expended. The number of strokes was not defined by law, being decided by the tribunal, but at bottom the life or death of the condemned depended on the executioner."—Salomon, *op. cit.*, p. 44, footnote.

Siberian town mark. This, which merely consisted of the name of the town to which the criminal had been sent, was stamped on the back. In the eighteenth century they branded in the following fashion: either VO on the forehead, and R on either cheek, or V simply on the forehead. By the code of 1845 branding was restricted to the convicts, but soon after runaways, exiles, and vagrants were included in the same category. The marks characteristic of this period are KAT (*i.e.*, *katorjnik*, convict), placed on the cheeks and forehead, SB (*i.e.*, *silni-bjegli*, exile-runaway), SK (*i.e.*, *silni-katorjnik*, exile-convict), and B (*i.e.*, *brodyaga*, vagrant). The last three marks are planted on the arm and shoulder-blade. Branding was abolished by the ukaz of 17th April 1863.

Dr Lansdell, who visited the Kara Penal Settlement in the summer of 1879, makes the following statement: "There were two or three veterans at Kara, one of whom, at my request, was brought to me, and whose cheeks and forehead were marked with the letters KAT, an abbreviation of *katorjnik*, a convict. This man had been marked in 1863, and the letters presented a tattooed appearance, though the operation of tattooing must be the more severe, since it is slowly done by hand, whereas, in the case of the prisoners, the brand was done by a kind of cupping instrument, or stamp, furnished with small points, which, on being tapped, pierced the skin. A liquid was then rubbed on, and so the convict was tattooed for life."[1] In the Nertchinsk Penal Settlement there is a station called Alexandrovsky, where all the aged convicts of the district who are unfit for work are collected and supported in almshouses at the Government expense; but though I watched carefully for such

[1] Through Siberia, p. 464.

curiosities when visiting that settlement, I failed to remark any one who had been subjected to the indignity. Later I learned that there were none—they had all died out. The illustration facing p. 222 represents a convict branded with the letters S, K, and A, the latter standing for *arestant*, i.e. prisoner. That facing p. 178 represents a *brodyaga* whose arm and cheek have been branded with the Russian B. I have other photographs in my possession, one of which shows a

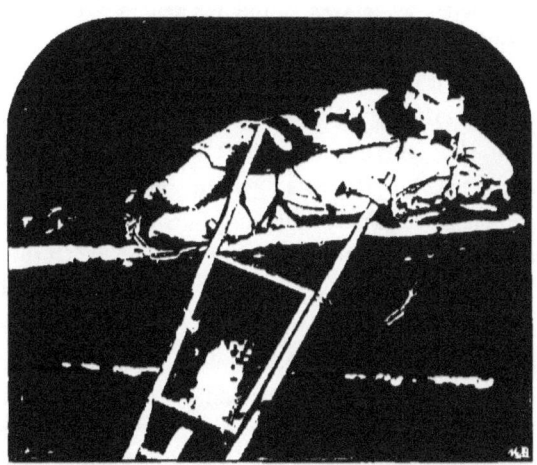

Convict chained to wheelbarrow, resting.

convict who has been branded eight times with the letters SK. The practice of chaining refractory life-sentenced convicts to wheelbarrows for months at a time is no longer carried on in continental Siberia, although Mr De Windt found it lingering in Sakhalin as late as 1894.

We next went to the extreme west end of the building, where the indoor labour is carried on. Here the prison stands very close to the courtyard wall, on the other side of which is a road that leads to the Peresilni prison and hospital upon the other side of the valley. Across the road is a cabbage-garden, where great quantities of the staple vegetable in *shtchi* are grown. The top storey of the building was laid out in a broad corridor, off which opened four *kameras*. In one of these several men were at work on ordinary prison boots and shoes, while a few were executing private orders for articles of a superior make. The excellence of the work in each case contrasted favourably with what was found elsewhere. In two of the other rooms was an army of tailors, who had overflowed to some extent into the corridor. Many had sewing-machines, while others sat tailorwise on the *nari*, where they sleep at night. In the fourth room was the cutter, who evidently took great pains with his general appearance, and enjoyed demonstrating the lightning-like rapidity with which he could cut two suits at a time from a pattern. Perhaps he had proved to be a little too sharp, as a warder is in constant attendance upon him to see that he does no mischief to the crowded shelves of linen that surround the room. Many of the tailors seemed to be in comparatively good circumstances, and the ornamental cushions that several of them owned for use at night looked strangely out of place.

Alexandrovsky supplies clothing for some of the local prisons in the neighbourhood, such as that in the town of Irkutsk. The prices received for making the different articles form a very considerable item of revenue. They are as follows: for a shirt, 3 kopeks; *kaftan*, 10 kopeks; boots, 10 kopeks; summer pantaloons, 3 kopeks; winter trousers, 5 kopeks. Regarding the work done from the point of view of the prisoner, we find that he has a very definite interest in it. For ordinary labour—such as carry-

CONVICT BRANDED S K A.

ing wood and water, cleaning up the rooms, and even keeping the village roads in condition—he receives nothing. For other work which is pecuniarily remunerative to the prison, such as any of the trades already mentioned, each man receives one-tenth of the value of what he does. If he has reached the stage of a "free-command" he receives three-tenths; the rest goes to the prison revenue. Of the money that he actually earns, one third is handed to him immediately, while two-thirds is laid to his credit till he has finished his term, so that he will have something to start with when he leaves the prison to become an exile settler.

Several of the Alexandrovsky men were working on the railway, and so well were they cared for that in the summer of 1896 three score ordinary navvies came and begged to be allowed to work on convict terms. They said that in that way they would be sure of good food and housing, and of getting their smaller wage with regularity.

In the prison *kontora* much of the work—*e.g.*, in the bookkeeping department—is done by ex-convicts. Further, the recent introduction into Siberia of trial by jury will involve the erection of a dozen large court-houses at various centres. As the price of labour is dear at present, it is suggested that the "free-commands" from the nearest penal settlement should be employed in their erection.

Till a quite recent period the aim of the governor of a Siberian prison was simply to keep the men under his charge in life, and some would have us believe that even this policy was not very vigorously pursued. Rational employment was not considered to be worth while.[1] Now all that is

[1] It might be possible to prove that it actually was not worth while, owing to "the expense of the carriage of raw materials, and the comparatively small demand for manufactured articles."

being rapidly changed, and the universal idea is that every man should do remunerative work. Of the prisoners at Alexandrovsky 26 per cent were doing no regular work —*i.e.*, work for which they received a proportion of its value. This figure includes those in hospital, and those who, amongst the industries engaged in at Alexandrovsky, found nothing to which they could turn their hands, and consequently did housework only.

Clemency joined with official decision in the *natchalnik's* unique conduct of everything concerned with Alexandrovsky Centrál. Not a man's head was shaven; the only fettered creature was in the secret cell. The humanity that permitted the unlocking of the beds by day, and the day-long opening of the *kamera* doors, let it be strictly understood that perfect behaviour on the part of the men was required in return. It is natural, therefore, that the men admire their *natchalnik*, who is more of a stern though kindly father towards them than a governor of jail-birds. A curious case occurred, in which a man had been transported from Alexandrovsky to another prison. But at a distance, as is most usual, he learned to appreciate the benevolent spirit of his former chief, and missed his gracious governance. And as he lay in his new quarters a great yearning came over him to see the old place, to live under the old conditions, and it grew upon him till it took the shape of a determination to return. One day the convict escaped, went straight back to Alexandrovsky Centrál, and presenting himself at the prison gate, demanded admittance. To the *natchalnik*, who interviewed him, he confided that he had had no intention of running away altogether—simply a desire to be once more at Alexandrovsky. Here was a difficulty, as the *brodyaga* who gives himself up or is recaptured becomes liable to punishment with the *plet*—and this man had run away. But the compassionate governor had not the heart to carry out the law—nay, rather took the side of the suppliant, and, under the very original charge of "voluntary change of prison," he arranged with the procurator that the *brodyaga* should go unpunished.

On the southern side of the valley are two series of buildings that demand attention—the Peresilni prison and the Alexandrovsky Prison Hospital. A Peresilni prison is simply a magnified *étape*, the main difference being that prisoners may often pass a considerable time there, owing to inadequate instructions in their papers, or to sickness, or, in the case of *poselentzi* (exile settlers), until a sufficient number has been collected to warrant the despatching of a party to the locality which is to be colonised by them. Crowds of vagrants are always to be found in the Peresilni prisons. How they chafe against delays.! We saw again in this instance the familiar long barracks, with the double *nari* in the centre: the prisoners stood with their backs to the wall, and looked very wretched and needy compared with those in the Central prison. Eight of them were engaged drawing water out of the 16-*sajen*-deep well in the courtyard, but the labour was light.

The hospital of the Central prison stood close by in two separate oblong enclosures. In the first of these were four barracks, and a little house which they called the Cottage. Accommodation was provided for 160 patients in all, the doctor being assisted by two *feldshers*. Siberian cottages have very commonly a double roof—*i.e.*, a tall sloping roof may rise above the flat inner one that forms the lid of the box-like cottage. Sometimes the second storey thus formed is used as a garret for storage, and may even be rendered

P

accessible by a wooden staircase outside the house. But one often notices that the outer roof is no longer the water-tight protection that it was intended to be, and sometimes it may be full of holes, and afford shelter to flocks of pigeons. This is considered no inconvenience so long as the inner roof is sound. The hospital barracks, which were overgrown cottages, had dispensed with the inner roof, and were excellently ventilated by roof-lights which could be opened at will. A few stout rafters spanned the place of the inner roof for strengthening purposes. The plan of the barracks was uniform. They were square buildings, of which the door led into a corridor. Off this, at the far end, opened the two main wards: on the left was the operation-room, and on the right a smaller ward and baths. The buildings were all of wood, but the English grates, built up with ornamental plaster-work, presented a very Western appearance. The usual iron bedstead was provided, and an extra sheet was characteristic of Alexandrovsky. The operation-room could hardly have been recognised as such, with its two beds and plain unvarnished floor. Another barrack was reserved for the military: they were treated, however, only to wooden bedsteads. One entire barrack was devoted to the purposes of kitchen. The arrangements here were not perfect, as the cooks have to sleep in the large kitchen, which thus presented a motley collection of coppers, beds, and private effects. The large caldrons shone in their brightness; but not even the pipes that connected their lids with the chimney, and so carried off the steam and vapours, prevented the atmosphere from being moist and oppressive. The food was excellent of its kind. In the other square were only two buildings, as remote from one another as was possible: one was the barrack for female patients, and the other that for all infectious cases. The former was, fortunately, at the moment tenantless.

In support of my impression that, while life at the large penal settlements of Siberia is quite passable, several of the bad features to which we have become accustomed from previous investigation still cling to the march and local prisons, I purpose to describe very shortly the prison at Irkutsk by way of contrast.

It lies on the outskirts of the town, separated from it by a little stream. There is the usual effect produced by the white-plastered building, and over the main entrance is built the church. On the left the hospital and laundry stand isolated within a wooden palisade. The first day on which we visited this prison happened to be a holiday, and as there was a special service in the church to which all prisoners who cared might go, we climbed up the wooden staircase that leads from the courtyard to the sanctuary, and hid behind a pillar to await developments. The transept into which the staircase led was railed off from the nave by a high iron grating, in which was a little gate. The wing thus shut off might hold 150 people. The decorations in the church were of the simplest. The *psalomstchik* was already in his place, and had begun his recitative in a low bass. The priest was meanwhile conducting his own private devotions, but soon disappeared into the sanctum behind the *ikonostas*. At the same time a soldier appeared at the head of the stair, and unlocking the iron gate, took up a position by it. Soon heavy steps were heard thundering up the staircase. A thief stood at the top for a moment like an apparition in his unbleached shirt and trousers. Then he marched sullenly across the transept, passed through the wicket, and stepped briskly to the back of the nave, where he prostrated himself before an *ikon*, kissed the ground, made the sign of the cross, and then stood erect facing the altar with his hands folded in front. Before he had done all this, the staircase again resounded to the tramp of feet, this time with the additional clanking of chains. But the repellent creature that emerged on this occasion merely sauntered up to the iron grating with a half-amused expression on his face, and, grasping a rail in either hand, supported himself as he stared dreamily through the partition at his more fortunate fellow - worshipper. Another and another succeeded. With firm determined tread the rebels against God and man stationed themselves either in the iron-bound transept or in the body of the church, according as they were chained or not. And now the recitative had closed, and in place there rose a prisoners' chorus, not indeed with the same *motif* as that which ends "Fidelio," but none the less a mighty unison, that followed one wellnigh all over the prison, breaking upon the ear at intervals.

The prison proper lies in a very large court, and is built round three sides of a square. The free ends of this single-storeyed structure meet the large front line of buildings which comprise the offices, guard-rooms, and church: the space enclosed is planted with birch-trees, and forms a sort of garden. The plan adopted is that of the single corridor with *kameras* opening off it. Beyond the prison stand numerous isolated sheds in which various trades are practised.

On the day of our visit there were 402 prisoners inside the gates: of these 157 were waiting to be judged. Those persons whose process has not yet been concluded may work or not as they choose. If they prefer to remain idle, they can only vary the monotony of their existence with sleep. As the library here, which was in the hands of a priest, hardly deserved the name, and the idea that one gathers from tales of the long periods that often pass before prisoners are put on trial and learn their sentences is in the main correct, one can well imagine the *ennui* of such a life: it is a bare existence. Of the rest of the inmates, 146 were detained for different numbers of months, sentenced for crimes of no great magnitude. The remainder—107 men and 8 women—were about to pass farther on.

The *kameras*, in which the men were grouped according to their crimes, were in a fairly presentable condition: they looked out on to the birch-planted square, and were lighted by four windows grated inside. They might measure 30 feet in length by 12 in height and 15 in breadth. Into each of them not more than twenty-four men were put, and sometimes only eighteen. From between the double row of *nari* in the middle rose great beams to support the whitewashed roof, with the result that the rooms seemed choked with woodwork, and there was only a minimum of space in which to move about. Each man had a straw-stuffed mattress with pillow attached, and a blanket which is changed every fortnight. In a smaller room were five men of noble birth, who, while they wore the ordinary prison garb, had better bed-clothing of their own. In those rooms where women, either under detention or serving their time, were lodged, beds with clothing as in the hospitals replaced the wooden *nari:* their children were beside them. In the workshops employment was given to joiners, cabinet-makers, bootmakers, and blacksmiths. In many of the rooms men were making cigarettes as a pastime: for the serious work they are paid as at Alexandrovsky, while women who work in the laundry get 2 rubles a-week.

Off one special corridor opened a series of single cells.

Indeed every prison is provided with such a secret suite, although solitary confinement is the exception in Siberia. They were of a uniform size—18 feet long, perhaps 12 feet in height and half as many in breadth—and lighted by a strongly barred window near the roof. A mattress in a corner was the main item of furniture. In one of them was a murderer on his way to Sakhalin. He was heavily chained, and unless my eyes deceived me there is more than one size of chain, although this is contrary to what one was told in several places. In another was a boy sixteen years of age under detention, on suspicion of having perpetrated a cruel murder. A third was occupied by a man, also in chains, who had been adopted into a family, and for some motive or other had burned the house and the whole of the inmates. Next to him was confined a gaunt old man, with long hair and in somewhat clerical garments, who rose hastily, removing his spectacles, from the perusal of some sacred literature. He had been arrested on the charge of having constituted himself a bishop of that interesting sect, the Old Creed. To do so is contrary to law.

The kitchen had evidently been hastily set in order: the bread and soup were poor, and the *kvass* was very sour. Each man receives $2\frac{1}{2}$ lb. of black bread daily. Twice in the week the prisoners were reputed to get $\frac{1}{4}$ lb. of flesh in their soup, while the sick are served with $\frac{3}{4}$ lb. daily, if they can take it.

If the above be compared with the Alexandrovsky diet, and it be further taken into consideration that the baths at Irkutsk are only at the disposal of the men once a-fortnight, and that just so often is clean linen given out, one will be able to perceive, from these three particulars alone, the enormous gap that separates the conduct of Alexandrovsky and that of Irkutsk Local. And Irkutsk Local is far better than many of its fellows.

The hospital was the best part of the establishment. Like that at Alexandrovsky, and unlike all others that I saw, it was built on the barrack system, each series of buildings (such as those for infectious cases, for men, and for women) having separate stockades. The inmates, with their peculiar striped dressing-gown covering a linen shirt and drawers, seemed on the whole contented. Floor, walls, and roof were all of wood, and the internal arrangements such as have been described elsewhere, although it was new to see even a strip of coarse cloth laid down in the centre of the room. The barred windows are as necessary here as anywhere. Commonly not more than fifteen men were in a ward, as in that for syphilitic cases, which was full.

The prison, then, might on the whole be described as clean; but from the points of contrast already stated, as well as from the numbers of petitions and complaints that were presented to my companion compared with those proffered at Alexandrovsky, the vast difference between the two places will be recognised. Perhaps this was as apparent in the quality of the food as in anything else.

The small amount of animal food supplied to prisoners all over Siberia may at first cause surprise; but after study of the peasant life in Russia one comes to a truer appreciation of the facts. In the south many of the peasants, owing to poverty, never eat flesh at all. Again, in the case of those who are somewhat better off, the long fasts accustom them to the want of it. In the south, then, the peasants rarely eat meat; in the north this is not so much the case. A southern landed proprietor known to myself on one occasion killed three pigs and gave them to the peasants immediately in the vicinity. They refused the present respectfully,—" We are unaccustomed to meat." With their ryebread, soups, and *kasha* (gruel) they feel quite content; but I have seen them sometimes put pieces of fat into their *borsch* (a soup). Russia is, however, essentially the country of contrast and contradiction. In the army the fasts, as they relate to abstinence from animal food, are not kept: in the prisons the authorities are only too glad to take advantage of them. Although, then, one impression may be corrected with regard to a part of the prisoners' fare, still it is the universal opinion of the prison officials themselves that the whole is barely sufficient. As one of them said, "If the men got more and better food, we would get more and better work out of them." Most of the governors see as the *natchalnik* of Alexandrovsky, although they may not be able to achieve what he has done.

. . . .

It was late in the evening. Outside the air was motionless, and in a clear sky the moon rose above the far side of the valley, and glinted down on the sombre old prison at Alexandrovsky, as it had done so often before. The village was at peace, and the single soldier, pacing up and down on the bare platform that embraced the courtyard wall at the corner, was cursing the monotony of his inglorious task. Suddenly he stopped short in his beat and listened. Strains of prayerful music had reached him in their gentle journey through space; but when he turned his head and quickly marked the spot whence they had emanated, he gave a significant nod and resumed his midnight watch.

The *natchalnik's* house stands across the road, almost facing the front entrance to Alexandrovsky Central. Each village home had long since been in darkness, but from the

open windows of the good man's home streamed rays of light
and waves of harmony, glad partners in their joyous mission.
In contrast to all this, a desperate struggle was taking place
in the heart of a "free-command," who had taken up residence in a deserted hut on the outskirts of the community.
The man had somehow convinced himself that he had been
seriously injured. His penal career calls for no comment,
except to remark that he had been dealt with very leniently,
and for a murder committed under provocation had been
allowed to pass his sentence of a decade and a half at Alexandrovsky instead of at one of the severer convict settlements. He had conducted himself well during his weary
term, in the course of which he had known the prison under
two *natchalniks;* but it was when the present governor came
into office with his generous influence that the unexpected
happened, and the "free-command"—still an inmate—was
alone but resolute in maintaining that a change for the
worse had set in. Sprung from one of the families of the
lesser nobility, he was essentially proud, and considering
that he was entitled to some consideration on the ground
that he had been resident at Alexandrovsky for several
years prior to the appearance of the new *natchalnik*, he
had felt hurt when some trivial concession that he had
requested had been gently though firmly refused by the
latter. This was the beginning of a suspicion that he had
been slighted, and the dignified and to him patronising manners of the governor gradually became objectionable. Dislike grew to contempt; this gave place to hatred, and in the
end a feeling of revulsion against everything connected with
his chief took complete possession of the man. Nor did it
lessen when he became a "free-command." We have seen
how men of this category do their daily round of work, but

live outside the prison walls with whatever members of their family have followed them. But this man dwelt alone, and nursed his griefs: on the other hand, his sensitive nature was often tortured by mental representations of the scene that had caused his banishment.

That evening the fire of hatred burned brightly, and the old instincts reawakened in the soul of the man. "He has injured me; I must be revenged." Once he had got on to this line of thought the advance was rapid. "How will it affect me? They can do little more to me,—a few strokes with the *plet*, and then resumption of the old life with a change of locality. But I shall have achieved my end, and his hideous smile will have lost itself in the kiss of death." He had surrendered. There are, after all, few things that a man can do once and remain satisfied therewith. The spirit that had ruled him one evening, now thirteen years ago, had returned: he went to the dresser, abstracted a long knife from the drawer, hid it beneath his coat, and slipped out into the night.

He hurried along the village street, and swore at the dogs beneath his breath as they bounded at him from courtyard gates. He hastened his steps—he ran. The prison church was now in sight, and he kept in the shadow of it: he saw the *natchalnik's* residence and the open windows, from which the road was partly illumined. He crossed it noiselessly, darted into the shade of the end wall of the house, and then crept round to the front. But the music had reached him ere this. He was conscious that he had slackened his pace, and his questioning mind demanded why. Nor was it content with the inward response that he must necessarily go more warily in approaching his prey. He knew there was another reason,—and he blasphemed the day of Jubal's birth.

Now he is crouching under the window: slowly he raises his head and peers cautiously over the sill. He sees a long room, neatly though frugally furnished, and lighted in part by a lamp set on a table in one corner. On a divan reclines the procurator; the Martha-like wife of the *natchalnik* and a nobleman are wellnigh asleep on their hard chairs. Four music-stands, resembling overgrown camp-stools with one edge of the seat considerably lower than the other, and a candle fixed thereto with wire, are planted in a semi-circle round the pioneer piano, at which the doctor's wife presides. Next to her is the man of physic with his 'cello, the student son of the *natchalnik* in command of a viola, a stranger with the second violin score before him, and then erect, the princely *natchalnik* hugging his loved violin. And the fiend outside at the window cowered and cursed. But as the leader's face became transformed in the union of his soul with the spirit of the theme, and he constrained his instrument to tell out the well-known melody in the Overture to "Der Freischütz," and the other strings soothingly coaxed, comforted, and supported the timid wayward air, the evil spirit departed from the man and he dropped his knife, muttering, "I cannot." And ere he slunk off like a whipped dog he cast one more glance at the quondam prison governor; and that tender face gazing upward, hidden in part by the iron-grey hair that would slip down over the ample forehead, and the grey eyes peering into other realms from beneath it, betrayed the secret of the man. For at that moment there flashed into the mind of the "free-command" the remembrance of occasions in the routine of prison-life when the same other-world expression had lit up the face of the *natchalnik* — and he saw that he had misjudged his chief. And as he glided back into the darkness, remorse seized him more overpoweringly than on the night that followed the last day of his innocency: the genius of Weber recalled a thousand memories that crowded in upon his mind.

Slowly he reached his cottage, overcome by the rush of thoughts that reviewed the past: but evermore he seemed to hear that theme. He flung himself down on his trestle-bed, and dreamt back to the old days in St Petersburg when he had first heard that beauteous strain; but when he awakened with a start to find himself in his miserable surroundings, it seemed more than he could bear. Once again visions of the occasions on which he had been used unfairly, although in innocency, by the governor rose before his mind like evil creatures, but with a final effort he repulsed them. And as the first rays of the rising sun stole in through the little window to the east, and lighted up the naked walls of the exile's home, a great peace entered his heart, for he knew that he had forgiven—and had been forgiven.

CHAPTER VIII.

THE SILVER MINES OF NERTCHINSK.

THE NERTCHINSK PENAL SETTLEMENT — HOW APPROACHED — THE CHINESE IN SIBERIA — THE VALLEY OF THE SHILKA — GORNI-ZERENTUI—CONVICT LABOUR ON THE RAILWAY—DESCRIPTION OF THE PRISON—THE CHILDREN'S HOME—THE SETTLEMENT OF VOLUNTARY FOLLOWERS—THE RELEASED CONVICT—ALGATCHI—WORK IN THE MINES—A TUNGUS VILLAGE—AKATUI—SLAVINSKI THE POLITICAL — DOWN THE MINE — ALEXANDROVSKY AND ITS HOUSES OF REFUGE.

THE penal settlement of Nertchinsk may be described in a general way as lying within the wedge of land enclosed by the rivers Shilka and Argun, immediately above the point where, by their union, the great Amur is born. It is thus spread over a vast undefined area, that at its broadest point measures 400 versts across, while nowhere can it be traversed under a journey of 100 versts. From the point of view of the prison inspector it is an institution by itself, under the direction of a special resident administrator, and divided, on account of its size, into two zones — the Zerentuisky and Algatchinsky. In the first of these are situated the Zerentui, Maltsevsky, and Kadainsky prisons, and the Kutomarsky barracks, to which last the "free - commands" are sent in summer for labour in the silver-melting works. They return again in the autumn to the stations whence they came. In the second zone are found the prisons of Algatchi, Akatui, and Pokrovsky, and the poorhouses of Alexandrovsky.

Formerly there was a third zone, but in 1893 the Kara prison district, round which Mr Kennan's work may be said to revolve, was closed. Towards the end of 1894 the great majority of the criminal "free-commands" were transferred to Zerentui. Kara is now but a name, and quickly the place shall know it no more. On the first of January 1895 twenty-three politicals still remained in "free-command," in addition to a few ordinary criminals. In the summer of 1896 the number of the former had fallen to thirteen, a decrease due to the fact that politicals condemned to hard labour are now despatched to Akatui.

The Zerentui, Maltsevsky, Kadainsky, Algatchi, Pokrovsky, and Akatui prisons are situated, then, at the silver-plumbago mines of the Nertchinsk mining district, while the smelting is done at Kutomarsky. In 1894 the average daily number of persons of both sexes located at these centres was 2800; but if we include all the stations in the district, the total number of offenders slightly exceeded 3000. During the year some 1100 new exile convicts entered the settlement, but if those are included who were transferred thither from other centres, the total influx is nearer 1700 souls. Of the different stations, judged solely by the numbers of convicts settled there, Zerentui and Algatchi are the most important. Regarding the convicts from the point of view of the length of their sentence, we find that while only 150 were under sentence for life, and the worst of these are slowly moved to Sakhalin, quite 1500 were suffering for a term of from twelve to twenty years. The maintenance of each offender costs about 85 rubles annually, while half a million rubles

OFF TO THE MINES.

are required to keep up the settlement. Again, only three-fifths of the criminal population were actually within prison-walls. The money earned by the convicts, on a system already explained, was barely 22,000 rubles. During the same year over 1200 patients were treated in the four lazarets of the district, in which the death rate was slightly over 4 per cent.

. . . .

While the town of Srjetensk is only 98 versts farther east from Nertchinsk along the great post-road, we must go nearly 300 to the south-east before we reach the centre of the Nertchinsk Penal Settlement. It takes a convict party nearly sixty days to cover the ground between Irkutsk and Zerentui. In leaving the town of Nertchinsk, we pass under a large white-painted wooden arch, which bears on one side the date of its foundation in 1653, and on the other the date of the visit of the present Emperor in 1891. We emerge from beneath it on to a wide wind-swept plain, on the edge of which the upper end of the town is built. Beyond it, in the vicinity of the Shilka, the country becomes broken up into little valleys, up and down which our horses drag us, till we come suddenly on the noble river that drains this region. Itself formed by the union of the Ingoda and the Onon, the Shilka descends through a course of 1700 miles before it meets the Argun as described above. At many points the bed of this fierce flood is confined by high cliffs, rising abruptly on either side. Even where these retreat, so that a little space is left for daring settlers to take up their abode, it almost seems a tempting of Providence to dwell so near its uncertain flow.

Here, on the granite cliffs, some Chinese coolies were at work, preparing a way for the Petersburg-Pekin express of the future, and chanting awhile their singularly unmelodious lays. The Chinese are overflowing into Siberia; and the Russians, who will in time be confronted with the same problem that engages the attention of Americans and Australians to-day, seem meanwhile content to look on. In Krasnoyarsk there is at any rate one Chinese tea-store; in Irkutsk there is at least one short street where the Celestials have planted themselves; but in Verkhni-Udinsk two sides of the large merchants' square in the centre of the town is hung with Chinese signboards, and farther east their quarter forms a conspicuous feature of every town. Already much of the small trade of Central Siberia is in Chinese hands. Advantage is increasingly taken of the cheaper coolie labour. This proceeds quietly at present. The patriotism of the Russian people manifests itself only after it has been thoroughly aroused. In time of peace it is at a discount: one day the crisis will come.

The Russian and the Chinaman seem to find equal difficulty in learning to speak one another's tongue. The worthy chief of police at Verkhni-Udinsk confessed to failure in his attempt merely to master the names of the natives of the Flowery Land who were under his baton. He had therefore dubbed them all with Russian names on a system known only to himself. But "pigeon Russian" attains its most sublime height in the pronunciation of the word "ruble," which the vendors of silk and tea roll on their tongues like some sweet morsel.

We crossed the Shilka in a pendulum ferry-boat, and crawled up a steep valley in the shade of larch and alder, spruce and birch. The cart-road, cruelly denuded by torrential streams even to the exposure of its deeply buried skeleton of close-set pine, together with the black-and-white painted posts that registered on one side an increasing and on the other side a decreasing tale of versts, was all of artificiality that met the eye. Soon we left this behind, and traversed country where the ground vegetation was absolutely dazzling. Talk of the Field of the Cloth-of-Gold! Look at that open strip guarded by a cordon of young trees. It is a natural carpet of orange trollius, into which groundwork the green grass works itself in natural light patterns, while bluebells form a straggling border. A little farther on a delicate pink willow-herb and pale-blue wild geraniums grow together in rich profusion. Or we pass a place where a burnet with rich dark crimson velvety head is dominant, and shortly after all these blend with purple and yellow ox-eye daisies, scarlet Turk's-cap and yellow day-lilies, peonies, milkworts, speed-wells, teasels, and grasses innumerable, in wealth of floral beauty.

Again and again the scenery strongly reminded one of many parts of Scotland. In the region of the Shilka it was as if one were travelling in a glorified Perthshire. Farther on, the heart of the Nertchinsk settlement was suggestive of an exaggerated Peeblesshire, or perhaps, more truly, the Sussex Downs were simulated in the long gently undulating billows of green pasture-land with their corresponding giant troughs across which our path lay. And yet again I have seen an exact reproduction of the carse of Stirling as one approaches it from the south, save that the hill whereon a castle might have stood was tenantless.

The stages are longer than in the west, with no intermediate villages to break their monotony. When you do come upon one, it shows no symmetry of form: the log huts are set down anywhere, and the bark of trees is often requisitioned to roof them. Once we have to halt till a small caravan of *telyegas* goes past. Four or five soldiers with fixed bayonets are in charge, and carefully watch the drivers. The freight is ammunition, and the rough untidy appearance of the Kossaks, often with torn uniforms, demonstrates forcibly how remote we are from headquarters. While we are driving across an open stretch of country, two large black birds rise out of a reedy patch of ground far to our right— too far for us to make out distinctly what they are. Our driver hazards the suggestion that they are black swans, and adds that there is a mineral spring at the spot where they rose. And so, now climbing wood-clad hills, now descending into the broad plains that they encompass, we gradually push on towards our destination.

Finally there comes a time when the last tree fades on the horizon, and we launch out on an immense sea of gently undulating hills, low and grass-covered, each of which is regularly succeeded by a corresponding trough. The child remarks how the scenery flies by as he gazes out of the window of the steady train that carries him from one place to another in our land; and if the same insensibility to motion had been possible in the jolting *kolyaska*, one could well have imagined that the great green billows that rolled past us, and the broad depressions that succeeded them, had a less solid consistency than they really possessed. It was late at night when we drove up to the prison of Gorni-Zerentui, and a watchman, enveloped in a *shuba*,—for the August nights were chilly,—directed us to the residence of the *natchalnik*. The large white building rose ghost-like out of a hollow: lights were still burning at certain of the windows, and one could hear the tread of the sentries on their beats at each of the four corners of the surrounding wall. Tomiline, the former *natchalnik*, has been, unfortunately for the prisoners, superseded in the chief command. With a kiss on either cheek he greeted my companion, his friend of yore, and we found Vassiliev the new chief, and the vice-governor of Trans-Baikalia there. The latter happened to be on his annual tour of inspection, which meant that one would see everything at its best, arranged with due care.

In and around Gorni-Zerentui there are some 800 or 900 prisoners and "free-commands," but many of them were away forming part of a contingent of 600 convicts from the Nertchinsk Penal Settlement who were at work on the railway. This form of labour has largely superseded employment in the mines. Of that large gang, which during the summer of 1896 was so poorly sentinelled that it was possible for every man of them to have escaped, only one had run off up to the end of July. At a certain village 100 versts to the east of Tchita, twenty-three convicts were trusted to work without a soldier in charge of them. How was this possible? Convicts were early employed on the railway, but the engineers considered their work to be poor and slow: the men showed no interest in it. The governor of Trans-Baikalia then made an arrangement whereby he engaged to provide the railway authorities with 600 men from the Nertchinsk Settlement, who would do a stated amount of work in a certain time, on the condition that they received one-tenth of the value of their work. I am not aware of the precise terms of the settlement; but if we assume that it provided that each convict was to do 70 kopeks' worth of work per diem (which cannot be very far off the actual figure), we see that this meant that each convict would only earn 7 kopeks daily. The convicts refused to do their part of the transaction, and, taking matters pretty much as they chose, did not accomplish more than

50 kopeks' worth daily. Naturally the railway authorities complained, and the usual prison screws were applied to the men, but without success: the whole movement seemed doomed to failure. Thereupon the governor conceived the idea of extending the arrangement, so that the full value of whatever work each man did over and above his 70 kopeks' worth should go directly into his pocket. The effect was magical: the men went to work with a will, and it was said that some of them actually cleared half a ruble on a day's toil. Here, then, was the secret of the extraordinary record given above. It did not pay a man to run away; on the contrary, it was distinctly to his advantage to stay and work. The vice-governor said further that in consequence of similar arrangements the number of escapes recorded in the Nertchinsk Settlement during the previous year had been considerably under the ordinary figure. He placed the total at seven, of whom two only had got away from under the military, while the other five were exile colonists who had decamped from their assigned places of residence. Of the seven, four had subsequently given themselves up again.

Tomiline was another type of *natchalnik* who is essentially popular with his men. His superior has not the same reputation for clemency, although his ability is undeniable. Last year, when Tomiline was returning from a visit to Russia, his *tarantass* broke down on the great highroad between two post-stations. Three men, who happened to be passing along, came up and gave assistance to him and his *yamstchik* in repairing the wrecked vehicle. This done with apparent success, the *natchalnik* slipped a few coins into their hands, asking who they were, and whither they were going. One of them replied casually that they were

travelling from one monastery to another, begging their
way. "Nonsense," said the now curious official; "you know
perfectly well that there are not more monasteries in Siberia
than fingers on my hands"; and becoming suspicious, he
added in an undertone, "Tell me, do you know anything
about Kara?" The men were silent, and then he noticed
a peculiar smile flitting across the face of one of them. The
truth flashed through Tomiline's mind in an instant, and he
demanded sharply, "Do you know who I am?" They said
they thought they did; whereupon, fully convinced of the
correctness of his judgment, he inquired from what prison
they had escaped. "From Gorni-Zerentui." The genial
little man was not in the least taken aback, but quietly
asked them how things had been going on in his absence.
The *brodyagi* set his mind at rest on a variety of matters.
Finally, overcome by the ludicrous side of the situation, he
burst out laughing, and said, "Well, you know, I can't take
you back with me in my pocket, and I don't suppose that
you will come." He then wished them good-bye. A little
way on his *tarantass* broke down a second time, and the
men ran back to help him again. Then they bade one
another farewell, and went on their separate ways.

The prison, which was finished in 1888, is a white-
plastered, T-shaped, three-storeyed brick building with a
red zinc roof, and is surrounded by a large, square, white
wall. One of the most modern of Siberian prisons, it lies
towards the foot of a gentle slope. The main hall was
located on the first floor of the prison building: it extended
the length of the T-head (some 50 yards at least), and also
constituted the prison church. At one end stood the altar,
and on the artificial dome overhead was a copy of the un-
rivalled Lord God of Sabaoth, by Markov and Koshelev, that

is the feature of the Cathedral of St Saviour in Moscow. The designs after which the woodwork had been executed were all from the hand of a young cadet who was serving his time for forgery. Possessed of a magnificent bass voice, he still continues to render active service in the choir, which forms an interesting feature of every prison. The best we heard was certainly that at Gorni-Zerentui, the main effect being due to a really fine quartette, while the others added little except in the way of questionable volume.

An iron gallery or balcony reached by a light iron staircase ran along one side of the church at the level of the second floor. On to it opened five *kamera* doors, with corresponding ones immediately below on the level of the church. In none of them, owing to the absence of so many men, was there the faintest trace of overcrowding. Each lodged from fifteen to twenty occupants, and the sleeping accommodation was on the same model as in the newer rooms at Alexandrovsky Central, except that the panels were much broader and admitted of two or three men reclining on each. Down the centre of the room ran a wooden table, covered (probably for the occasion) with a linen cloth. There was a general air of contentedness, and almost cheerfulness, about the men. The stalk of the T was filled with rooms where the old state of affairs still persisted. They were all of a good size, and the windows were thrown open to let in the fresh air. Carpenters, bootmakers, and tailors were at work in the various chambers: only the latter sleep in their workrooms. Everything had been scrupulously cleaned for the vice-governor's visit. In the largest room devoted to carpentry there were seven men at work, one of whom was engaged carving a screen for the church. The tailors worked with sewing-machines, sitting on their bed-benches in the orthodox fashion. The vice-governor described the place as a hard-labour institution where there was no hard labour, for each man was busily engaged with his natural employment.

The ground-floor was slightly sunk, and the first room we passed through was divided into two by a light wire partition. Here the prisoners are allowed to see their relatives on occasions: the close-meshed fence, however, separates them. Then we visited certain lesser storerooms, an adjacent lamp-room with a trusted man in charge, and, through the wall, a provision-room whose shelves groaned with the weight of many loaves. Five men were engaged in cutting them up and weighing the different portions. Then came a short passage, off which a minor vestibule opened on either side. The left-hand vestibule was lighted, and gave access in turn to a row of five narrow cells, each about 10 feet in height and fairly dark when their imperfectly fitting doors were shut. The other vestibule was not illuminated in any way, and off it opened larger cells: when their doors were closed, the occupant would be in utter night. They did not, however, give one the impression of being much used, and one believed Tomiline when he said as much, although he added that he sometimes put men in for an hour to frighten them. Under the circumstances in which we saw the institution, the impression that it gave was quite favourable, and tended to strengthen my main conclusion. Indeed—if the exaggeration were not so evident—the whole treatment of the prisoners might be compared to one man driving another along the street, cuffing him and subjecting him to every possible indignity, but once he has reached a certain house turning round and asking him in the politest manner to enter and sit down to some good meal he has prepared for him—in fact, to make himself absolutely at home. And the old stagers, knowing all this, hurry over the march.

In the yard, outside the main building, we found the laundry where employment was given to men. After being well washed, the linen is subjected to a special treatment. Wound round a roller, it is then rolled with another club-shaped piece of wood with a rough undulating surface: this gives the linen a peculiar glaze. The hospital and pharmacy, outside the courtyard wall, were in good order. Epileptics seemed to be more numerous than in any other station that we visited. The syphilitic ward is always full. It seemed strange to see the little doctor flitting about in uniform, with a great sword dangling by his side. Outside the walls, by the side of the prison, was a guardroom in which 11 men in charge of a sergeant were lolling about, waiting to relieve their comrades whose sentry-watch of three hours was almost over. Off the right side of the passage that led into this room were two cells, one with a window and sleeping bench, the other devoid of both. Incarceration in these chambers represented the two stages in the treatment of refractory guards. Higher up the slope were the barracks, and the gymnastic apparatus for the soldiers' exercise. Then came, parallel with these but farther away, a line of three large wooden storehouses. Here were heaped articles of clothing that are now familiar to us. We were shown a small house-shoe with flat wooden sole, which the prisoners detest because the sole will not give, and often ends by cracking right across. Elsewhere this tendency had been counteracted by making the sole in two pieces united by a hinge.

The village where the "free-commands" and some other

exile settlers live is almost *vis-à-vis*, nestling in a hollow of the hill opposite. On the same side as the prison, but about a verst farther up the main valley, is a long double line of miserable cabins, where the voluntary followers reside.

Immediately behind the prison stands one of a small number of children's homes that have been founded at each of the more important penal stations. These are supported by private subscription, and managed by a Petersburg com-

The settlement of the voluntary followers, Gorni-Zerentui.

mittee, of which the Empress is patroness, and Madame Narishkine the moving spirit. As we walked towards it, one could not help noticing what looked like gigantic rabbit-scrapings far up on the hillside. They marked the pit-head of other days. Thirty years ago the interior of the mine collapsed, and since that date it has not been worked. Tastefully erected in wood and surrounded by a neatly tended garden, the buildings that comprised the home were the most attractive in the place. In the front of the principal house was a large schoolroom hung with pictures of the saints. Towards the ends of the back wall of this apartment two doors led out into long narrow halls, the windows of which faced each other across the intervening space. Off the other side of these corridors opened dormitories. Down the length of the halls under the windows ran two narrow shelves, on each of which was a row of wooden bowls of soup, with a wooden spoon and a thick slice of bread lying by. A child stood opposite each bowl, the boys being in one hall and the girls in the other. One little fellow who had been left in the front room then rang a bell, whereupon the two lines filed in by their door, and closed up in two separate bodies. They then sang their "Grace before meat," and retired in the reverse order to that in which they had entered. As the space between the corridors, which were not very far apart, was vacant, the boys, when the windows were open, looked out on the girls immediately opposite to them, and *vice versa*. So they laughed and chatted across as they ate. The little girls, whose hair was close cropped, wore navy-blue serge dresses, and white aprons. In the dormitories each had a cot, with mattress, pillow, sheet, and blanket. The boys had suits of unbleached linen; but their beds were rougher, and grouped in fours, the heads being together in pairs, with a little raised partition between. The girls are taught to sew and knit, while the boys learn a trade—bootmaking or carpentry chiefly—in little workshops. At that time there were some seventy children of both sexes in the institution, of whom the youngest was a foundling baby girl. In spite of the obvious advantages of such a home, it is with the greatest difficulty that the prisoners are prevailed upon to part with their children, though but for a time.

THE YOUNGEST OF THE GIRLS.

After this we visited the strange settlement of those who had followed in the prisoners' wake—wives, children, lovers more rarely, husbands. The dwellings were primitive to the last degree, being largely composed of wicker-work. When an occupant no longer needs the scanty shelter offered by such a home because she can join her liberated mate in the

The best cabin.

"free-command," she attempts to sell it to some new-comer. Forty-five rubles is a common price in such a transaction. The majority of the cabins were slightly sunk, so that one stepped down in entering. From the outside the walls appeared to be made of birch branches carefully intertwined, with an occasional strengthening plank, the whole being filled in and daubed over with earth. The square roof was likewise covered with soil, so that it supported a thick growth of grasses and wild-flowers. The interior was divided into two unequal compartments. From the inside the wall of the larger room was seen to be as described, but the other chamber, which opened off it, contained the whitewashed brick stove, and was accordingly more stoutly bolstered up with boards internally, and in some cases was built entirely of brick. One had almost to get down on one's knees to enter this warm winter den. Even now difficulties did not end, for inside there was hardly room to turn, while it was necessary to stoop all the time, and the only places on which it was possible to recline were the stove or the floor. Clothes and goods were commonly stored in the outer room. Similar dwellings on a grander scale contained more rooms, and were not sunk, while the inner room was subdivided into two, and built partly of logs. About the door of each hut played a motley group of horses, pigs, cows, calves, hens, and dirty little children, under the eyes of the ill-dressed followers of the law-breakers. At the far end of the street one walked into rich pasture-land, where within 20 yards of this squalor were flowering edelweiss, yellow poppies, bluebells, and rich peonies. Farther down in the sleepy hollow some convicts were drawing water, and in the low scrub that clothed the base of the hillside stood four sentries, at corners of an imaginary square, watching them, their white jackets just rising above the green.

When I rejoined the vice-governor, who had been photographing the prison from the end of the line of cabins, he was engaged in earnest conversation with a middle-aged man. There was a quiet proud look about the latter that at once attracted one, dwelling as it did in a face with which, on the whole, Time had not dealt roughly, while his clear

GUARDING THE PIT-HEAD.

grey eyes glowed with suppressed emotion. " It was curious," he was saying to the vice-governor,—"remarkable. I declared from the beginning that I was not guilty, but somehow everything that I said seemed to turn against me. My innocency was clear as the noonday sun to my mind, and yet I could not prove it: whatever evidence I brought, by some remarkable perversion went against me." He had been sentenced to hard labour for life for the murder of a man who had mysteriously disappeared from a Russian village. Suspicion had fallen on him, as he was the last to be seen with the missing man; but at the trial, as he remarked, he was damned in some hideous way by his own evidence, do what he liked. And now, after ten years, the man who had so strangely disappeared, and who was supposed to have been murdered by our story-teller, had returned to his village in Russia, having himself run off conscience-struck on some account. Less than a week before, the man who faced us had received notice of his release by telegram: hence the triumphant calm that reigned in his countenance. One wanted to know if he would or could demand any compensation for these ten lost years. "No," he said, with a sad smile—knowing probably the futility of such an idea— " No; it is sufficient compensation to me that the world now knows that I spoke the truth. I am well repaid for the past in being vindicated, even if it is so late." Noble soul! the proudest man in the land, to whom the loss of ten long years was as nothing compared with the possession of a clean conscience, the misery he had undergone more than atoned for by the consciousness of the victory of truth—his truth— before the eyes of his fellow-men.

The character of the surroundings naturally makes the natives very sensitive upon the question of their ancestry.

Unfortunate suggestions are treated by genuine settlers with withering scorn. Thus my companion was unlucky enough on one occasion to mildly ask our driver how long it was since he had left Russia. The irate *yamstchik* turned round in an instant, and with stern emphasis replied that he had been born here, as had his father and his grandfather before him: whereupon there was an awkward pause.

We continued our drive to Algatchi, an important point in the second zone. About half a mile from Zerentui we passed a sentry-surrounded shed, in which convicts were making bricks. We still wandered through broad valleys lying between the grass-clad mounds, whose internal rocky structure was occasionally evidenced by the sharp outline of their crest. Indeed the underlying strata had sometimes so far forgotten themselves as to rend their green mantle, and protrude a long ragged edge. The floral wealth showed no decrease. Earlier in the season broad acres must have been covered by a purple cypripedium; at the moment a large blue campanula, umbelliferæ, labiates, and teasels in a hundred different shades, with the soft velvety burnet, almost buried everything else. We drove all night, and, being now beyond the sphere of post-stations, had to employ peasant horses, and still more peasant drivers.

After a continuous stretch of eighteen hours we reach Algatchi. The native Kossak population inhabit well-appointed cottages in one part of the village, which is built round the end and along the side of one of the two slopes that meet to form a valley. Near the head of this valley, about a mile above the prison, which happens to be the last building in the village, are the mines. Long before the settlement itself came into view, certain white dots high up on the slope suggested the existence of a cemetery there.

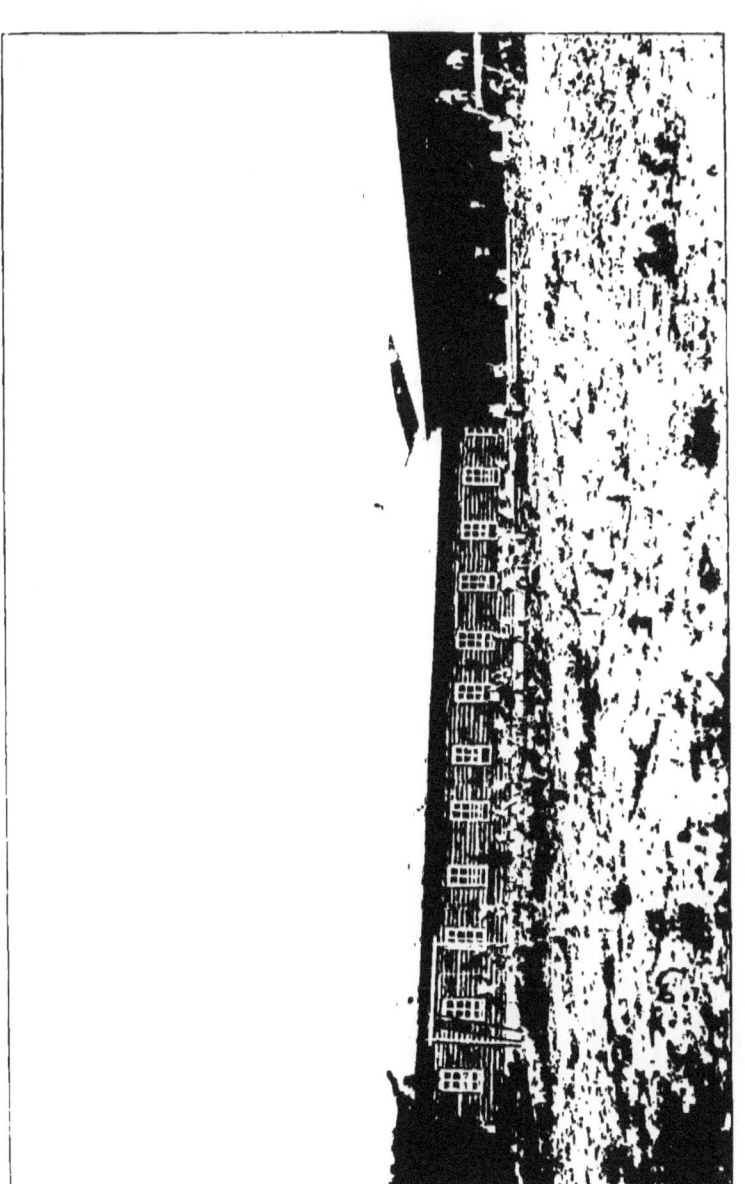

CONSTRUCTION OF THE PRISON AT ALGATCHI.

But on nearer approach they resolved themselves into the rude rough cabins and huts that form the homes of voluntaries and "free-commands." Many of these dwellings are simply holes drilled into the side of the hill; but the mouth of the artificial cave is built up, according to the means of the troglodyte inhabitant, either with wood or with whitewashed brick that shows up well against the green. We are soon surrounded by the life of the place. A new house is about to be erected, and four soldiers stand on guard, while the convicts dig at the foundations. But for many there is no such strict surveillance. It depends on the individual, and the stage of his prison career. Thus an additional labourer is marched down to work, closely followed by two soldiers with rifles and bayonets, while at the same time another convict in charge of a bullock-cart engaged in carrying stones to the scene of operations pursues his task unattended. Again, a dozen others may be seen at work in a distant garden, and no man heeds them.

The prison, built on the side of the hill within sight of the mines, is only six years old, but seems to have been badly constructed. A series of rough stone steps leads up from the road to its high-level. It is surrounded by an oblong white stone wall. The warder at the gate has to be prompted to recite the formula used in addressing a visiting-officer. The performance consists in reeling off, in one breath, a long sentence setting forth the condition of the prison on that day, and the number of people incarcerated. The barracks inside are all one-storeyed, of wood, with a stone foundation. There are half-a-dozen of them, and one with no special distinguishing feature avails as hospital; but its condition was poor. Most were long and narrow, traversed from end to end by a lighted corridor with *kameras* opening off the other side.

There were rarely more than a dozen men in the rooms, which were well aired at the moment by two open windows; but it was noticeable that holes had been cut in the corridor wall to assist the ventilation. The flooring was bad. One observed books lying about in several of the rooms. We unfortunately arrived late in the afternoon, only in time to see the men come in from their day's work in the mines. Several were in leg-fetters, but with the exception of the older men, one could not say that they looked very tired and worn out. They were a singularly unattractive lot of men: one felt distrustful even of the best faces.

Eight months of work in the mines is reckoned as a year of hard labour. The following are the regulation hours of work, which are thus seen to change with the seasons of the year:—

Month.	Number of hours' work in the day.	Number of hours' rest in the day.	Total number of hours spent at mines in the day.	Morning's work—Commences.	Ends.	Afternoon's work—Commences.	Ends.
January	7	1	8	8	11	12	4
February	$8\frac{1}{2}$	$1\frac{1}{2}$	10	7	11	12.30	5
March	9	2	11	6	11	1	5
April	10	2	12	6	11	1	6
May	11	3	14	5	11	2	7
June	11	3	14	5	11	2	7
July	11	3	14	5	11	2	7
August	10	2	12	6	11	1	6
September	9	2	11	6	11	1	5
October	$8\frac{1}{2}$	$1\frac{1}{2}$	10	7	11	12.30	5
November	7	1	8	8	11	12	4
December	7	1	8	8	11	12	4

But these regulations are enforced very much in accordance with the temperament of the *natchalnik*. I have said that everybody was busily employed; but it had been found too tedious to conduct the prisoners back and forwards between the mines and prison four times daily, and so, as I understand, they worked from six to two, with a shorter break in the forenoon, and then returned home earlier in the afternoon for good. It was my misfortune not to be able to visit the Algatchi mines: the men had just come in when we arrived, and we had to go on that night. The condition of the mines, however, was frankly stated as being none too good, the worn ladders and insufficient stays in the shafts and galleries making the labour by no means free of danger. Here also you find the type of *natchalnik* that many would have us believe is dominant throughout Siberia. Sour and severe are the two adjectives that one would have applied to him after six hours' acquaintance. And as I have discovered since my return that he has been lately denounced in Russian literature, I feel justified in the impression, formed at the time, that the one place to be avoided at present by the man condemned to residence in the Nertchinsk Penal Settlement is Algatchi.

Once more we were on the road. After a stiff climb over a more than usually steep hill, we ran down into country in no way differing from that on the other side of the watershed. The enormous green mounds still rose around us, but regular square brown patches on their sides betrayed the agricultural bent of the inhabitants, whoever they might be. We came to a village of the original Tungusian people. The main body of this tribe was driven to the north by the Buryats, but some were left in the south. The Southerners are a very gracious, gently spoken, clean, and thrifty people, who have always won the respect of travellers. The cottage that we entered was a great contrast to those of the Siberian people proper. We took it by surprise, only to find it a model of tidiness, and the goodwife further ingratiated herself by setting before us certain unsweetened cakes, such as we had never yet tasted in the land. Her husband drove us to the next village, and, judged by his garments, he would have been set down as destitute, for his coat had four rents in the body, and both sleeves were badly split; yet this dilettante beggar owned seventy horses and a like number of cattle.

Akatui has impressed all visitors unfavourably. It lies in a narrow, thickly wooded valley, the hills on either side of which are abrupt in their elevation. But I confess that when we rounded a corner, and drove into the clearing in the birch-wood where the settlement is situated, I felt for a moment that this was the choicest spot in the Nertchinsk Penal District. The surroundings were almost Swiss in their beauty and solitude. On a levelled foundation by the banks of the little stream that tosses down the valley stood a picturesque church, simplicity itself, with its dark-brown beams, white painted windows, green roof and spire, while three black-and-white kids had lain down in the cool shelter of the porch.

We had already passed an odd hut or two before we found ourselves between two rows of more substantial buildings. On the right in order came the house of the *natchalnik*, with the prison storehouses opposite; then a larger building—the residence of the under officers—with the prison buildings *vis-à-vis*, enclosed by a square whitewashed wall. The internal arrangements of the prison buildings differed little from those at Algatchi, and again there was no trace of overcrowding. The only unusual feature about the *kameras* was that an ante-chamber opened off each, which served amongst other purposes that of a repository for *khalats* and other clothing. Each man had his own little mattress,

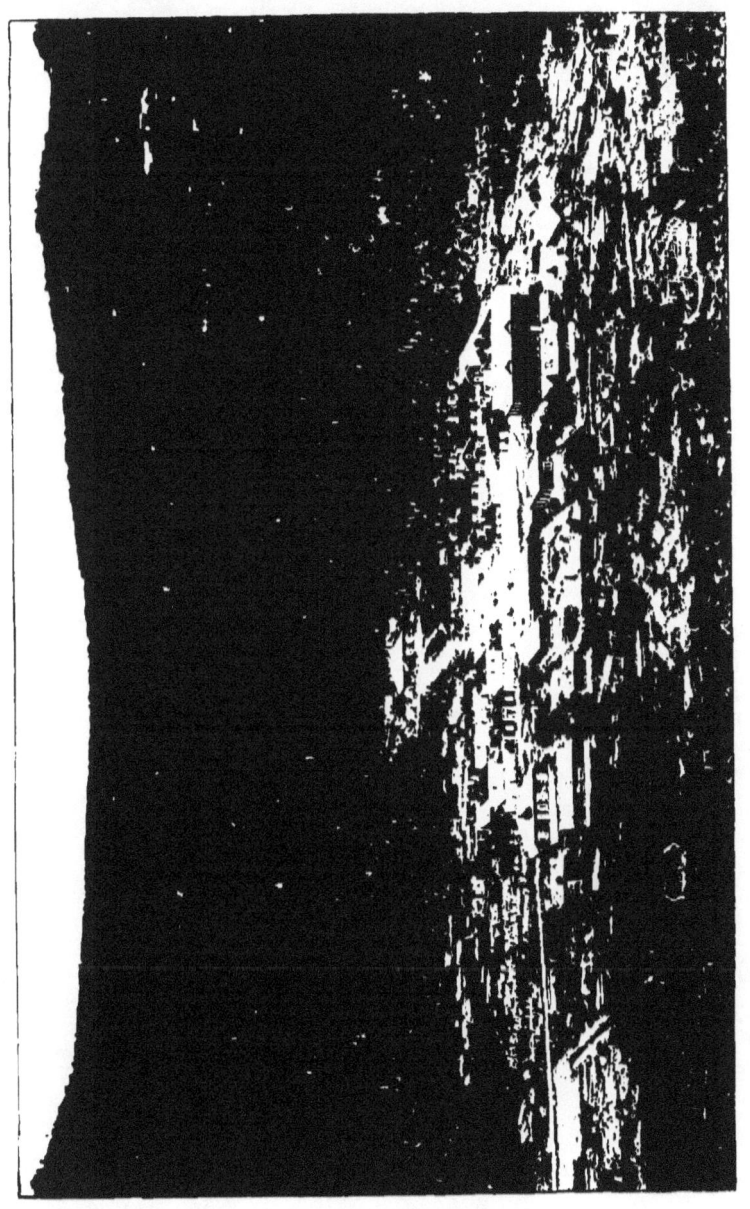

AKATUI.

although here especially they are supposed to lie on the hard platforms only. In the largest corpus a respectable library had been set up, of which the constituent volumes roamed all over the jail, being visible in several of the *kameras*. Across the corridor from it were two men in a room by themselves, under sentence for life for having sold plans of fortifications to the Austrian Government. One of them was binding a copy of Dostoievsky's 'Memories of a Dead House,' while the other spent his time in making small portmanteaus.

The lazaret, though set by itself in a corner, was within the same pale as the rest of the buildings. Infectious cases were lodged under the same roof as the non-infectious, but in a different room. At the end of the passage, in a room perhaps 12 feet long, 8 broad, and 12 high, lighted by a single window with the grating inside, Slavinski, one of the few politicals in Siberia at present supposed to be working in hard labour, was confined. Of medium height, with reddish hair—close shaven on the right—and beard, spectacled, and dressed in a rough grey coat, trousers, and cap, together with tall boots, he looked worthy of his career. He had been first arrested in Berlin, whither he had fled on being "wanted" for his deep implication in a conspiracy in Russia, and had known the interior of the Moabit Prison in that town. He was, however, extradited, and after trial was sentenced to death. This sentence was commuted to one of penal servitude for life, while, by the manifesto issued at the recent Coronation, the length of his term has been reduced to twenty years. He was able to give a very interesting comparison between prison life in the German capital and at Akatui, the verdict being greatly in favour of the latter. He maintained that while in the former place it was useless to expect any amelioration in one's lot, or any elasticity in the prison administration, at Akatui enforcement of the laws was tempered with humanity, and one could count on certain relaxations at times. I have since gone over the Moabit Prison, and any judgment that one could form from a single visit only bears out the truth of what Slavinski said.

The walls of his room were simply the outer logs, with their rough caulking very much in evidence. Through one corner broke the small stove that heats his and the adjoining room during the long cold winter. Another corner was filled by a large tea-chest: above it was a shelf and bracket covered with books and journals. Before the window stood a table with writing materials, and wedged in between it and the wall was his bed, with his own linen and a prison blanket, on the top of which crouched a tame pet rabbit. Round the walls hung various articles, from coats down to a spring-balance: one or two medicine-bottles lay on the window-sill. He had worked in chains in the mines, but his health broke down completely. First the fetters were removed, and then he was taken into the hospital and given this separate little ward to himself. His great interest is meteorology, in pursuit of which he is allowed to go out three times in the day to a little wooden observatory erected at a short distance from the prison, where he makes and records his observations. He proposed that we should come and see it. The *natchalnik* met us in the yard, and just as we were going out, Slavinski stopped, and with an amused sort of expression said to the governor, "You have forgotten something." "What do you mean?" "My guard." "Oh, that doesn't matter," said the lenient chief. "Come now," said the Terrorist, "you must do the thing properly. Give me my guard." And he refused to budge till a soldier came up and marched behind, when he stepped off in the joy of victory. As a matter of fact, Slavinski never has any one to look after him when he goes to his observatory. Further, this would-be overthrower of the Russian Government is actually in its paid service, as he receives a trifling salary for this work. He gave my companion (who told me that a man in an observatory at Sakhalin, doing more thorough work, is in a monthly receipt of 25 rubles) a written list of additional instruments that he wanted sent from St Petersburg at the Government expense. Here also another well-known political teaches in the village school, for which he receives 25 rubles a-month. Thus he has under his charge the children of the Kossak guards, who in the future will take the place of their fathers. My friend had brought out from St Petersburg one or two books of Polish poetry, which Slavinski's *fiancée* had given him, begging him to take them to Akatui. They were in due course handed over to the governor of the prison, who would after a formal inspection (for they were harmless) give them to him. But it will be several years yet before he can leave the prison to live in "free-command," when the girl will come out and marry him. Much had been done in the capital to get his lot alleviated, but he was stolid and obstinate, and refused to sign or countenance these petitions in any way.

Slavinski was eminently a practical man. He showed me a very neat geological sketch section of the hill through which the shafts of the mine were at present being led. He had filled in all the strata, with their approximate thicknesses and angles of dip. At Akatui, as at all the present convict-worked mines, the ore obtained is silver. At the moment the mine was full of water, and a horizontal gallery was being made to drain it off. He also had other drawings of a vertical shaft some 70 feet deep, which had been sunk already through successive strata of drift and soil (surface deposit), clay, sand, and mica, down to the crystalline rock, in the quartz veins of which it was expected that the noble metal would be found.

Besides Slavinski there were one or two other political prisoners in the prison. They are treated like ordinary criminals, having to work during the day in mines with the latter, and to pass the night with them in the same *kameras*. This presented a question on which one could very easily recognise the characteristic, and in part natural, difference between the outspoken political exiles and the reticent Russian official. The former had only one idea upon the subject—viz., that it was done on the principle of *abrutir pour détruire*. One or two of the latter, recalling the "hunger strikes" at Kara, suggested that the politicals would find their level quicker when mixed up with the ordinary criminals, from whom they would receive no sympathy in any attempted insubordination. There is probably as little in the one opinion as in the other, and I would be inclined to see in this procedure simply another example of the laxity and easy-going spirit that pervades the whole system, and that would ask in this case, What is the use of making any difference between four or five men and the other hundred condemned to the same punishment in a small out-of-the-way place like Akatui?

It is a dull grey morning, and a heavy shower has just passed off that leaves everything underfoot in a sodden condition, and yet does not relieve the intense humidity of the atmosphere to any appreciable extent. A thick mist overhangs the hill across the valley, and is creeping slowly

AT THE PIT-HEAD.

toward us over the birches. The range that hems in our side of the valley towers up behind the prison, and even from that level one can see above a belt of wood the treeless summit which is pierced by the vertical shaft. It is useless to attempt to descend the latter: one might as soon think of going down a well, for the rains of times recent and remote have filled the pit with water. In walking to the mine we first descend a little way, and then begin to climb. The track we follow is no better than a cart-road, and as it runs almost straight up the hillside, it forms a convenient conduit by which the rain of the previous night is rushing down to swell the valley stream. At last, after a verst or so, we come to a small clearing in the belt of trees. In it stand two wooden sheds, one built against the side of the hill, over the mouth of a horizontal shaft, out of which protrude the last few feet of a wooden railway for the trolley that rolls into the darkness of the cave. A sentry-box is placed at the end of the line, and the soldier, with white cap, grey coat, rifle and bayonet, is on guard without. Another military statue in grey watches by the side of the shed, and a petty officer has taken up a stand by the door itself. The other wooden erection, which is complete and only a few paces distant from the first, has its door likewise guarded by a sentinel. It is the blacksmith's shop, and four men are hard at work making and remaking tools for the toilers underground. The glowing fire within, hounded on by the roaring bellows, contrasts grimly with the gloom of the cloudy morning outside. A master workman supplies my guide and myself with a tallow candle. He leads, I follow with my conductor behind, while the petty officer protects the rear. We start along the trolley-track: it consists of three broad horizontal planks skirted by a stouter one on either side in the vertical, the two thus forming the rails. As the gallery is only about 6 feet high and 3½ across, one has to walk with bent head. Soon we are well in. How chill is the air, how damp, how quiet! The walls of the passage are buttressed by stout upright wooden beams disposed at intervals: some attempt also has been made, by means of planks, to keep the roof from falling in. Water continually drips down upon us; everything is clammy and moist. We have gone about 60 yards when suddenly the leader stops, steps off the rails, and we see a little wooden trolley on wooden wheels emerging out of the darkness, propelled by a dull grey figure who pushes for dear life. We all step to the side, and try to make ourselves as small as possible. As the low cart approaches us with a rumbling that rolls back into the night, the human engine evinces more and more difficulty in the performance of its task, and the freight-train comes to a halt immediately in front of us. With a sigh the convict puts his shoulder to it again; but the loaded truck refuses to move, so he creeps round by the other side to investigate the obstacle that impedes his progress. He wears the short cloth jacket, trousers, and grey cap that form part of the winter costume —as well he might, for the cold in that gallery pierces to the bones; but he walks in the water with his summer shoes, and his face is the face of a man in sorrow. At last he clears the line, and again struggles forward towards the light. But we press on into the darkness: an unlucky drop catches the candle of the officer behind me, and it goes out with a fizzle. We grope on. Will it never end? The noise of our splashing feet betrays the fact that we are wading through water. It rises and soaks through one's boots, and a chill creeps up one's back. Still on; but at last the end, an open space, wider than the gallery, in which are crouch-

FEMALE CONVICTS, ALEXANDROVSKY.

ing half-a-dozen astonished convicts, who have ceased from labour to gaze at the intruders. The light of their ill-burning candles, stuck on the damp quartzy rock in which they are working, just makes the shadowy creatures visible in the cold hazy atmosphere. One tall man with a long red beard —how pleasant his countenance looks since one can only see the outlines—stands, pick in hand, staring across in mute amazement at a smaller figure who leans thankfully upon his shovel. This is the hard labour—this is the price of blood.

As yet they had not reached the silver either by vertical shafts or horizontal gallery; and this long gallery in particular was being tunnelled, as already stated, to lead off the water from the main body of the pit. The convicts do not work here in the afternoon at all: the few that were employed were engaged for little more than form's sake. The reasonable *natchalnik* did not insist that the prisoners should do useless work. Even Gottze, a political who formerly worked in the Akatui mines, and whom I saw at Kurgan, admitted that the tax was nothing very serious. It all depends on the *natchalnik*: at Algatchi they are worked up to the last minute.

From Akatui we drove to Alexandrovsky, which we reached in two hours. It is situated in a broad plain enclosed by ranges of hills. As we neared our destination the rain came on again very heavily, and we saw things at their worst. Alexandrovsky is a straggling village in a state of decay, and full of people in a similar condition. All the infirm, decrepit, and aged have been collected from the various stations of the Nertchinsk Penal Settlement, and settled there—to die. We halted at the Zemski Kvartir,[1] through

[1] An official lodging, usually a couple of rooms in one of the best cottages in the village.

the porch of which the rain was descending in a stream. The streets were all now under water. As the *natchalnik* was not in the village, his lieutenant came, and we commenced the round in a downpour.

We first visited the women's prison (there are next to no women at Akatui or Algatchi), which contained 92 inmates including children, of whom 32 were too old to do any work. Situated on the outskirts of the village, it was surrounded by a palisade, and the sentry at the corner stood on a little erection made of pieces of wood, outside his sentry-box, as the ground was flooded all round. The stout matron soon appeared, carrying two large keys, and we entered the yard. The prison stood in the right corner, but the door was open, and we could see right in. The building had evidently consisted of two large *kameras*, but the partition had been taken down, and now one opened into the other. Further evidence of this could be seen, in that while the plank-beds were in the middle in the one case, they ran round the wall in the other. The stove that had in bygone days warmed the two rooms, was thus left stranded in the middle. From it a table covered with a linen cloth led down the centre of what had been the larger room, round the walls of which were shelves strewn with the convicts' effects. I understood that all the prison buildings in Alexandrovsky, being very old, were shortly going to be pulled down. The state of the women's prison certainly called for urgent measures, as the rain was coming in through the roof at five places, and at one—in front of the door—very badly. The women arranged themselves round the edge of the *nari*, dressed in sleeved brown coats, while each had a handkerchief bound round her head: in a few cases the prison garb had not

BLIND OLD CONVICTS.

been adopted. Some had boots; others were barefoot. Several of them had young infants with them; one woman had three. A couple of cradles were suspended from the roof. Cradles, Russian and Siberian, are rocked up and down instead of from side to side; and for this purpose one has seen all manner of appliances, from a regular steel spiral spring, a strong wooden bow (with the middle point of the cord attached to the ceiling), down simply to a pliant rod projecting from a wall to which it has been fixed at right angles, with the cradle attached to the free end. The only other buildings in the yard were a small kitchen, where two women were at work, while in another corner was a bathroom. I have already remarked how Tatars hang their heads: the female convicts seem to have the same peculiarity. Most of the young women had been sentenced for child murder: the elder ones it was who were the husband-slayers.

From this we went to two other houses, which were inhabited by men in "free-command" who were physically unfit for work of any kind. They were all in convict garb, mostly old, and a few crippled. In another house, which was guarded and had its own court, were all the old convicts who were unable for serious work. Several of them whiled away the time by making baskets or light cardboard boxes for tea, or even by wood-carving. Two or three of them were more than eighty years of age; one was over ninety. They seemed to be a little overcrowded. In a separate room in this building were nine blind men, mostly old, calmly awaiting death.

After this we visited the hospital. It took the form of a whitewashed brick building with barred windows, which opened into a stockaded courtyard, where stood also a kitchen and bath-house. Men and women were lodged in different wings of the house. In one of the wards a lady with beautiful white hair, refined face, and clean white muslin garments, looked sadly out of place amongst the other grey-clad females. She was the wife of an engineer, and had murdered another lady for her money. The prison proper had, again, a tall post wall, and in it was a single corpus with a long corridor, off which *kameras* opened on the right. The prisoners were mostly aged, and the doors are never locked during the day, so that the harmless old individuals can roam about their dwelling as they wish. Still, some were evidently regarded as being sufficiently wiry and determined to escape, if possible, as a man, who had been down in the village for some purpose, returned to the prison while we were there, convoyed by a soldier marching closely behind him. A bakery with a rotten floor, and ancient baths, also stood in the court. Alexandrovsky is a collection of dilapidated buildings, tenanted by decrepit old men and women.

During the course of our round, which had been made in the carriages of the *natchalnik* and his lieutenant, we were driven by "free-commands." This employment of the convicts as cooks, drivers, &c., is one of the peculiar features of the Siberian system. Cases have happened in which some man who was especially noted for his culinary accomplishments never saw the interior of his prison on arrival, but was immediately taken into the *natchalnik's* house, and retained with a fixed wage as his *chef de cuisine*. In the same way female convicts, when they have become "free-commands," have been taken into officers' families as maids and nurses. There is always a certain risk in such procedures. One officer who had thus chosen a woman to take charge of his only child, having on one occasion been away from home for the day with his wife, returned in the evening to find the infant murdered. The convict nurse was crouching in a corner of the room with a strange look upon her face: the old frenzy had returned with uncontrollable power.

CHAPTER IX.

SAKHALIN AND OTHER CENTRES.

SAKHALIN—HISTORY OF THE ISLAND—ITS CLIMATE—RUSSIAN POPULATION—NATIVE POPULATION—EXILE SETTLERS—CONVICT LABOUR—NERTCHINSK LOCAL PRISON—A MERCHANTS' TOWN—THE PRISON HOSPITAL AT TCHITA—SUNDAY LABOUR—LOCAL PRISON AT VERKHNI-UDINSK—KRASNOYARSK—TOBOLSK AND ITS PRISON FACTORY—THE GUBERNSKI PRISON AT TOMSK—INFLUENCE OF EXILE SETTLERS UPON THE SIBERIANS.

THERE still remain one or two penal centres without reference to which any account of the Siberian prison system would be incomplete, and it may at the same time be advisable to supplement what has already been said on the subject of the local prisons with yet farther illustration. Amongst the former the island of Sakhalin (which time alone prevented the writer from visiting) holds a unique position, and while the importance of the stations on the mainland is probably now on the wane, that of Sakhalin yearly becomes greater.

.   .   .   .

Administratively, the island of Sakhalin forms part of the maritime province of Siberia, from which it is separated by the Gulf of Tartary, a shallow piece of water, at one point barely five miles in breadth. The earliest information about Sakhalin dates from the commencement of the seventeenth century; but it was 1849 before Nevelski conclusively proved that it was an island. Its past history is concerned with Japan almost as much as with Russia, for the island of Yezo is but a score of miles distant from its southern extremity across the Strait of La Pérouse. But in 1875 these two countries came to an understanding, and Japan surrendered her claim to the southern portion of the island in exchange for the six-and-twenty islands that comprise the Kurile archipelago.

Already, during the joint occupation, experiments were made by the Russian Government in the utilisation of convict (necessarily "free-command") labour there. Muraviev-Post was founded in 1853; five years later forty convicts were working in the Dui coal-mines. It was gradually seen that the island possessed advantages that fitted it in a peculiar way to be a penal settlement. Its geographical position seemed to ensure the immunity of the mainland from the possible excesses of runaways. Punishment would necessarily receive an increased force, as exile to Sakhalin could be made perpetual.[1] On the other hand, there was plenty of scope for the activity of any offenders who might care to make a fresh start, and the exploitation of the coal-mines might be a highly remunerative undertaking. Accordingly in 1869 the Governor-General of Eastern Siberia received orders to send 800 men from Trans-Baikalia who were employed on certain farms organised for the purpose.

These ventures proved more or less successful, and as soon as the cession treaty was completed, Sakhalin began to acquire its present distinctive character. In 1876 the first

[1] Since 1888, however, the convicts have had the option of settling on the mainland, when once they have reached the stage at which they are registered as peasants. It is hardly necessary to state that full advantage is taken of this privilege.

prison settlement was established at Korsakov in the south of the island. During the following three years convicts bound for Sakhalin still marched across Siberia and reached their destination from Nicolaevsk near the mouth of the Amur. Consequently the exile population was comparatively insignificant—some 1500 souls. But since 1879 the convicts have been sent direct by sea from Odessa twice a-year,[1] and since 1883 all female convicts under forty-five years of age whose health is satisfactory have been transported thither.

The interior of the island is mountainous, and covered also to a very considerable extent by *taiga*, the home of the bear and wolf, sable and elk. The principal mountain-range runs north and south, and seems to be of volcanic origin. It culminates in Mount Tiara, which is barely 5000 feet in height, and often covered with snow as late as the middle of June. At places the basalt obtrudes through cretaceous beds: miocene deposits have also been found. The eastern coast is precipitous and wild, but on the west there is a long strip of low boggy ground between the shore-line and the hills. The central range forks towards the south, and the only rivers of any size—the Tim and Poronaï—take their rise in it. The climate is austere and raw, largely due to a cold ice-bearing current from the Sea of Okhotsk that flows round the north-east coast. At Dui on the west and warmer coast, in 51° N. of latitude, the average temperature throughout the year is $+0°.5$ C., as may be seen from the following statistics:—

Average winter temperature	$-15°$
Average in the coldest month	$-16°$
Average summer temperature	$+14$
Average in the warmest month	$+16°.5$

[1] See p. 143 and footnote.

The average temperature during the period of vegetation is 12°, which is really not sufficient for the growth of grain. At Muraviev-Post, farther south, the average temperature during the year is $+2°.3$; but while the winter is much less cold than at Dui (average = $-11°$), the summer is not so warm (average = $+13°$). In the Alexandrovsky district there were only five days free from rain, clouds, or fog in 1895, and in no year has there ever been more than nine or ten. The island is therefore almost unsuitable for ordinary settlers, and forms only a penal colony. The conditions are more favourable in Yakutsk.

In the beginning of 1896 the Russian population numbered 18,181 exile convicts and settlers, with an additional free population of over 8000 persons, some 2500 of whom comprised the officials and military of all degrees with their wives and families. Only one senior warder could be assigned to every seven-and-forty convicts, and one junior warder to every three-and-thirty, so that the reader can form an opinion of the possibilities of escape open to the Sakhalin exile, so far as they are dependent on the multitude of guards. These proportions are admittedly too small. The statistics also show that the number of male exile convicts registered at the beginning of 1895 was 32 per cent greater than the number registered on the same date of the preceding year, while the percentage of increase of female convict exiles was nearly 20. But this rise, being phenomenal, was succeeded by a trifling decrease the following year. In the course of 1895, some 800 convict exiles were transferred to the grade of settlers (*poselentzi*), and 196 escaped, of whom, however, 154 returned or were recovered. To sum up, the total Russian population of the island was divided thus amongst the different categories: free, 33 per cent; exile convicts, 31 per cent; exile settlers, 27 per cent; and peasants, lately exile settlers, 9 per cent.

To these have to be added barely 4500 of a native population composed of Gilyaks, Tunguses, Orotchons, and Ainus. Of these the Gilyaks inhabit the north of the island; the Tunguses and Orotchons have settled in the centre; the Ainus may still be found in the south. The "Hairy Ainu" of to-day is the survivor of an ancient race that once overspread Japan, and occupied great territories on the mainland. During the joint-occupancy of the island, the Japanese had fishing-stations on the southern shores. The Ainus served them, and imitating their masters in some points, came to like the grain foods that were given them. When the Japanese abandoned the island, the Ainus, who were no agriculturists, gradually became impoverished, and many of them followed the Japanese to Yezo. In small hunting and fishing communities, inhabiting pile-dwellings on the shores of the lakes of Sakhalin, or buried in the deep recesses of the forests of elm and poplar, birch and willow, these native races nurse their ebbing life. Disease and the knife of the escaped convict do not respect the traditions of a thousand years.

For purposes of internal administration, the island, which is under a military governor, is divided into three districts—Alexandrovsky on the western coast, Timovsky in the north, and Korsakovsky in the south: of these the first is the most important. Some Russian officials have a very high idea of the place that Sakhalin holds in the prison economy. One dignitary remarked, with a tone that was intended to convey the impression that he was overflowing with the milk of human kindness, "We send all our most severely sentenced prisoners to Sakhalin, because there it is possible to give them the greatest amount of liberty." But this is really too humane. He ought to have said, "Because, if they happen to escape there, the chances against them of getting right away are heaviest." At the same time he expressed a part of the truth.

The great majority of the exile settlers are engaged in agriculture. Reference has already been made to the physical conditions against which they have to wage unequal war. Thus while 2029 *puds* of rye were sown in 1894, only 4340 were raised, being an increase upon itself of 2·1. The corresponding figures for winter wheat were 4·1, for spring wheat 4·8, barley 3·4, for oats 4·4, for potatoes 4·9. There is, however, a slight improvement year by year. In the beginning of 1895 the number of settlers living in about one hundred communities scattered throughout the island exceeded 10,000. The Timovsky district was the most thickly populated, but this will not be for long, as the other two districts are in greater favour. There were amongst these some 5300 independent land- and house-holders, of whom the greater number were bachelor convict exiles. Some settled down as family men, and a few men "chummed" together in pairs. But this last arrangement has been lately prohibited. One way and another, there is left a balance of 1400 men, or about 25 per cent, who are land-labourers, but do not yet possess holdings of their own. About twenty new communities were founded during the year.

To the 5300 independent householders belonged considerably over 5900 *desiatines* of land, 4700 of which they had under cultivation. The fact of such a large quantity being untilled was due to the scarcity of seed, to its bad quality, or to poor crops which were all used up so that nothing could be spared for further sowing. Further in the older settlements the soil becomes exhausted, and the settlers either cannot or will not manure it, and to manure a field without cleaning it simply increases weeds. Indeed, seed had to be supplied to many by the Government. Very few of the old settlers cultivate as much as 15 *desiatines* of land, while those who are just settling down busy themselves mainly with the construction of their log-houses. Only 25 per cent of the settlers can be considered independent: the remaining three-fourths require Government assistance. Still for laziness, carelessness, or unwillingness to establish himself as a householder, the settler is liable to be sent back to hard labour for a year.

Cultivation is mostly done by the spade, though some of the older men are fortunate enough to possess ploughs. This will be the more readily understood when one takes into consideration that the amount of land cultivated by the average settler is not extensive, and that having been originally reclaimed from the *taiga*, it abounds in roots and requires time to develop into arable land of any quality. Nearly 700 *desiatines* were reclaimed in this way during 1895. Seed has to be sown thickly,[1] as it is not sufficiently protected in winter, and is thus liable to lose its vitality. The soil is mostly a heavy clay, such as is found in Russia to the north of the *tchernoziom* region. Those settlers who inhabit the northern or Timovsky district suffer most heavily of all in these respects. The severe climate does not affect the live stock so seriously, which accordingly thrive and increase.

The labour of the exile convicts is more diversified than in any of the penal settlements on the mainland. They always receive one-tenth of the value of their work, occasionally a

[1] In the Alexandrovsky district there are sown to the *desiatine* of winter rye 10 *puds*, of wheat 9½, of spring corn 8, of barley 8, of oats 7, and of potatoes 8.

OUTSIDE LABOUR AT THE OLD SMELTING WORKS, ALGATCHI.

little more. The Sakhalin Coal Company receives 270 convict labourers from the Government, paying for each of them at the rate of 20 kopeks per diem. The coal mines are situated at Dui—the oldest settlement—not far from Alexandrovsky-Post. Again, many are employed in building log-houses, and in procuring the wood for this purpose. During the winter the trunks of larch and spruce are dragged from the forests overland; in summer to a certain extent they are floated down the rivers. But the more the timber is felled, the farther are the distances that it has to be conveyed to any given point: to-day it is often carted 14 to 18 versts. In the Alexandrovsky district, some steam saw-mills are in operation: elsewhere the wood is sawn by hand. Road-making also is assigned to batches of convicts as their task. Although always lengthening and increasing in number, the present roadways are still insufficient to meet the wants of the growing population. Much of the difficulty connected with their construction is due to the almost impenetrable character of the *taiga* through which they are led. Hence, as it is the severest form of labour on the island, those convicts who are set to it receive additional allowances of bread, meat, and groats. As for the remainder, the vast army of locksmiths, blacksmiths, joiners, coopers, wheelwrights, bootmakers, tailors, bricklayers, plasterers, glaziers, and saddlers, no great power of imagination is required to conjure them up at work.

.   .   .   .

To return to the mainland: certain buildings in the towns of Nertchinsk and Tchita respectively furnish very good examples of the Siberian local prison. In the case of the former town, you must find your way as usual to the environs, where you will come upon three square plots of ground, each surrounded by a high palisade of rounded stakes. One of the walls thus formed is common to two of the squares, while the third and new one is separated by a narrow passage from the older block. Each end of this passage was guarded by a soldier, in addition to others posted at the different corners. A uniform plan of arrangement was observed inside the squares, of which we inspected the older first. The bath-house occupied one corner. In another stood the kitchen, now too much out of repair to be used as such. Floorless and otherwise decaying, it was utilised as a laundry by some of the cleanlier spirits. The barracks lay against the opposite wall, in the form of *kameras* opening off one side of a corridor that was bent on itself twice at right angles. Across the corridor was the log wall, out of which windows had been sawn, while a hanging shelf served, when fixed in the horizontal, as the dinner-table. None of the *kameras* lodged more than fifteen men: there was no trace of overcrowding, and of the fifty-seven men who were in ward at that time, the majority were passportless vagrants. Not a drop of whitewash had been expended on any part of the buildings—plain deal board or rounded log met the eye everywhere: still, while the older buildings were no better than *étapes*, in the more recently constructed one, hinged panel beds had been introduced. The prison was clean, but the men were very poorly clothed, and any one who could, or cared, was with pleasure allowed to retain his ordinary garments. This concession probably gave greatest relief to three Chinamen, who accordingly added colour to their surroundings. Here only did I see a man handcuffed in addition to bearing leg-fetters. There was, as is usual in the local prisons, little pretence of work. Two men were amusing themselves by patching boots, while in the kitchen of the new square several were glad to find the most trivial employment. As I walked through the buildings the pathetic comments of the *natchalnik* (who, by the way, was the only official I met that volunteered reminiscences of Dr Lansdell) were all in one strain, "Stari, stari, stari" ("Old, old, old"). He displayed, moreover (and in this he was no exception amongst *natchalniks*), a certain delicacy when referring to his wards both in and out of their presence, that one would hardly have expected under the Siberian system. True, there are words in the Russian language by which one can express the fine distinctions that we understand in the substantives murderer, robber, thief. But this *natchalnik* did not care to brand his men with such opprobrious epithets. He would point or go up to a prisoner and say, "This is a man who has committed theft!" This euphemistic tendency is pushed to an extreme in Sakhalin, where the convicts are not called *katorjniki*, but *rabotniki*—*i.e.*, workmen.

. . . . . .

Tchita is a quiet merchants' town. It has grown very quickly,—it is only since 1851 that it has ranked as a town, —and being more central than Nertchinsk, has become the residence of the governor of Trans-Baikalia. To winter there is not an enviable experience. Snow is a rarity, being seen once in ten years or so. But the severity of the frost is such that when one goes out of the mid-winter blazing sun into the shade of a wall or house, the change in temperature is almost unbearable. Otherwise the dryness of the atmosphere prevents one from feeling the full effect of the sharp cold. Moreover, earthquakes are not unknown; in fact they come a little too often to suit the taste of the more fearful inhabitants. The local prison has again been relegated to the outskirts of the town. Instead, however, of passing through the stockade of pointed posts, we step directly into the prison from the outside. A soldier continually stands on guard before this outer door. Once inside the corridors, we observe that the doors of the individual *kameras* are open, and that some of the prisoners are standing about smoking, whilst through the windows a few are visible strolling about the yard in other than prison garb. Again the bare log walls lack decoration or vestiture of any description; again there is an absence of overcrowding; again a spirit of general laxity seems to pervade the institution. The different barracks are distributed throughout the one large square, although such special quarters as the hospital and women's apartments are partitioned off by internal continuations of the surrounding palisade. The former subdivision demands more detailed description, because in its construction and administration it may be taken as representative of the ill-planned and more or less ill-conducted local prison hospitals. Imagine a log barrack of the character to which we have become accustomed. A door at one end gives entrance into a corridor that runs the extreme length of the building, and off it, on the left, open the various *kameras*, while on the right we skirt the window-pierced wall. The first *kamera* on the left—the pharmacy—is dignified with an anteroom containing two beds: the suite constitutes the *feldsher's* domain for the treatment of the sick. The next room along the lobby is reserved for infectious cases, and then follow three others, c, d, e, of which d is twice the size of the other two. The ward for infectious cases and ward e have a moss-caulked log-wall between them similar to that which separates any other adjoining *kameras*. The repulsive invalids, robed in magenta- and orange-striped dressing-gowns, look utterly wretched: for the first time I saw sick men in chains. This is, of course, a matter which the physician decides, as it is well known that men malinger in order to obtain admittance into hospital, where the chances are that their chains may be knocked off, where they get better food and no work, and where an attempt to escape is likelier to prove successful. The kitchen is on a sunk flat, reached from the outside, and so situated as to be, for the greater part, directly under the *feldsher's* rooms, but also separated from the infectious ward merely by the wooden floor.

The local committees in the different towns apparently have it in their power to very substantially alter the food rations according to the generosity of their hearts. At Tchita the men were said to receive one-third of a pound of meat daily; the soup, with a great variety of vegetables cut up into it, was as good as one had tasted anywhere, and the bread was quite of the same standard. In the bread storeroom certain of the loaves showed a round hole on the top, as if some one had shoved in a finger before the dough was yet stiffened, while in another set of loaves there were two such holes. It seems that the twice-punctured loaves had been baked by an ordinary prisoner, and the others by a convict, so that if any complaint was lodged by the men, it would be possible to find out at once who was the offending baker.

Although it is always possible to write out the table of rations for any local prison, it need not for one moment be supposed that in them all each man receives his due amount. The *starosta* of each *kamera*, in virtue of his position, levies a tax upon his room-mates, and the older men contrive to outwit their juniors in villany, while there is a certain peculiar aristocracy amongst the prisoners in acknowledgment of which all are not treated alike. Lastly, there is still the possibility of the *natchalnik* failing to do his duty. A political resident in Tchita to whom I spoke on the subject of rations, and instanced the local prison there as fulfilling all reasonable demands in this matter, merely remarked, "Do you believe it?"

In a preceding chapter reference has already been made to the external appearance of the prison at Verkhni-Udinsk. Although finished in 1886, it looked as new and fresh as if it had only been opened the day before we drove up from the banks of the Selenga through the pine-trees, and gained the open ground on which it has been so choicely situated. It is a brick building capable of accommodating about 450 persons, white painted, and with a high white-plastered wall surrounding its ample yard. On the north side of the wall are built the director's house, as also the guardroom and soldiers' barracks. It was Sunday — *i.e.*, a holiday — and several of the prisoners' friends and relatives were waiting about the gates till the hour when they might see their unfortunate kinsmen or acquaintances through the wire fence in the reception-room. On the question of Sunday labour the conclusion to which one came, independently of any communication on the part of the officials, was that it is not compulsory. One saw men engaged in work on Sundays, but not a sufficiently large proportion to warrant the assumption of any other custom than that maintained by more than one *natchalnik* to be in vogue, that if any man cared to work on Sunday he was not hindered, and that sometimes the authorities had work on hand that had to be continued during the first day of the week. Moreover, there are several other holidays on which the men do no work.

GRINDING CORN.

Once inside the yard of the new Verkhni-Udinsk prison, the visitor is confronted by what is termed the mill, whose capstan-like wheel turned by human labour is covered by a wooden shed, so that the weather cannot affect the numbers of *puds* that are ground. The prison buildings stand right in the centre of the yard, leaving as much spare room behind as in front. The backyard was in the possession of a gang of men who were busily shaking out pillows and mattresses. Everything inside the prison looked fresh and clean, and the only circumstance that suggested the possibility of age was the stone staircases, which were worn especially beside the iron balustrades, for which the prisoners had thus left evidence of being thankful. At the top of the first flight we stepped on to a broad well-ventilated corridor, off which opened a series of grey doors, each with a spy-hole. The beds were of that panel type described as introduced in the refurnished rooms at Alexandrovsky Central, except that they were maintained in the horizontal by long benches instead of the neat little stools that were provided at that station. But, like all innovations, this arrangement of bed is cordially disliked by the men. One looked in vain for overcrowding in this well-conducted prison, which was rather an exception to the ordinary run of local prisons. Rarely more than a dozen men were to be found in any *kamera*, sometimes only five or three. About half-way up to the second landing a recess is built off from the stairway on the side of the *kameras*, and in its three walls are three or four port-holes commanding as many rooms. Thus it is possible to watch the prisoners from above at night, and so dispense with the trouble of continually coming to the *kamera* doors to make observations. In the rooms on the second floor, which were identical with those below them, the old platform beds were still existent, and these rooms were fuller, apparently by the prisoners' own choice. The outlook over the Selenga, the town, and the plain beyond, from the two or three large windows that illuminated these *kameras*, was rare in a prison. The third floor was laid out as the hospital, an economy of space that is not uncommon in Siberian jails. The ward for infectious diseases formed one of a series in a natural order. One felt all through that least thought, care, and money had been expended on this department. Doctors more than once complained that they had not enough money to carry on their branch of one of these composite institutions with the care and thoroughness that was required. At the same time, the hospital is of course the place of ease in the prison, and the pains that are taken to prevent them becoming places that would possibly tempt a man can only be understood when one is thoroughly conversant with the loathsome and underhand devices to which some prisoners resort to obtain admission. All that one can say is that the authorities have succeeded amazingly well.

On the ground-floor were found the kitchen and bakeries, as also the carpenters' shop. A special feature of this prison was its school. This consisted of a nicely appointed room whose walls were hung with maps, while across one end stretched a huge blackboard on which were written up all the figures and letters of the Russian alphabet, thus showing the elementary nature of the instruction imparted. A rack for slates also stood against one of the walls. Teaching goes on for two hours every day, and all who wish may come. The attendance is remarkably good, as the movement has won the favour of the prisoners. This, and the fact that no one proffered a single complaint, are high tributes to one of those superior *natchalniks* whom you may find without difficulty in Siberia to-day.

The women's quarters were located in the west wing of the building, and were entered from a separate door in the yard. Here also a certain space was shut off by a special palisade where they might take exercise in peace and seclusion. In the same wing had been hidden the secret cells.

. . . .

The situation of Krasnoyarsk is its best feature. It lies in a hill-encircled plain, through which the Yenisei rushes after issuing out of a mountain gorge. On the north, south, and east these hills are wooded, but on the west nothing hinders the sun's rays as they slip over the grassy mounds, through whose bare sides breaks the ruddy marl of which they are composed. The wavy chains run mostly east and west, and towards the south their rugged grandeur and the clear-cut outlines of peaks indicate mountains of considerable altitude. The importance of the town cannot be overestimated. One glides down the river in less than eight-and-forty hours to Yeniseisk, whose future in relation to the Kara Sea route is established, even if one is disinclined to go as far as those who believe that the railway will be totally unable to cope with the export trade of the New Siberia, and that therefore this river-and-sea service will enter into keen competition with it. Only three weeks separate London from Yeniseisk, a valuable centre for the sale of agricultural implements. And even to-day they say that while the cost per *pud* of transport of commodities from Yeniseisk to Tomsk is 1 ruble, it is only 80 kopeks to London.

One had expected to see in the Krasnoyarsk prison the twin of the admirable institution at Verkhni-Udinsk, but was disappointed to find instead what was rather a depressing double of Tiumen. It seemed to be carelessly conducted. The schoolroom had fallen into disuse. The unbleached linen coat and trousers in which every man—with the exception of an "administrative" prisoner to whom reference will be made in a subsequent chapter—was dressed, were unspeakably soiled. As they stood in their *kameras*, red or green paper in hand, each prisoner looked more miserable than his neighbour. The rooms were uniformly smaller than in any prison I had seen: perhaps it was simply that the percentage of small ones was great, but, one and all, they were uncomfortably full. In connection with this prison a *prijut* is maintained for the children of the prisoners. As it is situated in a town, it is possible to introduce greater variety in the higher education of the children than, *e.g.*, at Zerentui. The two eldest boys were being trained as teachers.

. . . .

The convict prisons at Tobolsk, of which there are a couple, are quite unique, as General Bogdanovitch, the late Director of Prisons, has here attempted to carry out the ideal of making every prisoner work. The town, which was the ancient capital of Siberia, is situated on the right bank of the Irtish near its junction with the Tobol. The upper quarter, where the finest buildings—such as the citadel, Government houses, cathedral, and prisons—are to be found, is situated on the bluff, which, turning inland in the form of a crescent, leaves a level plain at its foot, part of which is occupied by the rest of the town. There is also a V-shaped break, probably cut out by some ancient stream, through which winds the main road from the lower to the upper town. The architectural disposition of certain of the buildings has been so arranged that in perspective the gap appears to be filled up by one of the nobler edifices. The most effective view is obtained from higher up the river, when the *coup d'œil* is exactly similar to that presented in approaching Heligoland from the east. As the steamer bears one slowly away from Tobolsk, its charm increases. For the red-tiled Chambers of Administration in all their outer whiteness stand shining on the edge of the bluff where it bends inland, and the cathedral, the roof of which is coloured with that peculiar Russian ecclesiastical green—the cheapest paint, some say—towers above them all. To the right extends a garden of dark-green spruces surrounded by part of the Kremlin wall: it contains the monument erected to Yermak, conqueror of Siberia. And as we steam away, the rising bank gradually obscures the lower town from view, till all that we may see are the seven or eight heaven-pointing steeples peeping above it, and the bold citadel against the sky. But when, in nearing the town from the north, one looks up to the top of the headland which rises sheer from the water's edge, the wooden paling that surrounds the prison first catches the eye—yellow and new where it encloses the factory founded by Bogdanovitch, grey and worn where it stands at the back of the old prison.

The lower town is not in any way attractive. Both pavement and street are laid with long broad planks, which are not kept in repair; hence it is perhaps a providential instinct that deters the Siberian from prowling about at night. Each shipping company has its own wharf, and as soon as any passenger steamer comes alongside, all those who wish to join the boat crowd on board in right Russian fashion before any one has disembarked. The path to the landing-stage is lined by a motley collection of cheap-jacks and hawkers, the name of whose wares is legion.

We drove at once to the prisons on the hill. The amount

of courtyard was rather less than one has usually found in the Siberian prisons, but there were sundry other characteristics that specially distinguished the administration of the Tobolsk prisons. In the first place, it was evident that the *régime* was strict. The head of every convict was shaven, most of them on the right, and a heavy percentage were in chains. The rooms in which they sat at their tasks were in good order, and one quickly perceived that this was the prison *par excellence* where work was being done. Every warder, down to the humblest female, was in spotless uniform of dark-blue cloth, with blue braid and gilt facings. Everything was scrupulously clean, and some humane ideas had been put into practice. Thus in the doors of the women's *kameras* the two upper panels had been replaced by iron gratings (at Gorni-Zerentui most of the wooden doors are taken off in summer, and light iron gates are substituted), so that the warders could see what was taking place inside the *kamera* without turning the ponderous locks, and a slightly wider range of view was accorded to the inmates. All the prisoners' garments here were made of light-brown rather than of dull-grey cloth. The women especially, in a jacket of this material and with a white handkerchief bound round the head, did not look so utterly forlorn as in some other jails. In one of the women's apartments were three of that remarkable sect the Skoptsi: two of the number were old hags, and the third was a girl of twenty-three, who had come under their influence.

The large prison was a conglomerate of tidy *kameras*, narrow corridors, and staircases, without a trace of overcrowding anywhere. The smart appearance of the men was greatly to their credit, and although many suits when more closely examined revealed patches of brown cloth, still these had been sewn on with a skill that demonstrated the thoroughness carried into the minutest work. In a roomful of *Peresílni* prisoners who had been gathered together in another part of the extensive buildings we saw three members of another sect, the Dukhobortsi. When the warder explained who they were, the expression of their countenances resolved itself into one of pride. It seems that they had been going on a visit to some famous Dukhoboretz who was in banishment near Tobolsk, but had been arrested as passportless. One had come all the way from the vicinity of Tiflis in the Caucasus, and the other two had tramped from the government of Kiev.

Thereafter we went over the tailoring department, where more men were engaged than in any other centre save Alexandrovsky Centrál. They were making not only prisoners' outfits but also warders' uniforms, ten or eleven completed suits of which were hanging round the walls of the room. The men were vociferous in returning the accustomed greeting, and seemed to be in immensely good spirits. For the third time I saw a prison schoolroom, which was only second to that at Verkhni-Udinsk.

The most remarkable branch of the institution, however, was the factory, to which allusion has already been made: it is to be found on the extreme right of all the prison buildings as one approaches them. At the head of it is an energetic *natchalnik* from the Baltic provinces with a genius for organisation. He said that he had over 300 men employed in the factory alone, which had been erected at a cost of only 4000 rubles. Bands of men were employed in the construction of another long building outside the palisade close to its entrance. With shaven heads and in chains they wrought with determination, seemingly un-

encumbered by their long brown belted *kaftans*. A single
warder sufficed to direct the work, but the sentry by the
gate in the palisade could easily have followed any deserter
with his rifle. Inside, all was a scene of labour. The
cloth-factory erected in prettily painted wood was the
principal building, but several men were busy making
serviceable paths between the various edifices that were
crowded within the wooden posts. A foundation of broken
fragments of brick, over which were to be laid hexagonal
blocks of wood similar to those that give such smooth
running on the streets of St Petersburg, showed that the
work was intended to be permanent. In one of the long
low buildings the handicrafts engaged in were chiefly remarkable for their variety. Every form of carpentry and
upholstery—from folding-tables to sofas, and portmanteaus
to shoes of birch bark sold at 10 kopeks the pair and
warranted to last—had its votary. The men receive the
tenth part of the value of their work. Under the same
roof were many delicate instruments and turning lathes;
outside, under sheds, stood several large pieces of machinery
—*e.g.*, corn-grinders, not as yet in use. The cloth-factory
contained a series of mechanical works from old-time
spinning-wheels up to more modern weaving-looms made
by the prisoners, in which case they were mainly constructed of wood, and although bulky, were yet tolerably
simple. The successive stages in the manufacture of cloth
could be watched, from the teasing of the raw material,
which was then twisted into threads, to the completed
web of prison cloth, of which several thousand *arshins*
are made here annually. The men looked interested in
their work, and none more so than the worthy *natchalnik*
himself, whose aim was to have every man employed. It

was only when one narrowly observed the men who were driving the spinning-wheels, that they were all seen to be maimed in some way—either afflicted with an injured arm or leg, or it might be entirely bereft of a member, and so unfit for hard work, although capable of this primitive form of labour. The directing overseers were all convicts, while one or two turnkeys stood about to see that no damage was done to the plant. Some of the weavers pursued their tasks in the solitude of proficiency, while others had to stop after each journey of the shuttle to rearrange a thread, either alone or with the help of some fellow-prisoner. I also met a prisoner here who could speak English. Twelve years ago he had returned home from America, where he had spent sixteen years in some trade. He was now an old man, and suffering a long term for having burnt his house to obtain the insurance money.

From this we went to a third house where were the workers in metal. A fine iron bedstead finished with brass stood at the door of the barrack, and might be taken away by any one for 5 rubles, while not far off was a fiacre which the men had made for the *natchalnik*. Inside, the anvils resounded to sturdy blows. One man was making rifles, for which work he had a special aptitude. He showed us a couple, to the excellence of which the *natchalnik* testified, saying that he had shot a sparrow with one of them. The bore was very small, similar to that of a pea-rifle. Another's specialty was the forging of daggers, the hafts of which he ornamented with pieces of carved mammoth tusk, daintily adding filigree silver work to the sheaths and belts. These were exceptions to the ordinary run of workers, but there were great differences in the individual handicraftsmen. Still it is a praiseworthy achievement to teach men to work, many of whom have never done an honest hand's turn all their days. And the sole ambition of the *natchalnik* was that he might not be left at Tobolsk for the rest of his natural term, but might be transferred to some other centre where he would have the opportunity of organising a like industry.

. . . .

We have now come back to one of our starting-points, but the local prison at Tomsk need not detain us long. One finds it on exactly the opposite side of the town to that on which the *Peresilni* prison lies. It is reached by a side-road, off one of the main roads towards the south, and in external appearance is not unlike Alexandrovsky Central, though smaller and with a wooden palisade enclosing the yard. In the same line, farther west, stands the women's prison, beyond which you are brought face to face with the entrance to the grounds of the *prijut*. The outskirts of Tomsk fill up the view at the far end of the road, with the river in the distance flowing in a divided course, and the shrub-covered plain behind all. Within the prison-door one was at once confronted with staircases and long dark corridors. We climbed one of the former till it brought us to a door inscribed with a gilt cross, presumably the church. At the end of a short passage to the right of the church was an iron gate which gave admittance to what was nothing else than a long broad corridor hedged in by an iron grating: here several of the prisoners dined. We passed in, and found ourselves in a large sanctuary which was one mass of colour, and of which the body was evidently reserved for officials, while the gallery and the sides under it were shielded off by a slight wooden framework painted a gaudy red. The interstices of this partition had been filled up with wire-netting, so that no unhallowed hand might sneak through and steal any of the goodly *ikons* or silver candlesticks that graced the building. One of the former, the halo of which was executed in lovely Moscow enamel work, seemed specially tempting. It was the most richly decorated prison church that one had seen,—but the idea of the prisoners' church was painfully evident. Still here only was the dim light that pervaded this prison at all in keeping: it crept in through beautiful stained-glass windows. What do the men of sundry violences think when they are marched within these sacred walls?

Built to accommodate 800 men, the prison contained 600 less than its complement; and of the 200 that were actually in charge a large proportion had not yet been tried. Those we saw in rooms which were not overcrowded and clean. The folding-beds had already been introduced, although they were not in the form of solid panels, but rather of light frameworks on which it was possible to lay a mattress. It seems that the type of bed constructed so as to admit of two or three men sleeping on each—*i.e.*, made with a breadth of some 10 feet—is considered better than those which are only large enough to hold a single man, as in the former case no one can disturb his neighbours by often raising a bed up and down, inasmuch as it is common to two or three men. In this prison a series of three or four beds was held up against the wall by a chain during the day, but one sometimes observed that the determining padlock was not closed. Many of the men awaiting trial filled up their time by making cigarette-cases and match-boxes, which they sold in quantities to local dealers for small sums. In a room full of murderers who were shortly to be sent farther on, the air assumed by the men was one of vast indifference — as if their deed was an everyday concern. The thieves were a far more cheery band; they were evidently not suffering under very heavy sentences. A small room contained five men who had served their term, but were detained until it was ascertained whether their communes would receive them back again; otherwise they would have to go east as exile settlers.

On the ground-floor the *kameras* were poorly lighted. In getting to them, one traversed long vaulted cellar-like regions, where the square slabs of stone that paved the floor had long ceased to have any regularity of surface, while the supporting buttresses of brick had been denuded of their plaster. The prison was gloomy to a degree; in fact it was the one Siberian building that of itself gave the impression of being a prison. The yard lay mainly to the back, the prison being, as it were, built round two sides of it: on a third side were the outhouses and baths. The top (third) storey of the main building had been converted into the hospital.

Finally, we went along a dark narrow passage on the ground-floor till we came to a large room, one wall of which was covered with *kaftans*, and at the foot of the platform beds that were ranged down the two long walls stood thirty to forty men. Some of them wore jackboots that showed white splatches of plaster, and other signs of labour besides that commonly attempted in a prison. These were the men who work out in the town. If a citizen wants a man to clean up, to pack waggons, or do some form of outdoor labour, he may apply to the prison authorities and will get as many as he wishes. The men before us had just returned from their respective spheres of labour to the prison for their midday meal. It is understood, of course, that these are men whose term is drawing to a close (no man is kept in such a

THE ROLL-CALL.

local prison whose sentence exceeds four or five years), and as they are in this way able to earn much more than they would working under the ordinary prison terms, they are generally anxious to reach the stage of such possibilities as soon as possible, and when they have attained, they are on their best behaviour. They are marched off to the scene of operations under warders, who stay by them and conduct them back again, in time for the evening roll-call.

The women's prison and the *prijut* call for no special comment, being like other institutions of a similar nature that have already been described. The latter was the largest of its kind, and in many ways the most nicely furnished and most ably conducted refuge that I saw. Slightly over 100 children were being cared for. It happened to be the vacation, and children must be pretty much the same all the world over, for when the kindly matron was asked what they did in the holiday-time, she answered with a laugh, "They romp about, and play all sorts of tricks."

. . . .

One question remains. What influence has this convict wave upon the inhabitants of the land? It is now nearly 250 years since the first exiles stepped across the boundaries of Siberia, and I do not know that it stands on record that in the earlier days of the system there was any determined objection made to constituting Siberia the cesspool of Russia. Latterly, however, this docile temperament has not characterised those who have been inundated in this way, and it would not be difficult to cull protests from newspapers, to collect representations from towns, and to quote the opinions of experts inimical to the present state of affairs. It should, however, be possible to disapprove of a scheme, and at the same time to refrain from magnifying the evil thereof. One naturally assumes that on the whole any influence the exiles may exert will be bad, but the question is, How much influence do they exert? I rather believe that through long experience the people of Siberia know very well how to deal with these exiles. Those of the exiles who do settle down and become good *poselentzi* are the best characters, and conversely the worst amongst them will not so settle down but lead the wandering life of tramps, do not marry, do not leave posterity, and living in drunkenness, in rioting, and in misery of every description, have their existences either cut short by the knife in some brawl, are murdered by the natives, or die from starvation in the *taiga*. Thus the unfit —those who would have a bad influence on the inhabitants— are weeded out and do not survive. Then, when one considers the great mixture of races amongst those convicts, one sees good omen for the future. There is the Little Russian and the man from the Baltic Provinces, the Caucasian and the native of Northern Russia. Now, the proportion of men who are accompanied by their wives is not very large, although much in excess of the number of husbands who accompany their convict wives; and when, in the state of "free-commands" or later as *poselentzi*, these convicts from widely separated districts marry amongst themselves, the children from these mixed unions are physically a magnificent race, and so the second generation do not make such a bad start as might be supposed. How exactly the bright intelligent Siberians have acquired their ability to manage the convict population thus thrown upon them it would be somewhat difficult to explain. Their success is by no means uniform. Thus the South Russian emigrants on the Ussuri who have not been out so long, want the knack of handling the convicts, indeed have signally failed in their relations with them;

and as the proportion of escapes, and therefore of *brodyagi*, is heaviest in the Amur region, it is just there that one finds the greatest amount of disaster on this account. It may be impossible to affirm that these convicts, settlers, and exiles have no influence upon the people of Siberia, still less that this influence is all for good, but at the same time its extent has been, I feel convinced, somewhat exaggerated. I have heard it urged that many of these exile settlers, by their ability to read and write, and by the adoption of pushing methods, seek to obtain important positions, such as *pisar* and *starosta* or *ataman*, in the villages, and that once they have secured these, they are able to do just as they like. But it is more truly the case that the exile settler knows that he has to comport himself with reason, as his life is not very safe with his suspicious fellow-villagers, amongst whom he and those of his kind are in the minority. Some of the Siberians are so fearless of these poor wretches who deserve rather to be pitied, that they will, when they are certain of a man's character, sometimes receive them into their houses if they are in their service. But it is really paying too high a compliment to the characters of these *poselentzi* to imagine that they are capable of influencing the native Siberian population for evil in the manner that has been so vividly depicted by certain writers.

CHAPTER X.

THE REVOLUTIONARY MOVEMENT.

ITS BIRTH—ALEXANDER I.—THE DECEMBRISTS—ALEXANDER HERZEN—TCHERNISHEVSKI—ABOLITION OF SERFAGE—KATKOV—NIHILISM—NETCHAIEV'S CONSPIRACY—LAVROV AND BAKUNIN—THE "GOING AMONGST THE PEOPLE"—FAILURE OF THE MOVEMENT—THE SECRET SOCIETY "LAND AND LIBERTY"—JAKOV STEPANOVITCH—THE HUNDRED AND NINETY-THREE — TERRORISM — HUNGER-STRIKES — SOLOVIEV'S ATTEMPT — CAMPAIGN AGAINST ALEXANDER II.— HIS ASSASSINATION — SECRET PRINTING-PRESSES AND BOMB-FACTORIES —WHAT THE TERRORISTS ACHIEVED.

LIKE other great social movements which have from time to time captivated masses of mankind, that one which from its later developments is known as the Russian Revolutionary Movement is unfortunate enough to have its origin—more peaceful than its end—wrapped in a certain measure of obscurity. The political secret society in Russia is not a thing of yesterday; it is a growth whose earliest stages reach far back into the eighteenth century. Sheltered behind the cloak of religion and organised upon Masonic lines, these secret leagues for long escaped official interference. In the last year of the reign of Katherine II., however, their real significance began to be appreciated if still winked at; but when persecution of the Freemasons followed, these other societies, such exquisite instances of mimicry, were subjected to similar treatment. A certain Novikov, who bore the brunt of these evil days, is in consequence regarded as the father of Russian revolutionaries.

Passing over the dull discouraging days of Paul I., we reach the kindlier reign of Alexander I., when the hopes of those interested in the higher welfare of their country began to rise. The times were auspicious. Pushkin's idealistic poetry was popularising Liberal ideas. Many of the young nobility serving in various capacities had, during the Napoleonic wars, come into closer touch with a culture which hitherto they had only known afar off, while there were officers who now learned to look at things from a new point of view. The ideas of citizenship, of freedom, and of constitutional rights laid hold of the livelier minds, and the men returned determined to realise them at home. In 1816 the first political society proper was formed; a year later another was inaugurated in which the secret element predominated.

From the beginning of Alexander's reign the Liberals had been almost confident of securing their wishes, but in 1822 there came that sudden and complete change in policy to which reference has already been made. Again all the Masonic lodges were closed; but so much the more flourished secret societies, especially amongst military men. Some of these had definite aims, such as the establishment of a Federal Republic or a Constitutional Monarchy. A crisis actually was reached when, on December 14, 1825, the troops in St Petersburg were required to take the oath of allegiance to Nicholas I. in place of his brother, desirous to abdicate; but the leader failed at the decisive moment, and the mutineers were readily dispersed. Any similar expression of opinion must have been doomed to ultimate failure, for only a small proportion of the privileged classes and of the army were in any degree enthusiastic, while in the heart of the people, as ever, there was no response.

The despair that followed finds its best expression in the poetry of Lermontov. This was in turn succeeded by that satirical literature of which Gogol's 'Dead Souls' is so eminent a type. Everything in custom and in civilisation that savoured of bureaucracy was subjected to its keen criticism: with grim, relentless, bitter humour were the inner workings of official Russia exposed. In numerous towns all over the empire like-minded individuals of every rank and class met to discuss the questions, political and social, that now had such an intense attraction for them. At these quiet reunions it was not merely the writings of their fellow-countrymen that they perused. Under the influence of such men as St Simon and Fourier, Russian Liberalism was coming dangerously near Socialism. Interest and ability were not wanting; yet this movement lacked one thing—thorough organisation. Even in its helpless infancy it was not left alone by a watchful Government. On April 23, 1849, thirty-three young men were arrested in St Petersburg, and twenty-one of them, mostly officers and officials, after being condemned to death, were put to hard labour with commuted sentences. The result achieved was satisfactory: Nicholas's reign was no longer disturbed.

While the Crimean war was yet in progress, Alexander Herzen came over to London and established there the first free Russian press. From that safe distance he welcomed Alexander II. to the throne in a letter remarkable for the comprehensiveness of its demands. In the forefront

of the latter he placed the abolition of serfage, without
which he felt that it was impossible for any future understanding to exist between Emperor and people. His journal,
'The Bell,' in spite of all interdiction, was to be found in
the palace as well as in humble homes: by means of it
he won a hitherto unknown influence upon Russian public
opinion. His line was mainly critical and denunciatory.
Himself a Socialist of the old school, he shared Rousseau's
high opinion of the inherent soundness of the peasant class,
and believed that they should be freed and exalted to the
seats of power: all future eventualities might well be left
to the resources of the healthy folk-instinct. His political
ideal was the Slavic Republic with the independency of
Poland.

To this foreign literary stimulus there corresponded an
internal activity, mainly promoted by Tchernishevski, who
consistently expounded the democratic-socialistic ideas
of the time through the medium of his journal, 'The
Contemporary.' If, thanks to the censor, the doses
he administered were almost homœopathic, they had the
most powerful effect upon the Russian youth of the day.
And through the mass of this more serious work still ran
the older satirical vein, shrinking in many instances into
mere pessimism. The air was now full of rumours regarding the probable abolition of serfage, and this momentous
issue served as text for criticism of all existing social
conditions. In addition to the Press, the supporters of the
movement found many helpful sympathisers amongst the
nobility, and in more than one of their district meetings
had the great question been openly discussed to their
hurt. Again, the young men and women who had come
under the spell of Tchernishevski, and felt that in his

Radical teaching lay the salvation of the land, opened Sunday-schools in various towns. From these as centres they sought to spread amongst the people the truth as they found it, in elements of learning, in the natural sciences, and finally in Radicalism. Such was the Liberal agitation of the day—spasmodic, often misdirected, extravagant when in the hands of the extreme Socialist wing, but peaceful, sincere, and with a firm trust in the goodwill of the monarch.

On the 19th February 1861 the serfs were emancipated by law, but the actual terms of the ukaz came as a blow to the Socialists. They had hoped that the land so long worked by the peasants would be in full distributed amongst them at a low price, or, if possible, in a free gift. They found that by preference the interests of the landed proprietors had been consulted in the allotment, and that the price the peasants had to pay in compensation was often fixed at a rate above the value of the soil. The peasants themselves looked on the land as the possession of the community: to them freedom meant the abolition of tax and of corvée. For some time previous, the Socialists had been led more and more to feel that their hopes would not be fully justified. An open letter had appeared in 'The Bell' (probably from Tchernishevski or some one of his circle) foreboding evil days. In it Herzen was upbraided for his optimistic trust. He replied on the old lines, maintaining that time was required for the favourable solution of the debated points; but from that day his influence declined with the hotter-headed members of the party.

The beginning of the year 1862 found much discontent awakened amongst several classes of the community at large. This was the result of severe repressive measures taken, not without reason, against the students and Socialists. The following year is memorable for the Polish rebellion, which might have been greatly complicated by significant risings nearer home. Demonstrations of sympathy with the oppressed Poles were actually initiated by the more extreme malcontents, but the body of the Liberal party was for a while irresolute. Then was it that Katkov—a journalist who had already distinguished himself by certain mild strictures upon Herzen and his ideas—appealed to the patriotic sentiments of the Liberals, and, enlarging upon the old-time oppression that Russia suffered at the hands of the Poles, showed that to succour them was nothing else than to weaken their own country and hinder the final union of the different branches of the Slavic people — a consummation most devoutly to be desired. He was wellnigh completely successful. All secret alliances with the Poles were immediately broken off, and the shrieks of still unconvinced fanatics were lost in the outburst of patriotic enthusiasm.

The period of comparative calm that followed this laudable decision saw the complete extinction of Herzen's influence upon the Liberal party. This was due partly to natural causes. With the greater liberty that was now accorded to the press, the demand for foreign literature of the type of 'The Bell' decreased. His appeals, his defences, his warnings were addressed to a shrinking constituency. The strange indecision that in many cases kept him from carrying out, so far as he was able, the lines of action that had commended themselves to him, had alienated the younger men. They could now find those who would express for them in black and white their stronger feelings —men who would, if necessary, lead them into action.

In one of Herzen's writings he gives us a description of this "young generation" who had disowned him. Assuredly the picture that he paints of impetuous youths sprung from the lowest classes of society, impatient even to boorishness of all existing institutions and customs, dwelling in the mist of their ill-conceived ideals, and absolutely inexperienced in the realities of life, is not attractive. It was partly coloured, we may suppose, by the bitterness that his fall had wrought in him. Not long after—it was 1870—he died in Paris, a disappointed man.

In Professor Thun's standard work upon the matter in hand, the decade from 1860 onwards is characterised as the age of Nihilism proper. This brings us to the necessity of defining, so far as is possible, this much-misused term. The term Nihilist has been loosely applied to those Russian democratic malcontents who were, to say the least of it, distinctly socialistic in their opinions, and who chose to force their wishes and ideas upon their country and its Government by violent means. To-day it is limited in Russia to the band of reformers whose achievements lie within the quarter of a century from 1860 to 1885. The name is due to the novelist Turgeniev. The character Bazarov in 'Fathers and Sons' is the typical Nihilist. They were thinking people, who denied all so-called prejudices relating to religion and government as they then existed in the land. They recognised little beyond the natural sciences, they criticised all things modern, and propagated their own opinions.

A somewhat closer scrutiny of the condition of things in Russia during the quarter of a century indicated shows that the party of unrest consisted of at least three somewhat diverse elements. Of these the Liberals or Moderates, drawn from all classes of society, were the most numerous. Their creed of popular self-government, of greater freedom in speech and in religious thought, of wider licence for the press and narrowed exercise of bureaucratic power, has never failed to commend itself. But they differed from the Socialistic or Revolutionary element proper in seeing that a man does not begin with a creed: he arrives at a creed. Accordingly, they were content to wait for the gradual accomplishment and development of their ideas; whereas the second group believed that the overthrow of the Government was a matter of such immediate moment for the realisation of them, as to justify all but the extremest efforts directed in pursuance of this aim. To the third and last group, the Terrorists, these violent measures were relegated,— more correctly, were appropriated by them,—with such results as will be narrated in the sequel.

Now, popular fancy has associated the name Nihilist with individuals of this last group in particular. But the term Nihilism may well describe, as it does, any philosophical system of negation; while the Nihilist is, as has been remarked, a thinking man, if anything republican from the political point of view, materialistic, democratic, yet intensely individualistic, who should ideally be a member of an honest *bourgeoisie*, carefully studious to lead a correct life and make the most of it, that so the good of the whole community may be best furthered. As such, the description might be applicable to a member of any of these three groups, but is misleading when applied to any one in particular, far more to all. And it is beyond dispute that genuine Nihilists were much more numerous amongst the Liberals and Socialists than amongst the third small section whose deeds are better known, and to which the designation of Nihilist is commonly restricted.

Karakosov's attempt upon the life of Alexander II. in 1866 furnished the Government with some excuse for again adopting severe measures in dealing with the malcontents. Radical journals were suppressed; but much cannot be said for the sporadic literature of foreign extraction that sought to take their place. Of more importance is the Netchaiev conspiracy, which may be said to introduce the Socialistic agitation that characterises the next few years. Originally a schoolmaster and a man of indomitable energy, Netchaiev appeared somewhat suddenly during certain local disturbances in the student world of St Petersburg (1869), and did his best to make them appear to have political significance. After matters had quieted down, he still continued to work amongst the students, and, thanks to remarkable gifts of organisation and an unusual power of influencing men, he surrounded himself with a band of like-minded agitators, forming a society in which the members were only known by numbers, and where by adopting the plan of different grades of initiation he succeeded in mystifying the less trusted conspirators. For them the old weapon of Nihilism—literary criticism—was an antiquated instrument. Something more concrete must now be employed, and they actually gave a date for the coming revolution. The story of the last stages of this short-lived machination has been often repeated in the case of its rich progeny — internal strife, suspicion of betrayal resulting in steps being taken for its prevention, if indeed it has not already occurred. And so it happened that Netchaiev convinced himself of the necessity of removing a certain obstreperous associate, and then succeeded in convincing four other members that they were the men to do the deed. The quartette of "numbers" performed their subtraction task, Netchaiev fled into Switzerland, the conspiracy was discovered, and at least one of the four lives in Siberia until this day.

The Netchaiev conspiracy clearly showed that the Russian youth were as yet ill prepared to put their revolutionary ideas into practice. But none the less, in the various university towns they sought to meet with one another, exchanged views upon every topic of interest, preferably in the region of politics and economics, and criticised everything in God's universe, beginning at home with their professors (the majority of whom were declared incapable), and culminating with the Tzar upon the throne. The Russian universities were thronged at that time with men drawn from humble homes. Poor in purse though not in spirit, they often affected to despise their obscure origin, to turn their backs with contempt upon the simple teaching of their tender childhood, and this as the result of—one year at the university. With the few general ideas gained in that brief space they advanced to the solution of all the problems that weighed upon their country, and evinced a supreme contempt for the study of details. It was only to be expected that such young men would not scruple to express their discontent when the Government attempted to prevent their gatherings. Accordingly, more than one year during the "sixties" is memorable for its student riots at St Petersburg. There was an unknown amount of latent activity waiting to be turned in some definite direction. This turn was given by the writings of Michael Bakunin and Peter Lavrov. The former, who was an uncompromising anarchist, had escaped from Siberia in 1859, and reached England in 1862, where he worked with Herzen. Now we find him in Zurich the centre of one of the various groups that existed in the Russian student colony of that town. His ideas were clear and concise. The existing form of Government in Russia must be overturned: it was merely an instrument for exploiting the people for the benefit of the ruling classes. Religion must be done away with, and Materialism and Atheism preached in its stead. The people must receive a thorough scientific education, and women shall have equal rights with men. To accomplish all this, only revolutionary agitation is required. The people are ready for this, and equally capable of organising themselves after the revolution. All that they want is some consciousness of their power. To this they must be roused by the revolutionaries, for whom it will also be a simple matter to excite their long-standing feeling against the privileged classes. The heart knows its own sorrows. Action only is required. Finally, by organising the people in equal independent groups, there will be no room for such centralisation and mystification as characterised the Netchaiev conspiracy.

More moderate was Peter Lavrov, originally Professor in the Military Academy at St Petersburg. He had known the loneliness of the exile banished by administrative order. He too escaped, and now (1873-1877), in connection with the journal 'Forward,' helped to furnish the Russian youth with the leadership that they sought. In common with Bakunin he urged the abolition of religion, demanded the rights of citizenship and equality of revenue, and advocated the claims of the individual and the community against the imperial centralisation. He differed from his fellow-workers by his belief in the sufficiency of a peaceful verbal propaganda amongst the people: the fiery Bakunin longed for deeds. The former saw that the people must be slowly educated to all this; the latter believed that they knew it already.

Lavrov was at once attacked by Tkatschev and others. He had said that it was absolutely necessary that the propagandists must know the people, their needs, their wishes. They must be experienced men and women, possessed of great energy, and prepared to devote the best years of their life to this great task. This was distasteful to the younger men. Why should it be necessary to wait so long before taking decisive action, and continue to suffer all the while? Lavrov showed in reply that it was a mistake to imagine that a revolution could be brought about at any moment. These things are not done in a day. The youth must prepare both themselves and the people, while the delay of a few years would not matter much. In 1873 the Russian Government forbade its subjects to study at the University of Zurich, and the colony returned prepared to go with their propaganda amongst the people.

The times were favourable. It was only some ten years since the abolition of serfage, and already many of those who had looked at the condition of things in Russia with greatest confidence were being rudely disillusioned. They were grieved to see that in the midst of numerous, though somewhat ill-connected, reforms the principle of autocracy remained unimpaired. They felt the present dispensation of justice to be nothing more than the expression of the will of an arbitrary administration. No rights seemed to be secure. In the provinces likewise there was discontent. The rights of the *zemstvos* had been curtailed, if not by law at least by the nobility, and the overburdened peasants were continually confronted with the thought of how they were to pay their taxes. Every resolution of the provincial assemblies had to be communicated to the governors, who now made full use of their practically unlimited powers. Initiative and enterprise were repressed, and the various assemblies became little more than administrative bodies interested in discussing general economic questions, but achieving nothing. Again, many of the lesser nobility who had been dependent on the cheap peasant labour in the exploitation of their lands, found themselves helpless after the great ukaz of 1861. Some were forced to sell their ancestral possessions, others were completely ruined.

Never perhaps in the pages of Russian history do we read of such enthusiasm as characterised the initial stages of the far-reaching movement described as *idti v narod*—"going amongst the people"—in order to make socialistic propaganda. The young people—the "noble revolutionary youth"—had indeed much in common with the peasants. Comparative poverty and experience of oppression gave them the needed sympathy with the subjects of their mission. They possessed a few of the qualities requisite for a good missionary. One of these—a high regard for the men and women amongst whom they intend to labour—they had in excess. They idealised the peasant, they saw in him the saviour of their land. They forgot that, after all, *vodka* was more to his taste than revolutionary agitation, and that they could sooner count upon finding him asleep in his miserable cabin than ready at his post in the event of any organised action. Beyond this, and an intense devotion to their cause, which in the broadest sense was the proclamation of Socialism in its extremest form, they were in reality poorly fitted for their work. This they attempted to carry on in different ways. Some remained in the university towns, and continued to attend their classes, but put their soul into the spread of socialistic doctrines amongst the working classes. Another group carried out the principles of the movement more literally. In the form of a society it sent its delegates throughout the land, who worked alongside of the peasants in all capacities, such as shoemakers, joiners, sawyers, weavers, teachers, or sought to win their confidence, and then instilled into their minds ideas about the abolition of taxes and of the standing army, about fair division of the land, provision of good schools, finance control, and other kindred matters. Thus a series of branch societies quietly came into existence, which were provided with funds and socialistic literature by the main body, and which, it was hoped, would be ready to come out on the day of the revolution and strike for the freedom of the country. How far off this day still remained depended entirely upon the efforts of the agitators.

This propaganda was carried on by word of mouth, with what assistance was given by the distribution of pamphlets and brochures. Secret printing-presses had been set up in some of the larger towns, and the works of men like K. Marx, Lassalle, and Büchner, as well as several broadsheets, were prepared for the benefit of the Russian peasant and the educated classes that the revolutionaries hoped to reach. All this was still supplemented by an imported literature coming from such anarchist centres as Geneva and Zurich. Many sympathisers from amongst the upper classes supported the movement financially; yet other enthusiasts devoted all their fortunes to the cause. The reason for this strange phenomenon of men actually contributing towards the maintenance of agitation partially directed against themselves, is probably to be found in a widespread feeling of embitterment against the Government: it was merely done as a protest against intolerance. It has been estimated that during the years 1872-1875, when this extraordinary wave of socialistic fervour reached its high-water mark, nearly 3000 young men and women went among the people in the manner above described.

In 1875, when most of the agitators had been less than a couple of years at work, numerous arrests took place, and the whole organisation was broken up through the careful and strict measures adopted by the Government. Coming so soon after their spirited commencement, this severe blow wellnigh reduced the party to despair. It is true that certain of them were undaunted by prison walls, and cheerfully carried on the programme amongst their fellow-prisoners, feeling that in them they had material —if won over—that would be ready for all emergencies. Otherwise the movement had been a hopeless failure. The peasants had not in any considerable numbers been converted to the doctrines of Socialism. One aim of the movement had been to instruct the more intelligent of the factory-hands in the towns, and then send them back to their villages to teach their fellows. This line of action had generally been successful wherever it was tried. But the Socialists who had gone amongst the people were too young, too imprudent. They overestimated their capabilities, and thought that the peasant had only to be told their truths to accept them. The growing size of the societies only laid them the more open to betrayal, and the centralisation and discipline were not strengthened and improved in proportion. The attitude of the peasants themselves towards their would-be benefactors caused greatest disappointment, because most unexpected. In many instances they betrayed the agitators to the police, and even gave them up bound hand and foot. More commonly they entertained a most reasonable suspicion of the new-comer to their village, who assured them so repeatedly of his love and devotion to them, for a long while after his arrival. Then the circle of ideas of the peasant and of his tutor were very different. The latter had only recently left the benches of the Political Economy, Philosophy, and Natural Science classrooms, but he knew little of the needs and difficulties of his pupil's daily life, and nothing of his point of view. Moreover, the peasant was seldom able to read the pamphlet secretly pressed into his hand; and even if he could, it might be questioned whether he had either the time or the inclination so to do. But the chief cause of failure probably is to be found in the fact that the idea underlying the whole movement was absolutely foreign to the traditions of the people.

We find, then, that by 1875 this enterprise was practically wrecked by the assiduity of the police. The majority of the socialistic propagandists were arrested, while those who were more fortunate in this respect retired to the larger towns, especially to St Petersburg, where they gave themselves heartily to the unpleasant task of discovering the reason of their avowed failure apart from police interference. The most important result of these lively seances was that the opinion of the majority took a distinct turn in the direction of abandoning the diffusion of cosmopolitan Socialism in favour of more definite attempts to carry out the will of the people, feeling that henceforth their agitation must be expressed in deeds rather than in words. There was nothing unnatural in all this. Their short experience of peasant life had taught the Socialists that the men and women upon whom they had expended their labours were not so ideal as they had imagined. Further, they were poor and ignorant and full of prejudice, retaining, in spite of their dislike for officials and the landed proprietors in general, a deep love and respect for the Emperor, that has ever proved one of the greatest stumbling-blocks to revolutionary zeal. The Socialists had also seen with what affection the peasants regarded the old system of the village commune, where the principle of equality was dominant, and how their desires were mainly centred upon the acquirement of more land and the abolition of the paralysing taxes.

About this time a secret society was gradually forming itself, which, under the name of "Land and Liberty," was destined later to play a great, if not the greatest, part in the revolutionary movement. It was composed in the first instance of the remnants of one or two of the older revolutionary circles, with the addition of some remarkable personalities. Its abettors considered that it was needful to continue the old plan of settling amongst the people, but rather now with the intention of organising them into bands for the ostensible purpose of appearing united and determined in their insistence upon the setting right of local wrongs, and in securing attention from the authorities to their needs. But some of the Socialists went further, considering this to be merely the means for inducing a general revolution. It is noteworthy how the South Russians were ever the more hot-blooded and the more extreme. Success in achieving the wishes of the people was the dream of the revolutionary of the North. But the Southerner had an ampler vision, of which his sterner brother's dream was but the phantom.

Accordingly, we now witness the remarkable scene of a second "pilgrimage to the inner sanctuary of the people's life," begun under far less auspicious circumstances than those that heralded the first. To begin with, the participants had been profoundly impressed by the manner in which their old comrades had been arrested in droves, and often detained without trial, seemingly with no regard to the extent of their implication in any given case. Then, again, their activity was greatly hampered by the increased alertness of the police, while the old peripatetic propagandism, under which whole provinces used to be fugitively visited and roused by the more intense spirits, was strictly prohibited. The agitators were now required to settle down in one place and carry on their work of organisation there alone. The personal sacrifice was consequently greater, and the return was again not in proportion. The story of Jakov Stepanovitch's league can hardly be taken as typical, although it illustrates the hollowness of much of this movement. He possessed considerable talent for organisation, and resolved, for purposes of propaganda, to take advantage of certain riots that had occurred in the end of 1875 amongst the peasants in some districts of the province of Kiev, consequent on attempts to do away with their communal system. In consequence of these disturbances some hundreds of peasants seem to have been imprisoned, strong in the belief that what had occurred was contrary to the wishes of the Emperor. Stepanovitch got into communication with the unfortunate rustics, and offered to take a petition from them to the Tzar. After experiencing considerable difficulty in overcoming their suspicion, Stepanovitch was dismissed as their representative, with many devout wishes for his success. After several months he returned with forged documents of imposing appearance, in which the peasants were commanded in the name of the Tzar to form a secret society with a view to latterly rising against the nobility, the clergy, and bureaucracy, who had joined forces, the manifesto went on to explain, since 1861 to prevent him (the Tzar) from giving not only liberty but all the land to his faithful peasants. The guileless creatures accepted the authenticity of the document. It agreed with their ancient preconceived ideas of the Emperor's attitude towards themselves, although, truth to say, many of them were not a little amazed at this strange admission of his powerlessness. In the spring of 1877 the peasants were released from prison, returned to their homes, and forthwith, under the leadership of the wily Stepanovitch, entered upon this Solemn League and Covenant. The movement grew steadily if secretly, and the chances of betrayal correspondingly increased. It was somewhat characteristically betrayed by two drunken members. Nine hundred arrests were made, including the leader, but the rank and file were treated rather as dupes than as important political conspirators. Stepanovitch made a wonderful escape from the Kiev prison in 1878 by the help of a comrade, who entered the service of the institution in a menial capacity, and gradually worked his way up till he came to have charge of the political prisoners. And this work of assisting in the flight of imprisoned leaders formed another branch of revolutionary enterprise during this otherwise somewhat quiet period, and provides the most entertaining reading in all the annals of the movement.

From 1874 to 1878 there were continual "processes" against the arrested propagandists, which culminated with what are known as those of the Fifty and of the Hundred and Ninety-three. In some respects the revolutionaries almost looked forward to their trials, as they then hoped to be able from the dock to rouse their country to the miserable condition of the people, and to the complete failure of all so-called reforms, thus seeking at once to justify their tactics and do a little self-advertisement. The trial of the Hundred and Ninety-three remains in some ways famous. The accused adopted from the beginning the lofty course of disputing the competency of the court to judge them, feeling ran high on either side, and the prisoners at the bar were literally choked into silence by the *gendarmes*.

The last of these years may be said to mark the transition to Terrorism. Socialistic aims gave way to those of a purely political nature: peaceful propagandism, even the later revolutionary agitation, were abandoned — but all at the cost of a great split in the Revolutionary party considered as a whole. Those — and they were the majority — who had no heart for the centralised Terroristic line of action held back, and were powerless to control their headstrong comrades.

The Hundred and Ninety-three had been barely sentenced when Vera Zasulitch made her unsuccessful attempt upon the life of General Trepov, the St Petersburg chief of police. She gave as motive for her crime his alleged mistreatment of a student, personally unknown to herself, who was at that time lodged in one of the city prisons. Her trial by jury, final acquittal, and the consequent dismissal of the Minister of Justice, are matters of history.

The series of assassinations, more especially of spies, that followed hard upon the resolute action of Vera Zasulitch, was still only the harbinger of the systematic course of murderous action that characterised the period of Terrorism. Partly done in self-defence, and partly from the desire for revenge, these offences were more than justified in the eyes of those who committed them, by the situations that seemed to necessitate them. In the South were first seen the earliest developments of the Terroristic phase. Secret societies were rapidly formed under the influence of Valerian Ossinski—a man of an intensely sympathetic nature, who was one of the first to look on Terrorism not merely as an instrument of revenge, but as a legal weapon of offence. The native revolutionary press showed also marked signs of a reviving spirit, and in proportion the influence of the foreign pamphlets and journals waned. The times were too stirring: each day brought forth some new development, and men no longer wished theoretical discussions of the questions and issues at stake.

Towards the autumn of 1878 rumours went round the Revolutionary party that certain of their number, lodged in the Fortress of St Peter and St Paul at St Petersburg, and in the central prison at Kharkhov, had been driven to initiating "hunger-strikes" as the last resort to compel better treatment of themselves. These reports appealed to the inflamed feelings of the younger members of the party, and on August 4 General Mesenzev, chief of the secret police, fell by the assassin's knife in broad daylight, in one of the streets of the capital. He was supposed to be directly responsible for the misery that had forced the imprisoned politicals to take their lives. In the explanatory pamphlet that was usually found in some city letter-box after each of these outrages, the writer, after attempting to show justification, demanded the following course of action on the part of the Government: discontinuance of the persecutions, an end to all arbitrariness, trial by jury in all political prosecutions, and a complete amnesty for political criminals. The Government naturally replied by instituting still sharper measures. The secret society "Land and Liberty" was thoroughly broken up at this time, but seems to have been as quickly re-established by the strong personality and organising talent of one of its earliest members, Alexander Michailov, who was perhaps of all the revolutionaries most importunate in urging the necessity for centralisation and more discipline in the Terroristic movement. Latterly he achieved both of these desired results, and, as a member of the executive committee, became one of the principal leaders of this wing of the party.

Numerous arrests took place after the murder of Mesenzev, although the actual delinquent escaped at the time. The party replied by other attacks, successful in the case of Prince Kropotkin, governor of Kharkhov, but not so in that of the new chief of the secret police, General Drentelu. In each instance it was a prominent official who was the victim of these unscrupulous onslaughts; but reflection showed the revolutionaries that, after all, they had not yet got to the kernel of the matter. And so, from tactics that were originally adopted in self-defence, and from the desire for revenge on spies and on officials, there was gradually evolved the scheme of assassinating the Emperor.

At once the party of discontent proceeded to put their new plan into action. A mine laid near Nicolaiev on the Black Sea was early discovered by the police. But at the time that Goldenberg, Kropotkin's assassin, was thinking of adding to his former glory by this more stupendous attempt, it was strongly borne in upon the mind of Soloviev, a provincial schoolmaster, that his mission in life was to kill the Tzar. The two men came to St Petersburg and confided their intentions to Michailov, and both were so determined to carry out the project that a small arbitration committee of arch-Terrorists was appointed to mediate between the rival candidates. In the discussion certain disadvantages were pointed out that would arise from the fact that Goldenberg was a Polish Jew—*e.g.*, reprisals would fall heavily upon the people of his race. Thereupon Soloviev rose to his feet, declaring that Alexander II. was his prey, and that he would give place to no one in attempting his life. Remonstrance was vain, and the arbitrators had to yield. On April 2, 1879, he calmly fired five shots at the Emperor as he was promenading, but failed to injure him. Michailov quietly looked on from a distance.

All European Russia was immediately placed under six governors-general with extraordinary powers. Every inhabitant of St Petersburg was put under observation, and the sentences on arrested revolutionaries were extended. The society "Land and Liberty," by the ability of its leaders, no less than by its similarly titled journal issued from a secret press, now came into great prominence. Before the annual meeting in 1879, which was fixed to be held at Voronesch, the extreme Terrorist clique — still in the minority—met together at another town not far away to consider what course they should adopt at the general gathering. They drew up their old programme, with its chief item of State-administration by the people, to be attained by any means, including assassination of the Tzar, and resolved to press its acceptance upon the Voronesch assembly. This they found to be far from easy, and the abler men, including Michailov, devoted all their energies to averting the rupture that was continually threatened. Finally, a compromise was reached: it was decided that the fight against the Government should be carried on with greater vigour, and the society agreed to adopt extreme measures if everything else failed. The Terrorists were, however, far from pleased. They departed to the larger towns and rediscussed the whole matter among themselves. On August 15, 1879, they broke their connection with the society, whose other members had meanwhile returned to their life amongst the people, and less than a fortnight later they had condemned the Emperor to death. A whole campaign was planned against him.

We have seen how the Terrorists realised the impossibility of peacefully propagating Socialism, owing to the insecurity of personal rights and the lack of freedom in the expression of opinion. They felt that the first step was to gain political rights, and in this demand Socialists and Liberals were one. The Terrorists believed that it was impossible to attain political freedom by any quiet organisation of a party of the people. Under the circumstances, in which every means they had as yet tried had proved a failure, they felt justified in trying this extreme course of assassinating the Emperor. This is perhaps the point of view of the moderate Terrorists: others, like Morosov and Tarnovski, were still more illogical.

The executive committee of the Terrorist wing had existed since the spring of 1879, and was composed of members from different little revolutionary societies. Now it was perfectly organised, and had its troop of agents divided into three ranks, those of the first being members of executive, and thus in full confidence, while those of

x

the other two had lessening degrees of trust reposed in them. This ensured secrecy of plan and a firm discipline. Financially the committee, like the whole movement, was supported by rich members who devoted all their fortunes to the cause by contributions from outside sympathisers, and by the proceeds of those "confiscations of State capital"—their euphemism for theft and robbery, which, as perpetrated on Crown property, they recognised as a legal means of warfare.

The committee lost no time in attempting to accomplish their miserable task. At three points along the railway line over which Alexander II. was to pass on leaving Livadia in the Crimea, mines were laid which could be discharged by electricity. One was not required owing to a change in the royal route, the second refused to explode at the critical moment, while by means of the third—that near Moscow—a wrong train was wrecked. About the same time (autumn of 1879) Khalturin, a revolutionary who had laboured much amongst the working classes in St Petersburg, offered his services to the executive committee in connection with the scheme they had on hand. As it had been agreed that, in the event of failure of the plans already made, he should attempt to blow up the Tzar in the Winter Palace at St Petersburg, he entered the imperial dwelling-house in October, having found employment as a varnisher, and at once proceeded to make a careful study of the situation, and fixed on the dining-hall as the most convenient and assailable point. It is difficult to conceive mental agony greater than that endured by this wretched fellow during the long nights that preceded the completion of his plans. He was in an advanced stage of consumption, became increasingly nervous, and was often unable to sleep on his pillow of nitro-glycerine owing to headaches brought on by the escaping gases. On the 5th February 1880 the explosion took place. Ten men of the guard were killed and fifty-three wounded. The Emperor had been detained from coming to table at the usual hour by the late arrival of an important guest.

The organisation of the Terrorist party had now reached its zenith. In addition to the supreme executive committee elected from amongst the members of the different local groups comprising the party, those branches perhaps showed the greatest activity which devoted all their energies to work amongst the soldiers, students, and factory-hands. As these three classes of society were more intelligent than the mere peasants, the attempt to win them to the side of discontent was felt to be more worth while. With the agitation amongst the working classes Jelyabov, who all along played a leading part in the Terrorist movement, specially identified himself. It has been computed that the membership of the wing was 500 in all.[1] But this is evidently a vague statement covered under a round number.

The winter of 1880-81 was a period of unwonted excitement and enthusiasm amongst the party, terminating with the assassination of the Emperor on the 1st March. The deed was carefully planned by the executive committee, and forty-seven members answered Jelyabov's call for volunteers. Grinewizki, who threw his bomb straight —the details are known to every one—was carried to the hospital to die. He opened his eyes for a moment before closing them for the last time, and was immediately sur-

[1] Thun, Geschichte der revolutionären Bewegungen in Russland; but see p. 346.

rounded by a group of people eagerly anxious to ascertain who the assassin was. With a bitter smile he briefly replied to the question "Who are you?" "I do not know," and passed away. The subsequent history of the party is best studied in Siberia.

. . . .

No less interesting are accounts of the Revolutionary movement that deal more particularly with two of its great aids — the secret printing-presses and the bomb-factories. Situated on the top storeys of the highest houses where few might hear the rolling cylinders, composed of machinery so simple that in a quarter of an hour the whole apparatus could be taken down and stowed away in a large cupboard, the secret presses continued to unburden themselves of sheets of lettered wrongs and challenges, warnings and consolations, at more or less regular intervals. And if, on the day that an issue had been published, you had known to stand about the railway station of the town, you would have seen a man or woman, with pockets stuffed full of propaganda, carefully deposit a somewhat heavy portmanteau in a second class carriage, and disappear with it when the next town was reached. Thus by a travelling post copies of the journal were distributed in all the centres of Revolutionary movement along the railway line, and the different branches were kept in touch. And if, again, you had gone with the police, to whom by treachery or chance the existence of the hidden press had become known, you might have seen the counting-house defended with revolvers, till every shred of compromising matter had been destroyed. But how much more dangerous in every way were the bomb - factories! The noxious fumes of the chemicals, the unpleasant way that the explosives had of going off in course of preparation or even afterwards, and the almost certain chance of discovery in that event, would have been enough to deter most men from working at least in this department of the Revolutionary movement. But Kibaltschitsch, their great chemist, was not dismayed even when on one occasion he poured so much sulphuric acid on the floor that it ran down and dissolved the gilt wall-decorations of the room below. On the contrary, hearing the tumult below, he went out of the secret laboratory, and meeting the anxious proprietor on the stairs so as to prevent him if possible from coming to see—and to discover—told him calmly not to worry, as he would pay all the damage.

Perhaps no task is more difficult than to estimate this movement at its proper value, far less to tabulate its results. We have seen how its aim was the freedom of Russia, how by means of secret societies the Revolutionary party tried to organise itself, and succeeded to a considerable extent, and how the Government at once began the struggle with it. We have seen that the Revolutionary society was well organised up to the death of the Tzar in 1881, and that so long as Alexander II. continued his reforms all went well. After a time other things occupied his attention more than the State, and this led to renewed activity on the part of the Revolutionary party. They were, however, checkmated at every point. When they found themselves powerless, they resolved to frighten the Government. They thought that by killing the Emperor they would get power into their hands, which they would use to develop the peasant communities, and so make Russia a country of organised communities, which meant progress. They only exchanged didactic for hysterical measures when the first were rendered impossible. The Revolutionary party took the law into their own hands, and gave to what followed the character of a life-and-death struggle. In such a case it is not natural for the vanquished to expect quarter, and the Russian Government was firm in dealing with their opponents.[1] So the Terrorists were conquered, captured, and banished for the most part, while those who remained free or escaped saw that the realisation of their ideals was but a dream.

Again, the history of the inner workings of the Revolutionary party may be summarised as one long tale of internecine strife, of mystery sometimes and of deception, of the struggles waged by different individuals desirous to be lord and master over their less gifted fellows. What has been the result? What did they achieve? In one particular, at least, it is easy to show that something was done. In all, up to the year 1882, when the Terrorist wing was finally broken up—and with it disappeared the vitality of the old party—six attempts had been made upon high officials, in three instances with fatal results, and four upon chiefs of police, with one death. As many attempts at least were made upon Alexander II., with what success is known; and while nine spies and traitors were assassinated, two only were wounded. No less than four-and-twenty times was armed resistance made to the authorities. But these are not results of which to be proud.

To the general question it is more easy to give a negative than a positive answer. The result was, to put it plainly, complete failure to obtain the principal objects in view—viz., an insurrection of the people, or a constitution, while the attempts to bring workmen and students into touch with one another met with less than moderate success. At the same time, he would be rash who would deny that after so many

[1] From 1878 to 1882 alone, thirty-one politicals were executed.

years of activity the Revolutionary party left some slight impression on the people, could point to some poor peasants prepared to discourse on the glorious theme of liberty, could cite communities educated in advance of their times albeit with sinister purpose, could secretly rejoice in an opposition press meagre in quantity if not in quality, that, in spite of all coercion, survives unto this day. So much for the past: we turn now to the present, to see, if possible, what effect the movement has had upon the politicals themselves.

CHAPTER XI.

THE POLITICAL PRISONER.

PAST OPINION—EXILE BY ADMINISTRATIVE PROCESS—POLITICALS ON THE MARCH—AN "ADMINISTRATIVE" IN PRISON—LIFE IN A YAKUTE ULUS—A POLITICAL OF THE SECOND CLASS—SCHLÜSSELBURG—THE EX-POLITICAL NEWSPAPER EDITOR—TERRORIST COLONIES—STRENGTH OF THE TERRORIST PARTY—LIFE AT KARA—MANIFESTOES—A GIRL POLITICAL—THE NETCHAIEV CONSPIRATOR—THE ROMANCE OF THE POLITICAL'S LIFE—RUSSIA AND FRANCE—PRESENT-DAY SOCIALISTIC MOVEMENTS—RUSSIAN JUSTICE—GROWTH OF THE REVOLUTIONARY IDEA—TERRORISTS AND THE PEASANTS—THE WATCHMAKER AND THE PHOTOGRAPHER—POLITICALS AND SCIENTIFIC WORK—THE BRIGHT SIDE OF THEIR EXISTENCE—DO THEY REMAIN IN SIBERIA?—CRITICISM—THE FREEDOM OF RUSSIA.

ONE is well aware that the most difficult and delicate part of the subject has now to be faced. In criticising a system and its workings, a man may be pardoned if he shows evidence of having misconstrued or failed to appreciate the significance of certain points—nay, even of having totally overlooked yet others. For this there may be various reasons, and at the worst it can only be said that he is no critic. But when it comes to be a question of dealing with one's fellow-men and fellow-women, then, even if he be no critic, his judgment somehow does not pass into the oblivion that it deserves, but helps somewhere to form or strengthen a false impression of the people under review. No pages of Mr Kennan's work are more fascinating than those in which he deals with the political question. Strong in the conviction of the justice of the cause that he has championed, he presents pictures of palpitating interest, and sketches careers of suffering and endurance that make the reader hold his breath in the perusal of them. And the query that the world has made ever since is, How far is all this true? My interest in Siberia and its exile system is not sufficiently old to have enabled me to master all the criticism and discussion that succeeded the publication of Mr Kennan's story, but my impression is that he came out of it with some success.

One method of retort, employed, for example, by Mr De Windt (and likewise exemplified by the description of Slavinski in Chapter IX.), was to question the different politicals whom he visited in confinement. But the result for the object in hand is, comparatively, worthless. What you get is an idea of the man and his surroundings, an impression of his present condition more or less accurate, but nothing more.

How can it be otherwise? A proud political rises one morning in his cheerless surroundings with certain well-defined feelings against the human race in general surging in his breast. At some time or other in the course of the day his cell door is flung open, and he is set face to face with a travel-stained unkempt stranger (I speak for myself), whose sole efforts must be directed towards repressing the air of the naturalist that he is in danger of assuming as he gazes—it may be for the first time—on a specimen of this Russian specialty. Is it to be expected that the sensitive political will unburden himself to any visitor? Will he reveal his inmost thoughts, and tell the story of his life, especially enlarging upon its latest developments, in a brief half hour, however intensely he may feel? No, if I judge the man aright; and if he did I should respect him the less. Talk to Slavinski if you will about some subject that interests him—his meteorology or geological sections—or even hazard a comparison of his prison experiences in different lands, but beyond that nothing. It is in far different circumstances that one learns about the political exile. In the upper chamber of some log-house in Nertchinsk, when the lights burn low; in the back-room of a Tchita dwelling-house, during the small hours of the morning; in some sequestered garden by the side of an exile's home in Irkutsk,—these are the likelier places. Meet them as fellow-creatures, in little companies or singly, and they, having passed through the harder phases of their experience, and being now calmer and more dispassionate, will bear with you even when you ply them with questions; and according as you win their confidence or not, you will succeed or fail in the object that you have in view.

Mr Kennan's too felicitous method consisted very largely in relating the experiences of individuals as given by themselves, or by their friends and sympathisers. However accurate these may be, it is, nevertheless, obviously a one-sided method. When one reads the account of Dr Weimar's life as given by Mr Kennan and Mr De Windt respectively, it is difficult to believe that the same man is the subject of both sketches, although the purer narrative in the former case suggests that it is probably the more accurate estimate. Still that man only can confute Mr Kennan who takes up each incident that he has related, and proves credibly and lucidly that such and such details have been grossly exaggerated.

I am not aware to what extent this has been done. I believe that circumstances now render it impossible that it can be done. And yet I have the well-defined impression that there was a considerable amount of exaggeration (apart from all side-effects that seem to be the natural accompaniments of sundry forms of journalism) in Mr Kennan's literary treatment of the political prisoner, even if one is not prepared to go the length of saying with Mr De Windt that he became "the unsuspecting mouthpiece of scheming and untruthful individuals." My reason for believing this should be plain after a perusal of the following pages; if it is not, the judgment goes for nothing. I, too, have heard heart-stirring tales of personal experiences, but prefer to attempt to describe the exile's life at the present moment, so far as I know it, from different points of view. Even if one is unsuccessful, it is at least eminently the fairer method.

At the threshold of this inquiry it is useful to consider how the politicals may best be classified. Perhaps the simplest method is to divide them into two great classes— those who have been exiled by administrative process, and those who have been condemned by a court and sentenced to hard labour. Of these the former are numerically the greater body. It is also probably true that politicals form only one per cent of the entire yearly "export" of prisoners.

In considering each of these two classes, we remark, first, that the mere existence of exile by administrative process is the darkest blot on the whole Siberian system: of this the writer will make more or less according to his temperament. It simply means that any man, woman, or child, who, owing to information received through what is probably the most perfect system of espionage in the world, is considered "politically untrustworthy" by the local authorities of any part of the Russian empire, may be arrested, detained during such time as the Goverment makes further inquiries, and finally banished to some other region, usually Northern European Russia or Siberia, for a period that should not exceed five years, but which not unusually and often quite arbitrarily is extended at the end of that term. Formerly the limit was five years; to-day the term never exceeds a decade, though it is often eight years; but, again, there are many who do not suffer the statutory five. Such exiles do not lose all their civil rights. I suppose it would be impossible to catalogue the misdeeds for which this treatment is considered the correct expedient. Many of them would seem harmless enough to us, but to be a propagandist of socialism, to have forbidden books in one's possession, to be a member of a secret society which may limit its activities simply to discussion of the political questions of the day, down even to merely being an avowed sympathiser with such persons, was and is quite sufficient to merit such procedure. The secrecy with which these "processes" are conducted is one of their appalling features. During the investigation of a case, in which the unfortunate "administrative" can do nothing in his own behalf, he is lodged in a House of Preliminary Detention, commonly that at St Petersburg, and there alone he may pass months, or even years. Then, some day, his case is taken up, judged quietly, and he joins the next gang of exiles *en route* for Siberia.

Of the treatment of such prisoners on the march something has already been said. When they start from their native town, a collection is generally made for them amongst their friends *sub rosâ*. We have noticed the option that they have of travelling alone by post at their own expense, but advantage is rarely taken of this concession owing to insufficient means. There is no doubt that, as the natural result of their difference in birth and upbringing, the march presents hardships for them such as the ordinary convict never experiences. Again, it must be confessed that the attention (of a kind) bestowed during the march upon the politicals is largely in excess of that extended to the ordinary criminal, insomuch that one is almost tempted to say that while the taker of human life might slip or arrange to slip away on any day, the man who belonged to some innocent society would make such an attempt in vain. The politicals have almost always separate rooms in the *étapes;* sometimes the women of their party have the additional luxury of a *kamera* to themselves. Their allowance is one-half again as great as that of the ordinary criminal, and *telyegas* are always supplied for their use. Politicals, even more than the convicts, form clubs or unions, the wealthier members of which, with rare magnanimity, often take their needier brethren into equal partnership. In spite of all this, and of the fact that one of their number has in print declared that his existence on the march was simply that of a dilettante prisoner, it seems to me wholly unnecessary, except from the point of view of economy, that politicals exiled by administrative order should ever come into any contact with ordinary convicts, far less be sent along the road with them. And even the club has its limits. The private means of the last party that passed through Irkutsk two summers ago came to an end at Krasnoyarsk, and they suffered great privations: one of them died on the road, and a second expired in the former town. The friends of the "cause" throughout Siberia watch well the numbers of those who are sent along the great highroad. Thus one learned that on such and such a day, shortly before our arrival at Irkutsk, a party of sixteen had passed through that town, of whom four were bound for Nertchinsk, while twelve were going to the province of Yakutsk. Again, the extraordinary methods by which the political exiles can keep up a correspondence with almost any one displays an ingenuity that only such circumstances as those in which they live could develop. With regard to letter-writing, there is probably less restriction made in Siberia, at least upon the frequency of this privilege, than in most countries. Prisoners may write as often as they like, but as only a small proportion of the ordinary criminals know how to hold a pen, they are unaffected by the privilege. The politicals indulge in the practice more, and their correspondence also is subject to the revision of those under whose immediate authority they are. But in any case, letter-writing is not much cultivated as yet amongst the Russian people. Also, all money sent on behalf of a prisoner is generally taken in charge by the *natchalnik*, and given to the recipient as he may need.

One short chat with an "administrative" *en route* remains graven in my memory. It was at Krasnoyarsk, where the *kameras a* and *b* of the prison were reserved for men of that class spending a few days there in their journey to some farther destination. There was nobody in *a*; but *b*, which was an oblong room about 15 feet high, with *nari* along the wall opposite the door, was occupied. The windows were placed high up on the wall above the platform, which also seemed to be much more elevated than usual. On this, at a point between two of the windows, a couple of rugs with a white sheet and pillow had been made up into a bed. Not far off were two dozen fresh eggs and a *krinka* of sweet milk; a teapot, basin, kettle, and two metal cups were also lying about, together with two or three tins of preserved meat. By one side of the shake-down were ranged a couple of portmanteaus, one of which was open, and a few odd garments were strewn about. There were also several books, from the perusal of one of which—poems by one of the lesser Polish writers—the occupant of the room arose, and turned slowly round with a surprised look as we entered. He was a somewhat short man, dressed in a dark-coloured blouse, dark pantaloons, and boots. Beneath a deeply-furrowed brow shone out a pair of clear grey eyes keenly penetrant; a thick growth of sandy hair and beard concealed the greater part of his features. When he saw the not unfriendly character of the intrusion a faint smile broke across his face, and the right side of his mouth curled up. He was an "administrative" political going to Siberia for the second time. His sentence was eight years in the province of Yakutsk, but as he had heart disease he felt sure that he would not be sent there. He spoke of the *étape* life as hard, but said that many of the prisons through which he had passed were in good order, and if I remember rightly he singled out Omsk in particular. In the far corner of the room were the belongings of another "administrative," who was not, however, in the room at the time. Both had an amount of liberty that I had not seen equalled before.

There seems to be much arbitrariness exerted in assigning destinations to the different persons thus exiled, even if we grant that the remoteness of the locality does, to a certain extent, depend upon the nature of the individual's crime and on his social position. And once a man has been arrested, he, or rather his relatives, generally direct their endeavours to getting some mild and not too lonely spot selected as his place of exile. This arbitrariness is one of the pervading weaknesses of the system, for if we leave out of account for the moment all that is involved in separation from one's home and relatives, it may still be little worse than a pleasant holiday to be set down in a village on the highroad near Lake Baikal, while it is tribulation to be banished to a Yakute *ulus;* and even the exquisite monotony of life in Yakutsk is much less to be desired than residence in towns like Irkutsk, Tchita, or Nertchinsk, which has its compensations. As to the life in a Yakute *ulus*, opinion seems much to differ. The politicals would have us believe that it is one of the most terrible experiences possible to imagine. Alone with the *taiga*, or surrounded by unsavoury Yakutes, the political frets under the mere inactivity of an existence that offers him no possibility of employing any talents with which he may have been dowered. If he desires to converse with his rude neighbours, he must first learn their language. One sympathiser concluded an exposition of the utter dreariness of such ostracism with this climax, "The exiles sometimes marry Yakute women, because they have nothing else to do."

On the other hand, one has seen people who have come back from these surroundings. And while one of my informants would have led me to believe that, on immediate return from a Yakute *ulus*, the politicals look like wild men of the woods, and have in many cases forgotten their mother-tongue through want of practice, still, if I may judge from those I met, it does not take them long to throw off all traces of the savage, or to reacquire their own language; and, moreover, they all had a robust healthy appearance that their town compatriots often lacked. At the same time, I do not seek to minimise the darker aspects of the situation. Lately the question has occupied the minds of those in high places. The main difficulty in the way of the abolition of exile by administrative process is that the Russian villagers would, in that event, have no defence against the numbers of evil-doers whose presence they no longer desire in the community, and who have in consequence to be sent out to Siberia as settlers. In comparison with this class of exile, the number of politicals banished administratively is small. With the advance of the railway, much of the unlovely character of Siberian exile will naturally vanish. In the minds of many the *eidolon* will still remain, but the difference in the lot of two politicals exiled respectively to Samara and to Irkutsk will be merely that of longer travel in a railway carriage. For every reason they might as well be at one place as at the other: they could leave the one as readily as the other.

Politicals have a Government allowance of 12 rubles a-month for their support in the Province of Yakutsk, but the amount varies with the latitude, being only half as much in Trans-Baikalia. As soon as a man can support himself by any trade it is withdrawn. The exiles are very much restricted in the methods by which they may endeavour to maintain themselves by their own labour. They may in no way teach, and, if resident in a town, may take no part in connection with any public society or institution, while any form of employment that bears on literature, even if it be the mere printing, is closed to them. It is necessary to obtain special permission from the Minister of the Interior to practise medicine. In fact, all work that brings them into contact with a fellow-being is denied them by law; and while they are at liberty to practise any handicraft or artisan's pursuit, yet even in the matter of trade there are limitations, for merchants are always members of a guild, and this would not be permissible in the case of a political. Also, as most "administratives" are students, journalists, or teachers, the courses left open to them are of little purpose. Again, it often happens that the only Russian-speaking individual in the Yakute *ulus* to which the political has been banished is the police officer, who has the right to search his hut at any time of the night or day, and to whom he is supposed to report himself daily, while he may not leave the spot without special permission. Such is an idea of the law on paper, but I am bound to confess that in practice it is a different thing. There are, it is true, some petty officials who find sincere pleasure in carrying out all these and other like details to the last letter, and with whom it may be either a matter of fiendish cruelty or of a shadowy conscience that they take such care not to fail in the application of the last jot or tittle of the regulations. There are such cases, but their number grows yearly less, and it is as often that one finds the contrary. For to take, even that Yakute *ulus*: the police officer presumably has children whom he desires to have educated to the best possible advantage, and as even in many southern Siberian villages the most intelligent man is the banished Russian student, the sensible officer does not scruple to invite him to teach his children, while it is he of all men who should see that the exile has intercourse with no one. And of this there can be no stronger instance than that already related as existing at Akatui, where a well-known Terrorist is actually engaged as master in the village school. Again, the same police officer soon learns that his exile is of all men most peaceable, and while he may in accordance with instructions begin by demanding that his ward report his presence daily, this soon becomes a weekly occurrence, then fortnightly, and in time that section of the law falls into complete abeyance as regards the exiles in that village. One does not deny the other side of the picture, but there is this side also, which is as true.

The political of the second class is a man of quite a different order. He has been tried by court, and condemned either for having attempted, intended to attempt, or belonged to a society that was organised for the purpose of attempting, to overthrow the present state of government in the land, or for having circulated, or secretly abetted the circulation of, seditious literature. In addition to exile and hard labour he loses all his rights. The number of those who belong to the second class is not nearly so great as that of the administratives. They are the people simply who have adopted extreme measures, and have attempted or intended to attempt to gain their ends by violence. The tendency of the Government during the last decade has been to include all political offenders, so far as it was possible, in the first class, as thereby the difficulties of a trial are obviated, and they are thus better able to do with them as they like. At the same time this arrangement has not altogether been to the disadvantage of the politicals. The printing of forbidden literature was formerly considered to be punishable with exile by administrative process only; but recently, inasmuch as there have been no Terrorist movements (nor are there likely to be), this crime has been included in the category of those subject to severer measures. The punishment is a long term of hard labour, at the end of which the political has been generally despatched to the province of Yakutsk, there to dwell in a *ulus* for a period not so much less than that passed within the prison walls. Like the " administratives," they maintain themselves on the monthly grant rendered to them by the local authorities, in some cases simply the village policeman. After ten years, commonly, of such a life, they are enrolled as members of a peasant community, and then allowed to settle in a town in Eastern Siberia, where they pass the remainder of their lives, supporting themselves by some trade, or, if unable or unwilling to do so, subsisting on the Government allowance. Of individuals of this class actually in hard labour at the present moment there are not many; indeed I do not remember to have seen a dozen. Formerly, when there was no lack of Terrorists, they were sent in droves to Kara, there to perform hard labour; and it is around their life at this station that the thrilling pages of Mr Kennan's stories mainly circle. A few were sent to Nertchinsk.

It is well known that in the fortresses of Schlusselburg and Petropavlovsk many of the more dangerous politicals have been incarcerated. Not many of those who are once escorted within these iron-bound doors ever retrace their steps to the world without. The man who enters Schlusselburg is practically buried alive. Little is known about the dread place. The mother may not learn whether her daughter yet lives or not; the father is ignorant as to whether his son still renders his earthly account or has been called to a higher bar. One or two have come out, but upon them is the silence of the tomb. As the man leaves, he is put on his honour to disclose nothing of what passes within the walls. Well do such creatures keep their trust: the alternative is too heavy. If anything were divulged, the authorities would then equally visit with condign punishment all who have been let out, careless to find the tale-bearer—this, I understand, is the arrangement—and their last end would be worse than the first. Vera Figner, who is perhaps best known of all Terrorists, and whose brother was a renowned singer, was imprisoned there for life. Her mother, presently at Kasan, happened to be living in Krasnoyarsk when Mr Galkine Vraskoi, the late Director of the Prisons, passed through that town a few years ago on a tour of inspection of the Siberian penal stations. She begged an interview with the potentate, and when ushered into his presence asked if he would tell her how her daughter fared. "Oh," said the Director, "she has her own room, goes out every day for a walk, reads books, and even drinks her tea with lemon." Now there was a (false) impression abroad at the time that the girl was already dead; and as Schlusselburg is a military fortress, and therefore did not come within Mr Galkine Vraskoi's sway, it is possible that he never was inside the prison. This little incident is narrated for what it is worth, being the sort of tale that one hears in profusion from the afflicted politicals, but which should influence a man in no possible manner in forming a judgment on the question of their treatment, unless he knows the other side. There is said to be a man at Krasnoyarsk at the present moment who has lately been released from Schlusselburg, but so well does he keep his oath that his most intimate comrades can learn nothing from him upon the subject,—which made it useless, as they suggested, for any outsider to talk with him.

In illustrating the first class of politicals, we may take the case of a man who is now the editor of perhaps the most influential paper in Siberia. He was arrested twelve years ago in St Petersburg because he happened to know certain workmen who belonged to secret societies. As he had previously married the daughter of a wealthy merchant in Kiakhta, he offered to go to that town in banishment before the final decision was arrived at in his case; and as it was so much farther off than the north of Russia, whither he would naturally have been sent, he was released from the House of Preliminary Detention at St Petersburg after eight and a half months, and proceeded to the Chinese frontier. Here he was employed in a quiet way by his father-in-law; and after his term of four years had expired, his former profession of tutor being now closed to him, he went to one of the large towns in Siberia, where he settled, and now edits a newspaper. Thus he has immeasurably more influence, and a far better position, than he ever hoped to have gained at home. When he is away in Russia on business (which, now that his term is over, he is free to do as often as he likes) his wife conducts the paper for him. I grant, of course, that the censorship exercised over it is truly remarkable. The word "people" is regularly deleted, and the wholly unequivalent term "population" is inserted instead. It is wrong to speak of the Russian people,—they are not supposed to exist, or even to be recognised in a journal. Again, in discussion of some labour question, the word "workman" was used, for which the insipid phrase "people who work" was substituted with the same intention. In an article descriptive of Northern Siberia there occurred this sentence: "During the long winter the Tunguses and Ostyaks come nearer the Russian villages." The word "Russian" was stroked out, as the censor would brook no such division of the empire. But it is ridiculous to learn that the same man actually on one occasion expunged a couple of sentences standing in inverted commas, which he did not recognise as being a direct quotation from a manifesto issued at the Coronation of 1896. One therefore has some sympathy with the editor's wife when she describes the atmosphere in which they live as "stifling."

IN THE GOLD MINES AT KARA.

In addition to her ordinary work in connection with the journal, which is not merely limited to the seasons of her husband's absence, this lady teaches from 10 to 5 P.M. in a Sunday-school, of which there are two in her town. These Sunday-schools are so called from the day on which they are held. As a body, politicals show more than mere indifference to religion, although, as they number many Jews, it cannot be said that they are atheistical as a whole. They regard religion as a thing that should be done away with, a superstition fit only for the children of the past. On this point they are as intolerant as they imagine those to be who are in authority over them. Thus, if they gained all that they wish, religious instruction would almost certainly be dispensed with—one idea of liberty of conscience. Liberty of conscience with the political is—not only to be atheistical, but actively to combat all belief in such superstition as religion and theism. So one can understand that politicals have absolutely no sympathy with, e.g., Stundists, not even to the extent that one might have imagined from their both being sufferers: they leave them severely alone. They would also fain make out that the religious beliefs of the peasant people are insincere and of no account. Much can be found to support their general attitude in the inefficiency of the Russian clergy. They wish to help their fellow-men, so that the world may become better. Of course there is nothing very original in this view. "There are a great many churches in this town," said the editor's wife. "It would be much better to take most of the money that is lavished on these buildings and spend it on the poor—in fact, to do something for them, instead of merely praying for them as they do in these churches." But to return. The schools in which this intensely practical lady assists are for girls who are at work all the week, and whose ages are about fifteen—*i.e.*, even if they could, they are too old to enter the Government schools. They are taught elementary subjects—reading, writing, arithmetic, and sewing. This work is a distinct self-sacrifice on the part of the busy woman, who, in consequence, feels herself forced to give up the personal education of her little son, who was at Kiakhta with his grandparents. But this spirit overwhelms her at times—" I am lonely without him: he always slept in my room, and had no governess, for I taught him everything."

But not only does the man of whom I speak edit a newspaper—he has also been appointed curator of one of the best museums in Siberia. In all this there is a certain inconsistency that marks much Russian official procedure. Cases of this sort are by no means so rare as one would suppose. The man who owns the largest book-shop, with printing works attached, in Siberia, is another old "administrative." The number of plate-glass windows in his establishment is greater than would represent the years he spent in exile. Again, one evening I met a technical engineer who had been banished for a few years. Being a sharp young fellow, he had obtained a good position on the railway, and admitted that he was now almost making as much in four months as he made in a year at home before he came out. Everything considered, he was content with the turn that affairs had taken in his life, and his intention was to stay on in Siberia even when his term had expired. He was essentially of a buoyant disposition, otherwise it would have been impossible for him to speak in such a light-hearted manner of his present circumstances, so as almost to be thankful for the fact that he had been found with an illicit book in his possession, and was sentenced accordingly.

But it is amongst the prisoners and exiles of the second class that we find the relics of what is popularly known as Nihilism and Nihilists. In all the East Siberian towns there are little colonies of such exiles who are passing their latter years amidst more restful surroundings than those in which they started on their careers. And the method in which they spend their time differs with the intellectual strength and depth of character of the individual. Some, for example, are well content to receive Government support, and while away the day in idleness, except when they are denouncing the hand that provides for them. More have found reasonable employment, and by honest work, often under the most depressing circumstances, have rendered themselves independent of the powers that be. Lastly, there are a few particularly energetic ones who put the best of their ideas into practice, and by not only doing sound work themselves, but by helping others to work and giving them employment, have earned the respect of all their fellow-citizens of low and high degree.

Evenings passed in the company of such people could not easily be forgotten. Often the seance was prolonged to the early morning; and where a more liberal official spirit prevailed, such reunions were quite possible during the day. In one of these towns there is a large central square, on one of the sides of which you will find a photographer's shop. We can walk in to supper one evening and hear about the life at Kara from the photographer, and some of his comrades whom he is kind enough to invite for that purpose. That part of the broad unpaved street which is reserved on either side for pedestrians is separated from the rest of it by a series of short, stout, wooden posts set down at somewhat wide intervals. The thoroughfares are completely deserted as we wander along one of them, till it opens into the square, when we see our signal in the form of a lamp burning brightly by an open window. We are the first to arrive—punctuality is rare in that country. The other guests drop in slowly, and as each enters he quickly salutes his friends. Soon we are all seated by the table. After general conversation, in the course of which one quickly learns that the company is composed of highly intelligent men and women, we confine our attention to one man in particular.

"In time past," said the ex-Terrorist, "all political prisoners who had been condemned by court" (*i.e.*, those of the second class) "were sent to Kara. For the last five years none have been sent there; they are now transported to Nertchinsk and Sakhalin, or shut up in Schlusselburg. A new model prison" (this with a sneer) "has been erected at Akatui, where criminals and politicals are mixed together." Seditionary propagandism amongst the soldiers rouses the authorities almost more than anything else: for this, offenders are sent to the most remote parts after trial. In the Akatui prison at the present moment an officer is undergoing ten years' hard labour for distributing seditionary literature amongst his men.

One thing that I gained in particular from this man was a truer conception of the size of the Revolutionary party. When one judges the organisation by what it actually accomplished, it is natural to imagine that it must have numbered many hundreds. But of members of the Terrorist order my informant could not count one hundred. "At Kara there are, I believe, about twenty in free command, at Akatui four, in Sakhalin thirty. We know that since 1883 forty people have been sent to Schlusselburg: eighteen of these are dead, and one is presently living at Krasnoyarsk." In another town there is one other Terrorist exile, and in a second the colony consists of more than twenty. So that even if we double his total to include all those who succeeded in escaping, we get the number of active members at the moment of greatest activity to be two hundred. In what country could two hundred men do so much? It was the method they chose to adopt that gained for them a prominence out of all proportion at least to their numbers.

"Their trials were conducted in more than one large town of the empire—Kharkhov as well as St Petersburg. The political condemned by court lost all civil rights; university degrees were forfeited, likewise all honours and public position; even his wife could get divorce for the asking, while all his property passes to his heirs as if he were no longer existent. After leaving Kara the political was commonly despatched to the province of Yakutsk for a season. Indeed he was permitted to ask where he would like to go, although the procedure commonly followed implied ten years in the province of Yakutsk. But advantage was rarely taken of such condescension except in cases of sickness, for it really made little or no difference to the man where he went. Often, however, parents and relatives would try to obtain some amelioration of the exile's fate, especially if they had any position at home."

Since 1893, although the old law is still in vogue, the greater proportion of politicals have been sent, either through the intervention of friends or the growing humanity of the Government, to some place in Trans-Baikalia. For ten years after leaving his place of punishment no rights and no liberty of movement are granted to the exile. At the end of that term he may ask to be inscribed in a peasant community, and if it accepts him, as is usual, he becomes a peasant, and has the rights of a peasant. After some years he may become even a citizen, but he cannot leave the town where he has settled without permission, and that only for a season. There are four classes in Russian society, and there is the man who belongs to no one of them—viz., the exile after he has left Kara, or the place where he has passed his term of imprisonment. The system forbade the possibility of there being any one at Kara with a sentence of less duration than four years, although in the case of minors even this was shortened by one year and four months.

According to my informant the treatment of the politicals at Kara was very variable, there being both good and bad times. This depended partly on the state of feeling at headquarters, where the keynote was given, but much more on its expression and the little variations played thereon by local authorities. For long periods the politicals were allowed to subscribe to papers, and although certain journals were always forbidden, they received books without a very strict supervisal, while there were other times when they were, denied any form of literary luxury at all. Again, for months they were only granted an occasional magazine, while papers in foreign languages were always withheld. The politicals had a separate prison of their own, acquaintance with which has been made by all those interested in the subject through Mr Kennan's work.

"With regard to employment, we had nothing to do: they gave us nothing to do"—*i.e.*, the hard labour at Kara consisted in doing nothing. At first they tried to set the politicals to wash gold, but the outlay exceeded the income, and this was discontinued. They were allowed to spend their day as they chose. "There was," he said, "during the time that I was at Kara, no *régime* worthy the name: we had nothing to do." The prison consisted of five large *kameras* (one being used as hospital), in each of which generally from eighteen to twenty people were confined. In 1828 there were 120 political prisoners in Kara: this would make twenty-four in each room. Gradually the number decreased to sixty in 1868, and then to fifty, and so on, till we reach the condition of things to be seen there to-day. The proportion depended on the total number of persons in confinement. "When I left, there were still sixty politicals in the prison." During the latter part of his stay the number of those leaving owing to expiry of sentence had been in excess of those who entered. He maintained that there was overcrowding even when he was there, although he did not remember exactly how many exiles there were when he first joined the circle. Ordinarily they were allowed out for exercise in the yard for an hour or two—*i.e.*, their *kamera* door was left open for that time. But that was only during the very severe epochs; and, more commonly, when the warders knew that those in command were not specially anxious to enforce the law, the doors were left open during the greater part of the day, and thus free communication between the different *kameras* was possible. The regulations were practically alike in the good and in the evil days: it was rather the enforcement of them that varied. The strictest period fell between the years 1882-84. In the former year some prisoners escaped, and the rest were divided up into different parties and distributed throughout the various Kara convict prisons.

About the food he did not seem to be very clear. They were allowed to receive supplies from their friends and relatives. "Soup, 23 *zolotniks* of meat, and 2½ lb. of bread, daily," if he remembered aright. They had their own *samovars*, made a common fund out of all their money, and elected a *starosta* or elder to act as treasurer. Each man had to go in turn to the kitchen. They divided themselves up into little companies of three, four, or five cooks, each with a *chef*, and one party did all the cooking for a week in turn. For clothing they received two pairs of boots in the year, the grey cloth suit, overcoat, *shuba*, four shirts, and four pairs of drawers, with the privilege of a bath every fourteen days. While he was at Kara they were permitted to wear of their own clothing only blouses and shirts; but one has noticed politicals in other than prison trousers, and ordinary criminals in their own jackboots.

The manifestoes issued from time to time help considerably in reducing sentences, and consequently the misery of many lives. The principle is uniform. The man condemned for life thereafter joins those whose sentence is one of twenty years, and so on through all the categories previously set out at length. The net result may roughly be summarised as the reduction of the term by a third. But if two manifestoes follow closely on one another, the man who has benefited by the first is affected by the second only to the extent of one year. My informant illustrated their advantage in a fascinating and naïve account of his past. "I gave, —oh,—it was a shoemaker, a good smack with a stick," on the suspicion that he had been supplying underhand information against a certain society to which he belonged. His defence was that the man was not killed, but the prosecution urged a knife in place of the stick. He was sentenced to fourteen years' hard labour. In 1883 Alexander III. was crowned, and the manifesto issued on that occasion, together with a second which celebrated the journey of Nicholas II. through Siberia in 1891, reduced the Terrorist's sentence by a third. In November 1894, the date of Nicholas's marriage, my informant's ten years in Yakutsk (on which term he had entered) were reduced to four, and he had not yet heard how he would be affected by the last coronation manifesto. He is employed in some capacity on the railway, which has proved a perfect godsend to many politicals of both classes, as otherwise, he said, there was nothing to do.

By this time a young woman has joined us. Outwardly she corresponds exactly with one's fancy-begotten picture of a Terrorist, and yet she is so merry withal. Her high forehead, strongly marked features, large dark-brown eyes, and tremendous head of short coal-black hair, give her such an imposing appearance that even her comrades call her Nyam-Nyam in jest, after some swarthy African tribe. She was always bright and brimful of fun when you spoke with her, but in the intervals she relapsed into a sad pensiveness, and a distant wearied expression brooded upon her countenance. She was sent out originally as an "administrative," but got severely implicated in the revolt known as the "Yakutsk History," and was accordingly sentenced to twenty years' hard labour at Kara, which term was latterly reduced to fifteen. Finally her case was re-examined, and she was treated with further leniency, being allowed to come and live in a town. She laughed at all her prison experiences: on this question she would not be serious. "My first day in Kara was the happiest day in my life; everybody was so kind to me, and I was quite content all the time I was there. The men played cards; I liked to play chess better. We had to find employment for ourselves. We women usually spent our time in sewing and making costumes," and she laughed across at my more serious male informant, who watched her steadily, evidently well accustomed to her little vagaries. In Russia she had been a teacher of drawing, and now was in the employment of the railway, drawing diagrams and plans. She could not be got to look at the gloomier side of things, and when one asked, "Now, what was hardest in the life at Kara?" she replied with evident truth, "Well, it was simply the want of liberty—the feeling that you were shut up, and could not get out. Otherwise I had a happy time: everybody was so good to me." Then she gave me a very racy account of the past history of some secret societies, and the really brilliant way (whatever else one may feel) in which the Government was able to descend upon them through its too well-organised system of espionage. "Some secret societies," she remarked with a smile, "were broken up even before they had time to choose a president."

And now our host comes over to our corner. His political history dates from the Netchaiev "Process." But Kara and all its woes are passed, and to-day he pursues his quiet photographic profession, in which he is assisted by three fair daughters. He is a remarkable man, and there are moments when in his unbleached linen coat and long white cuffs he looks many degrees above his social position. A high forehead with much black hair carefully brushed back, a long beard finely streaked with silver, and cold steely grey eyes,— and you have one of the party of young men who persuaded a fellow-student to go a walk with them in Moscow, and, having reached a lonely spot, murdered him there, on suspicion of having acted as spy upon them and reported their secret doings to a university official. At times the photographer seemed to be lost in thought, and often he sat motionless on his chair for several successive minutes, gazing at the floor in front of him, and grasping the tip of his beard in his right hand while he supported the elbow in the palm of his left. And again he would start out of his reverie with his face all lit up, and discuss questions with impassioned

FEMALE CONVICT LABOUR AT KARA.

warmth, only to relapse into that attitude of vacant insensibility that almost gave one the impression that he was a man living under a curse. Later we found that he had only too good reason for his exceeding pensiveness, and I am bound to say that I too in the sequel felt something of the regard that is entertained for the man by his more liberal fellow-citizens, and which showed itself practically in appointing him as curator of the museum. This position is filled by him to great purpose, and in that capacity he had the honour of conducting the present Emperor round the building when he passed through the town on his Siberian tour, and actually in courtesy shook the hand from which at one time he would have preferred to strike the sceptre. "Have there ever been such cruelties perpetrated under the present system, that individuals would have preferred death to living under it?" He smiled at the question, and said that without any doubt they preferred life under the system. "Every convict knows that sooner or later he will gain comparative freedom. Certainly they prefer the present system." I was then of my own accord in ignorance of the "Hunger Strikes" at Kara, and so did not know to ask his views upon that point. While there he met a young girl, also a prisoner, whom he subsequently married. There could be no possible doubt about his ability and culture when one saw him in his museum determining minerals by the most approved methods, chatting about the habits of animals, or particularly interested in the identification of a large tooth that constituted one of the latest finds of some other politicals who were on his working staff.

There is a wild infectious spirit of romance about the whole political question that catches many of the younger men and women and carries them off their feet, before they well know where they are. To understand this it is necessary to picture to oneself the lonely, circumscribed life of the average political exile's home in a Siberian town. For whatever else be stated to the contrary, there is sometimes undeniably a certain boycotting of old politicals by the other inhabitants, even if it is often to their own loss. Then there is the effect produced on the youthful mind by constantly repeated tales of that great past, characterised by so much cruelty on the one hand and so much nobility upon the other. Thus the second generation early experience in imagination the excitement, the constant general uncertainty, and the peculiar sensations engendered by the secret union of a body of men and women persecuted and yet determined to set right the affairs of their beloved country. From the days of their childhood they have been taught to regard the struggle as a field for the exercise of prowess, self-denial, and self-sacrifice. Many of them become fascinated with the idea of the reckless uncertain life of the poor students, which is nothing more than a protracted tussle from first to last, the hand-to-mouth existence of men watched by the police, and little able to call themselves their own, yet always full of hope that the day will come when the arm of the oppressor will be broken, and the desire of their hearts be fulfilled, and, what is best, they too will have played a part in the glorious work of freeing a great people. The romance of this life! How it appeals to the young, how it stirs their blood, till, for the "cause," they are prepared to undertake the long journey from Eastern Siberia alone, and to choose this terribly doubtful, unknown lot in a university town, exposed to privation of every sort, in preference to remaining quietly at home and doing some honest labour. No wonder that the photographer was moody, for had he not lately buried a child without any hope, and now his favourite daughter had announced her intention of going to St Petersburg to plunge herself right into the centre of this vortex whose tremor she had felt afar off, even if it meant that she was leaving her home for ever. And yet what right had he to complain? He had brought them all up in the belief that there is no God, that morality is a mere illusion, and that there is no need to pay any special regard to parents. But when the pinch comes, he is querulous. Still he is honest—"I see that I was wrong, and now I try to persuade her otherwise." But it is all without avail, and, after a while, the old spirit of resignation steals over the man, he goes to his writing-table and lays on it an additional photograph of the wilful Tatyana, being strengthened by the assurance of the younger Shura that she will not leave her father.

This spirit of wild unrest that comes over the younger members of politicals' families in this absorbing fashion is a peculiar phenomenon, probably hereditary. Tatyana had a position under her father in the museum, and in addition to this lent him valuable aid in his profession, so that far from being a burden to him, she was his staff. But, in answer to this inward call that she feels must be obeyed, she knows not why, the girl is content to undertake a fierce struggle with poverty, and, probably in the end, to play at the political game. She wants to support herself, but is not pleased to do so in the simple manner that lies to her hand. Indeed she can only say, "Perhaps I shall return in six years," and this in face of the fact that the initial steps entail a heavy outlay on the part of her father. But the neighbours gossip, and the wise ones shake their heads and say, "No, the girl has no serious intention to study, but there is a certain young political with whom she wishes to share the hardships of student life, and she will go to him in St Petersburg." Again, it is not the young women only that catch this fever, for the lady from Kiakhta also related how her brother of nineteen had set out from that town with his young bride and sister to study in St Petersburg, but now she doubted the sincerity of their intentions.

It is wellnigh a fashion with some of the younger people to affect the political. They are sent off for a few years into exile by administrative process, and then they return covered with glory. This view of things of necessity obtains only in rare instances, but it does occur.

I had more than one long talk with my Kara informant. A considerable interval of time separated two of these meetings, and in the meanwhile his wife had returned from Paris. One evening he held a "house-warming," and this lady, being the latest addition to the colony, was the centre of attraction for the time being. She said that the French idea of Russia was summed up in three words, "Tzar, knut, samovar." She was loud in her ridicule of the Russo-French alliance, remarking how painfully obvious it was that Russia was using her confederate merely as a cat's-paw, being quite prepared to throw her over so soon as she had gained her ends.

The man himself was one of the more bitter "comrades," but a very intelligent fellow. He returned time after time to the unfairness of putting politicals and ordinary criminals together, as at Akatui. Having been away from Russia for so long, his knowledge of any present movements was limited, but many of his reminiscences were entertaining. Referring to the universities, he said that in his time the proportion of students who were of humble parentage was not particularly large: that then, as now, there was a Conservative majority, only it was not organised, while at that time the revolutionary minority was a well-disciplined body. However that may be, nothing could be more complete than the disorganisation of the party as a whole to-day. During the period of its great achievements, the organisation of the party left little to be desired. To-day no two men agree entirely in their ideas and wishes, and they seem to reckon him the greatest amongst them who has spent the longest time in prison and at hard labour. They can point to no one as a leader amongst the exiles now in prison or in free command. Each tends to regard himself as the principal exponent of the party programme.

To-day there are no Terrorists of the accredited brand in Russia outside the grasp of the law. Their place has been taken by a host of Socialists, Radicals, and other milder reformers. Formerly the revolutionary movement was intellectual to a certain degree—*e.g.*, during the Terrorist period. It now resembles the socialist movement of Western Europe, but is still poorly organised. "There was a time," said my Kara historian, "when it was believed that a bold advance would put everything right." But in the death-struggle the Terrorists were conquered. Even from their point of view, the assassination of Alexander II. was one of the most stupid performances in history. After Peter the Great, he was the greatest Russian revolutionary in the best sense of the word. The most reasonable of the Terrorists whom I met admitted this. Still, others defended the action by maintaining that they were in duty bound to try every means of bringing about their ends, and that it was impossible to know that the assassination of that great monarch was not the correct way till they had tried it—*i.e.*, the affair had negative results.

The modern movement, then, attempts to get the working people as its basis of operation—to make them Socialists. It takes the form of organisation of socialistic societies, and the propagation of socialistic ideas amongst the workmen in the factories. At St Petersburg, Moscow, Kiev, Odessa, and Riga, and indeed in all the great labour centres, this goes on quietly. But there is no general organisation of the whole, the leaders are only local, and there are no funds. The difference between the modern movement and the past activities of the revolutionaries proper is so immense that at first one fails to grasp it. At the same time, such an incident as the large strike in the St Petersburg factories in June 1896 is significant as being the first concerted strike in Russia. Many recruits to the cause are still drawn from the universities, and of these the sons of *tchinovniks* and priests constitute the largest proportion. The education even of the women of the party is extraordinary. Every one knows the works of Spencer and Buckle, Darwin and Comte: Carlyle is not so much read—he is too religious. The policy of an "administrative" is largely negative : he criticises, and often does little else. Of course one cannot get past the facts that there is much to criticise with all justice, and that action along certain lines even of genuine philanthropy has been promptly checked. But the political of the first class really takes the one impracticable course.

It was only natural to find that the politicals were very strong in their denunciation of the methods of procedure in cases of arrest and trial. In Russia to-day there is still abundant evidence to show that, even if exaggerated, such censure is in part deserved.

My informant maintained that those persons comprising

the second class were arrested mainly for propagandism and agitation. Prosecution was limited to endeavouring to prove that a man belonged to a party that had attempted to overthrow the Government by violent means. The personal action counted for very little—it was enough that he belonged to a party, and so might have done this or that. And, according to this biassed witness, the penal courts worked somewhat after this manner. If it was known that a man had spoken with a member of a secret society, little more incriminating evidence was required, and the authorities then attempted to prove a more intimate connection on the man's part with the society. To have known, or even to have spoken to, a member of a secret society, was held to be proof that a man belonged to the society in intention. So some fifty persons being arrested in company, it was easily proved that they all belonged to the party. The party, being revolutionary, must be judged and punished in accordance with statute 228, say: A, B, and C were in that party, and so must be punished according to that column in the penal code. Such was a political's account of Russian justice in the Terrorist period.

It would be an interesting study to try and trace the growth of the revolutionary idea in the mind of the Russian political. Differences of temperament play a great part, and while some men join the "cause" for one reason, others do so from different motives. Certain questions and issues appeal more to one mind than another, but in many instances it is possible to discern the following sequence of thought. In Russia, perhaps more than in any other country, there are broad distinctions of class. Amongst a certain number of those who were better educated, and perhaps by nature more impulsive, there arose a growing tendency to assert opinion on behalf of freedom of the press, of speech, and of conscience. Orderly attempts to bring about these laudable conditions having failed, and the impression having gained ground amongst those most interested that it would be impossible to obtain the fulfilment of their desires, keen dissatisfaction arose, which was perhaps expressed most openly amongst the students, as young individuals with no great responsibilities. Many of the older generation shared the same opinions, but were unwilling to risk anything on behalf of them; while the youth, who had nothing actual to lose except freedom, and with it the power of agitation, were willing to run all risks.

Russia is a great peasant realm. The majority of her people are given to agricultural pursuits, so that it will be many years before the people become an active factor in advancing liberal ideas. In 1872 the revolutionaries believed that they had the people with them, but, finding they were mistaken, they had to carry on their self-imposed conflict alone. The outcome of this failure to carry the people along with them is that as a class they entertain a low view of their less fortunate brothers. They say that the peasants were too dull and ignorant to understand anything, and that it was all the same to them whether they were under Sultan, Pope, or Tzar.

Accordingly it is a surprise to observe the change of attitude of the Terrorists themselves towards their past history. Fifteen years ago everybody amongst the sentenced was eager and proud to be able to say that he was the man who had committed such and such a bomb outrage. The fashion has changed: to-day no one wishes to be connected with dynamite. A higher Anarchism has replaced the lower Terrorism of the past. The Terrorists themselves demonstrate this. With few exceptions, they were willing to give very succinct accounts of all that happened to them after the moment of arrest: they were commonly a little hazy as to what had occurred previously.

On a subsequent occasion I met in the same town another man of a type of mind quite different from any of those hitherto described. He was a quaint, uncouth creature, with small ears, low forehead, and dreamy eyes that, before the end of every third sentence that he spoke, sparkled as he broke out into a kind of heartless chronic smile. Nevertheless, he was a man with a clear sense of the proportion of things, and had rigidly made up his mind as to what course of action he would pursue during the rest of his day. He and his wife were involved in some plot, and both passed many years in Kara. But he learned much in that time. "I shall not take that Government allowance of 6 rubles monthly. It comes from the peasants: it is wrung out of them. I have had a straight fight with the Government and been worsted: I intend to have nothing more to do with it in future." He is almost alone amongst his comrades in taking up this position. The result is that he is respected by the community. He works all day at his watchmaker's trade, except when he does a little electrical engineering as a recreation, and, in addition, gives employment to a qualified assistant and two boys. Being an enterprising man with ideas in his head, he wants to bring machinery for making watches to his town, but has not the capital. He would like to train other men in his art. He spends little money, living partly on his garden produce, and has purchased an adjoining hut where his chief assistant works and sleeps. There are Russian officials who help this man financially in a quiet way, because he is genuine, sensible, and serious. His wife looked rather unattractive in a short ungainly print skirt. Her greyish hair and the dark lines round her eyes showed how the prison life had told upon her.

Listen to this remarkable confession from this no less remarkable man. "From a mere lad I recognised that in work lay the salvation of mankind; but during these earlier years I did not work, far less teach others so to do—I wasted my time. Since then I have known better, and now no one interferes with me when I am seriously employed." While many of his comrades loaf about in idleness, unless when engaged in talking socialism, he works and gives employment, and is the true socialist of the lot.

With him I must couple another man who also impressed me by the reasonableness and common-sense with which he spoke. I spent an evening with him in the town where he follows the business of photographer. He was the only man who recognised that the whole question had two sides, or rather who was willing to admit as much. Accordingly, one considered that his judgment of Mr Kennan's book would be more valuable than that of the average political. In reply to an expressed desire for his opinion he said, "Except in some minor descriptions and details, which show that Mr Kennan did not altogether understand our Russian customs and suchlike, his book is true *quant à moi*"—*i.e.*, he recognised the possibility of another point of view.

He had been involved in some process of which he did not seem anxious to give any very succinct account. After arrest, he passed two and a half years in Kharkhov. The first year seems to have been very hard, as he was left absolutely alone in a little cell with no one to whom to speak and with no books to read. Latterly he was provided with literature. He said that it was ten times harder in

Kharkhov than during the strictest time in Kara, and he arrived there just after the escape of the prisoners. A good many of the politicals spent their time at Kara in learning foreign languages by means of dictionaries. Thus many of them could read English and French, although totally unable to speak it: some, however, could talk a little French. This man had a few back, very back, numbers of the 'London Illustrated News,' and even ventured to speak English, but after a sentence in reply, he modestly said in French, "Your pronunciation is different from mine," and that was the end of the matter. The poor fellows had taught themselves a pronunciation, but to little or no purpose. Many of them could speak German, especially the Jews. In talking of bygone days, this man of great height, long hair almost reaching to his shoulders, small eyes, poorly developed cranium, and prominent under-jaw covered with a thick beard—a poor man making a sparse living by desperately hard work with dry plates and lenses—said of himself and of his fellow-students: "We were too naïve. We thought that all that was necessary for the freedom of Russia was the removal of the Tzar. Now we see that we were wrong in that, and although we still hold the opinions of our youth with regard to the liberty of the press and of speech, we see that it requires a great deal more and a method quite other than that which we adopted, to achieve our ends. If we killed thirty Tzars it would make no difference." During his time, he said, "the students belonging to the class of the nobility who attended the university had not so much influence as they have now." According to him, fully five per cent of the students were Jews; and with the great number of Jews in the Revolutionary party it never could have been very popular. He also added that in his day a student could wear his own blouse if he wished, but that now ¦they must don a uniform, the cost of which is one of a series of things that debar the very poor from entering the university. To-day the majority of the students are, as ever, Conservative.

Once more let us slip into a little garden in another town situated at the end of a road behind a house. It is a well-known rendezvous, and some of the people who are there on this occasion we have already met. As we sit under the shade of the trees and drink tea, while listening to varied experiences of prison life and political exile, it is difficult to believe that the men who have once passed through such tribulation should now be recounting without fear their stories in broad daylight. During the conversation one of those present, distinguishable amongst the others as much by his stiff frock-coat as by the softness of his speech and his unobtrusive thoughtful manner, hands me a slip of paper. On it are inscribed these words, "The East Siberian Branch of the Russian Geographical Society will be obliged if they may receive information from you as to whether you have received their publication which was sent some time ago." The man, whose bold though deeply-lined forehead is half hidden by the hair that is allowed to fall down on one side of his sad, firm face, cannot speak a word of English, and asks in German if I will correct the language of this communication, which is to be addressed to some defaulting English-speaking Geographical Society. The incident is typical of the manner in which this country of the future is developing its resources, and largely undertakes its own scientific work; as also of the fact that in connection with such work, especially when it takes the form of scientific expeditions, the educated politicals are often employed, numbering as they do amongst their ranks a heavy proportion of the men in Siberia who have had the necessary training for such research. This man had spent many years at Kara in hard labour, and thereafter passed the usual term in a Yakutsk *ulus*. Now he was living in a Siberian town, but had a presentiment that he would not be allowed to remain there long. Here, again, one stumbles across a circumstance that helps to bear out the impression one has received of the arbitrariness that pervades the system. So much of the welfare of these exiles depends on the character of those who are over them in high places. And if, for example, a governor-general, as in one well-known instance, is unfavourably inclined towards these people as a class, not only do the governors under him who may, from instinct, wish to act otherwise, cringe under him owing to that serfdom of spirit that since 1861 has merely moved from low to high estate, and so consequently violate their own feelings, but certain laws that are honoured in the breach by most of the governors are strictly carried into force by a ruler of this type. Thus Russian Jews, after serving their term, are supposed to return to Russia. But this law is only put into practice over one large region by a man who would fain clear his town of all politicals, if it were possible, and who does his best to achieve this, as the geographer would learn to his cost. To return to the latter: his modest retiring disposition prominently marked him out amongst his fellows. His knowledge of the Yakute language was invaluable for scientific purposes. He also professed Russian and Italian, some German and some French. In virtue of this he was retained by the Geographical Society. He had also taken part in one of M. Sibiryakov's expeditions. This gentleman, who owns several gold mines, has given handsome sums towards organising expeditions for the exploration of Siberia. On one occasion he gave 15,000 rubles towards an expedition for the exploration of part of the province of Yakutsk. As this province is more than seven times the area of France, such an undertaking demands a numerous staff, even to carry it out in part. But who amongst the Russians know the Yakute language? Here comes in the exceeding usefulness of the politicals.

The life-history of one other individual in that gathering verged on tragedy. His was a curious eager face, out of which peered strong, staring, protuberant eyes, generally spectacled. His thin black hair was scrupulously brushed back, and a straggling beard crept down his threadbare coat. In the centre of his forehead was a red-and-black mark — a long vertical scar, intersected at right angles by three shorter ones. They were the souvenirs of a self-inflicted wound, when in a moment of acute depression he had thought to end his life with a revolver. For participation in some bomb conspiracy he had passed eight and a half years in Russian and Siberian prisons, but his term in the Yakutsk province was reduced to four years by a manifesto. Now he is a member of a peasant community, and is free to travel about Siberia.

I have said that few of those with whom I had the pleasure of intercourse were disposed to recognise that there might be two sides to the question. Even into the literature of the exile system our nineteenth-century specialism has so much entered, that while Mr Kennan has been at pains to master one side in his own fashion, Mr De Windt has appropriated the other in a no less uncompromising manner. But even if the politicals likewise have eyes for but one point of view, it does not follow that their nearest relations always think accordingly. Thus Gottze, a political to whom reference has been made in a previous chapter, was all along treated with clemency, and, his term being almost finished, he had been allowed to spend the last two or three years in Kurgan, on the western confines of Siberia. I have already related how his parents, and younger brother whom he had not as yet looked on, happened to be fellow-passengers with us in the train. The former were going out to see him after a separation of ten years. The scene at the reunion could leave no one in any doubt as to the strength of the affection that united father and son, and yet in a discussion of the whole situation previous to arrival at that town, he who of all men might have been expected to have been in full sympathy with the movement for which his son had suffered summed up his view of the whole matter with the laconic and almost cruel remark, " Now, I hope, the brain is better."

I have already quoted instances of men who have confessed that whatever agony they went through at the moment of separation, they have in the end made a better thing of life in the land of their exile than they ever would have done at home; but no one will, of course, imagine that such cases form the majority, or even any considerable fraction, of the total number. At the same time, it is also true that most of the scientific work in Siberia is being done by political exiles. In one town the principal banker came out in 1863 as a political, but now all that is forgotten, and he is on friendly terms with the governor. The excellent high road from Krasnoyarsk eastward was engineered, at any rate as far as Kansk, by an old political, who received a salary of 4000 rubles per annum, and by his work so pleased the Governor-General of Irkutsk that he went to his house to thank him in person.

Again, the gold from all the Imperial mines, to the extent

of several hundred *puds*, is collected at Irkutsk, where it is smelted—and from that point the famous gold-caravan makes its way to Krasnoyarsk along the great highroad. The freight is conveyed in *tarantasses* strongly guarded by the military. The Administration of Mines generally finds that it has a few spare places in these *tarantasses*, and offers them free to needy individuals who wish to go to St Petersburg or Moscow for purposes of study. They are always given to girls, of whom many more apply than there are seats available, for they thus get safe-conduct over the only dangerous part of the road. The daughters of politicals often find transport in these Government conveyances, and our photographer intended to despatch his restless daughter by this post. Further, his principal assistant in the museum was also an old political of the second class. This man was given a place on a scientific expedition to Manchuria, and on his return, in addition to his salary, he received a bonus of 200 rubles.

I found it difficult to obtain exact information as to what proportion of the politicals remain in the country after they have come to the end of their term. Very different answers were given in different quarters, depending on the point of view of the informant. My own impression is that the numbers are about half and half, but there were several who said that the majority do not return. In Siberia there is a much greater approximation to a normal life than in Russia, and it is the country where money is to be made. Even the worst politicals have the possibility, however remote, of being allowed to return to Russia. But of the more heavily sentenced "administratives" (which is the class that the question really concerns), the younger men commonly return. Even if they were sent off in the middle of their university course, they sometimes return, at any rate to finish it, even if they choose to go back again to Siberia for good in the end. At the same time, considerable reluctance is shown in letting "administrative" exiles go back to university towns. So it may be said that generally all the young men return: they wish to get back to their homes and the associations of their youth. All the literary life, for example, is in the capitals of Russia, and those young men who wish to make a name for themselves in that department come back. But the older men, who have during their exile settled down to some trade, and now have wives and families dependent on them, find it more to their advantage to remain; and it is on them that the doom has fallen most heavily, being visited upon them and their children even unto the second and third generations.

It is tolerably certain that one day there will be a revolution in Russia, but when it comes it will not be from any revolutionary party, strictly so-called. Individuals who are minded to spend their time in that fashion have not at present, and will not have in the future, any chance of organising themselves sufficiently to do lasting damage. When the revolution does come, it will come from the mass of the people. It is possible to imagine that it will be hastened by some *faux pas* on the part of the Government, unless before that time there arises a Tzar who has strength of character sufficient to present the people with a constitution. I do not think that the Government is likely to make that *faux pas*, nor do I say that the country is yet ready for constitutional government: what has been said should make it clear that it is not. The reason of so much of the past and present discontent is that Russia has no safety-valves. St Petersburg has no Trafalgar Square; Moscow has not her Glasgow Green. Accordingly it is only in the nature of things that at times there should be little explosions.

Regarding the political question as a whole, and judging simply from personal experiences, one came to the following definite conclusions: (1) The present condition of the political exiles is not as bad as many would have us believe. This conclusion is largely based on their own evidence. (2) The past of the Terrorist party is not looked back on by its members with the pride that one would have imagined and expected from them. Many are willing and frank enough to speak of the foolishness of their younger days, and there is a marked eagerness to disclaim all connection with dynamite. (3) It is an undoubted fact that many of them have made a better thing of the remnants of their lives in Siberia than they ever dreamt of making of the whole at home.

Further, they speak a great deal of the ways in which they desire to help their country. The question naturally arises, Is the only way to help your country by endeavouring to upset the present form of Government? Regarding the politicals as a class, one would feel sorry for Russia if the dreams of the Terrorists had been realised, and they had got the power they sought into their hands. They have too high an opinion of their own capabilities to do much good work, but their experiences have made them sympathetic to a degree. Many are most intelligent men from whom one could learn much, but the ideas of the majority, beyond certain narrow limits, are cloudy in the extreme. They talk much about what they want to do for the peasant, and what they would do for him in certain eventualities; but they are not of the peasants, and do not know them, nor do the peasants care especially for them.

There seems to be a strange perverseness and want of balance about many of them. It was pathetic to listen to their tales of the past. "There were moments of great enthusiasm," said my Kara informant as he thought back upon them, but now all the spirit has died out of the survivors, or rather they have come to see that they went on wrong lines. But how they could ever have imagined that they were the men to set Russia right passes one's comprehension. Their interest in those of our fellow-countrymen who are most in sympathy with them was very marked. Mr Stopford Brooke and Dr Spence Watson are names with which to conjure in an exile colony. Still it seems to me that a British Society of Friends of Russian Freedom can only rightly rouse the same feeling in Russia as the existence in that country of a Society of Friends of Irish Freedom would in ours. Russia is the one country with which it is most urgent that we should be in alliance, and it seems a pity that any possible cause of misunderstanding should exist. Besides, after all, the great majority of the politicals would far rather stay on in Russia than escape to any so-called land of freedom. What lies before Russia is the education of her people, not only the peasant but also the middle classes. Before this has been achieved, freedom is impossible. Teach the people the elements of morality—they have yet much to learn; give them to understand the larger questions that touch humanity and the world at large; show them the possibilities, and let them feel the obligations, of a larger life. And the well-tried bureaucratic system, fit type of arrested development, but till then not antiquated, will be sloughed off, unequal to the expanding life within, and Russia will be free indeed. The day belongs to those who feel the pressure, provided that they refrain from one thing—resisting it with violence.

CHAPTER XII.

CONCLUSION.

CRITICISM OF THE SIBERIAN EXILE SYSTEM—THE FUTURE OF THE COUNTRY—ITS INTERNAL DEVELOPMENT AND UNITY.

In attempting a very brief criticism of the Siberian exile system as a whole, one would remark *first*, that in its best features it is eminently worthy of imitation, but that it presents opportunities of abuse of which it might be difficult to deny that advantage is still taken in some localities, although in ever lessening degree. In the nature of the country itself lies the occasion of the relatively large amount of liberty that it is found possible to accord to the convicts. But when one hears authenticated tales from those who have been within ear-shot of the conversation round the fire in some "free-command's" cabin of an evening, in the course of which the villains cap each other's recitals of cruelty, murder, and lust, and when one thinks of the possibilities that still lie within the reach of such creatures, one is tempted to question the advisability even of this otherwise admirable feature of the system. If, however, a psychological examination of each criminal were made, so that liberty could be granted to an individual who had slain his fellow in a sudden fit of jealousy or passion, whilst the man of homicidal tendency could be kept under constant restraint, a step would be taken towards approximation to the ideal. *Secondly*, it is too arbitrary to allow so much to depend merely upon the character of the individual *natchalniks* and other officials. Arbitrariness is so engrained in all Russian affairs that it need not surprise us here: it is the blemish that will take longest to disappear. *Thirdly*, while in the large stations, such as Alexandrovsky Central and the Nertchinsk Penal Settlement, life as a whole is quite passable, yet in all the circumstances connected with the march, and in many of the small local prisons, that state of affairs which one may euphemistically style "the old *régime*" prevails to some extent. The railway will, however, revolutionise the march —in fact do away with it as a march; and it is not to be expected that the local prison management will long lag behind in the progress which all branches of the system are making. It might be possible to bully ten men, but it is different when you have a thousand. A *natchalnik* might succeed in hushing up the death of five men from asphyxia or starvation, but it would be difficult to account for the death of a hundred. The tolerableness of existence at these great centres is due to the numbers of the convicts there, to the fact that provision of a sort must be made for them in consequence of their numbers, but still more to their being under the charge of the best directors. *Fourthly*, the hospitals perhaps constitute the weakest point all through, owing to insufficient outlay. The doctors complained more than any other officials. Theirs is probably the least enviable of all positions. *Finally*, the criticism of former days as to universal idleness of the convicts and absence of serious purpose in providing work for them is no longer in place. Both theory and practice in these particulars have been entirely altered, and, as I believe, a better era in the history of this remarkable system has been inaugurated under the new director, Mr Salomon.

. . . .

The circumstances which invest the Siberia of yesterday with an interest for some minds are far other than those which now invite attention to this country of the coming century. Reference has been made on more than one occasion to the untold wealth of gold, iron, and coal that lies as yet concealed in Siberian territory. Hitherto many of the gold mines and most of the Ural iron-works have been in the hands of large capitalists, who, with few exceptions, are open to the charge of leaving in the country very little of the money that they take out of it, preferring to pass the winter in St Petersburg, in Paris, or in Moscow, rather than to stay on and help to develop the country that has done so much for them. And so the foundries are always smoking, but the old machinery remains, and though the output increases slowly, still the general progress is not what it might so easily be. The gold-mine owner forgets how Siberia has been the saviour of Russia, and though there are Sibiryakovs, yet they are sadly in the minority. But recognition of Siberia and of its value is fast spreading, and its position as one of the greatest countries of the future is assured. Moreover, the twentieth century will see the solution of a problem whose terms are even now being laid down. After reflecting on the peasant immigration, of which some account has been given, one is inclined to question if, after all, Siberia is not being converted into a nation of *mujiks*. Two opinions obtain in Russia to-day upon the situation. One is, that in the industrious, easily-controlled peasant you have the best element with which to seriously commence the work of building up and unifying a future empire. Then at a later period attention can be directed to bringing out representatives of the other classes of society, and centres of intellectual life will arise in the towns, from which education will gradually spread throughout the country. From the other point of view it is asserted that this procedure is radically wrong, that under it the country cannot make any great progress, and that, on the contrary, higher elements — representatives of every force that is potent in human society—should be there from the first.

But there is a still more important question. As one looks at the map of All the Russias, and attempts to comprehend the size of that vast empire, the different peoples included in it, the variety of education, of tribal and other constitutions, of economies, and of creeds, it seems impossible to believe that the heterogeneous mass can hold together long. If the Yenisei be taken as a rough dividing line, on the east and south-east of it are Mongolian peoples, to the west of it the Slav. Is it not possible, nay, rather probable, that the races to the east and south-east of that great river, being akin in almost every relation, should become welded together in the course of the next century into a powerful empire that could throw off allegiance to the Slav? To my mind the continuity of the empire in its north Asiatic dominions depends entirely upon the rate at which the new railway Russianises Siberia. Much more will be conditioned by what that railway carries in than by what it bears away.

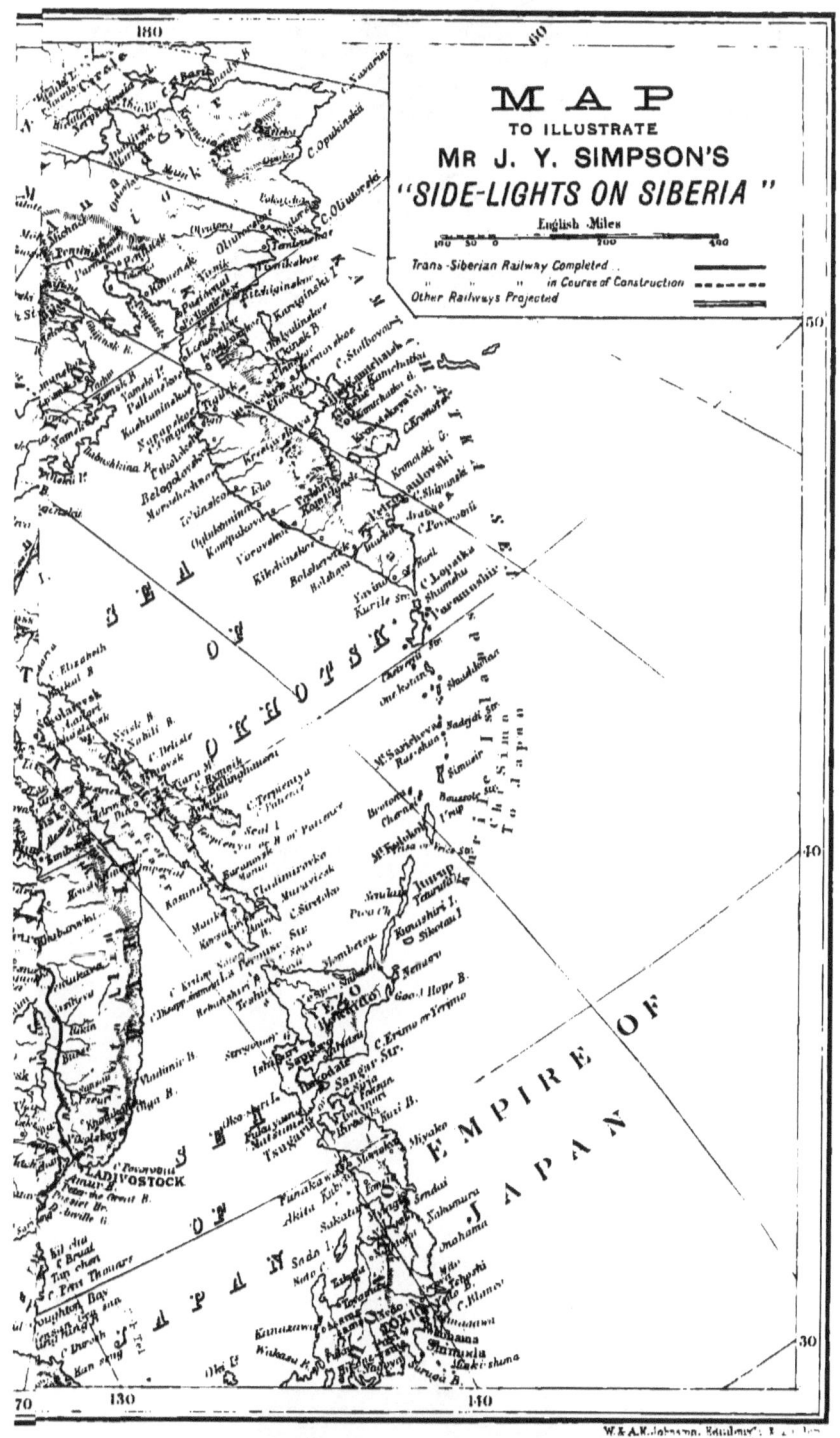

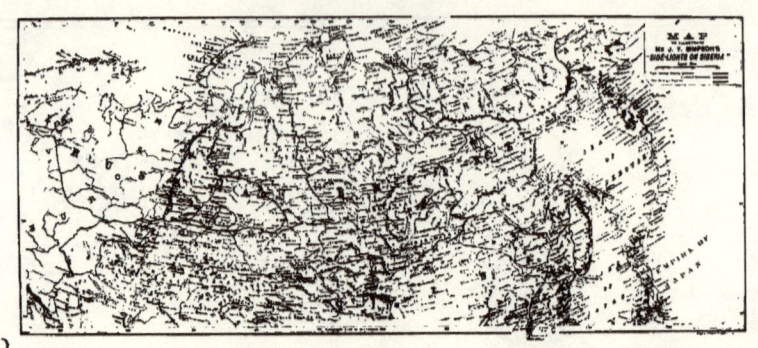

GLOSSARY.

Arshin	Russian lineal measure = 16 *vershoks* = 28 inches.
Artel	A strong co-operative association.
Ataman	Headman of a Kossak village.
Barin	Master.
Borsch	A soup commonly composed of beetroot and bacon.
Brodyaga	Vagrant, vagabond.
Desiatine	Russian square measure = 2·7 acres.
Dobrovolni	Lit. "voluntary," and so of those who of their own freewill accompany relatives or friends into exile.
Droshky	A one-horse carriage. (The single hood is a later improvement.)
Duga	The shaft-bow, to which bells are attached.
Dvornik	Name applied to a servant attached to each town-house, whose duties include that of watching at the gate of the yard.
Feldsher	A partially qualified medical officer.
Ikon	Russian sacred picture.
Ikonostas	The screen adorned with *ikons* which separates the altar from the body of the church.
Intelligenti	Educated men, those who have passed through a university or one of the higher schools of the empire: almost all politicals can be so described.
Ispravnik	Chief of the police in a district.
Isvostchik	Driver of a hired carriage with not more than two horses.

Kabak	Tavern, public-house.
Kaftan	See *Khalat*.
Kamera	A room, and so of a prison-ward.
Karaúlnaya	Guardroom.
Kasha	Gruel.
Katorjnik	Hard-labour convict.
Khalat	Lit. "a morning-gown," but used of the summer overcoat to which the name *kaftan* is also sometimes applied.
Knut	A whip or scourge with weighted tails. See p. 219.
Kolyaska	A carriage in shape and build like a landau, but with only one hood as in a victoria.
Kontora	Comptoir, office.
Kopek	100th part of a ruble, slightly under one farthing.
Krinka	An earthen pot.
Kvass	A non-intoxicating drink made from the fermentation of rye-bread soaked in water.
Nagaika	A whip (especially of the Kossaks).
Nari	Guardroom beds, sleeping platforms.
Natchalnik	A general term for a superior or commander of any description, as, *e.g.*, the governor of a prison, the captain of a convoy, &c.
Oblast	Province. See p. 3, footnote.
Palatch	Executioner, flogger.
(*Na*) *perekladnikh*	To travel by post and change carriage at every station.
Pilmeni	A form of mince pâté.
Pisar	Lit. "writer," and so (postmaster's) secretary.
Plet	A whip or scourge. See p. 219.
Podorojnaya	An order for post-horses.
Poselentzi	Exile settlers.
Prijut	An educational home for children.
Progon	Post-fare.
Psalomstchik	Psalm-reader.
Pud	Russian weight = 40 lb. Russ. = 32·24 lb. Eng.
Rozgi	Species of birch-rod.
Rubashka	Shirt.
Ruble	In value two shillings.
Ryabtchik	Gelinotte, or hazel-grouse.

Sajen .	Russian measure: linear *sajen* = 3 *arshines* = 7 feet; square *sajen* = 49 sq. ft.
Shtchi .	Cabbage-soup.
Shuba .	A fur coat; generally of sheepskin, as worn by the peasants.
Starosta	Senior or headman.
Taiga .	Primeval or virgin forest. See p. 6.
Tarantass .	A long travelling-coach.
Tchernoziom	Lit. "black earth"; the rich black soil characteristic of South Russia and certain parts of Siberia.
Tchinovnik .	Person who has a certain *tchin* or rank; an official.
Teleyga .	A shallow, four-wheeled, springless cart.
Trakt .	Highroad.
Troika .	Lit. "threefold," so of a team of three horses.
Tundra .	The swampy, treeless belt of land that skirts the Arctic Ocean. See p. 4.
Ulus .	Originally a nomad village of tents, and so of a Yakute village.
Verst .	Russian measure: linear *verst* = 500 *sajens* = ·66 Eng. miles; square *verst* = ·439 square Eng. miles.
Vodka	A spirit made of rye.
Yamstchik .	Postboy; driver of a post-carriage with more than one horse.
Zolotnik	96th part of 1 lb. Russ., which is slightly less than 1 lb. Eng.

INDEX.

Abolition of serfage, 302, 309.
Administrative Process. See Exile.
Ainus, 274.
Akatui, 238, 258-265, 338, 346, 356.
Alexander I., 132-137, 299, 300.
Alexander II., 300-306, 320, 322, 324, 325, 357.
Alexandrovsky (near Irkutsk), 202-204 ; Central Prison at, 203-217, 221-226 ; Peresilni Prison at, 225 ; in Nertchinsk penal settlement, 265-269.
Alexandrovsky Post (Sakhalin), 273, 274, 277.
Algatchi, prison at, 254-256 ; mines at, 256, 257, 265.
Altai, 4, 104.
Amur, region of, 3, 8, 28, 237 ; government of, 44.
Angara, 3, 11, 12, 81, 82.
Annexation of Siberia, 2.
Area of Siberia, 2.
Atchinsk, 9, 46-48.

Baer's Law, 9.
Baikal, 3, 4, 11, 13, 24, 51-53, 81, 85 ; Trans - Baikalian Railway, 86, 91.
Bakunin, 307, 308.
Balkhash, Lake, 3.
Barabinsky steppe, 39.
Barge, convict, 153-159, 164.
Bomb factories, 324, 325.
Branding of prisoners, 219-221.

Brodyaga, 88, 90, 176-181, 224.
Buryats, 13, 72, 82, 85.

Capital punishment, 216.
Censorship, 342.
Children's homes, 205, 249, 250, 286, 292, 295.
Chinese, 239, 278.
Civil rights, loss of, 197, 198, 332, 347, 348.
Coal, 58, 271, 277.
Communal exile, 151, 200, 201, 337.
Convict, labour on railway, 43-45, 243, 244 ; punishment of, 149, 152, 196, 197, 217, 221 ; voluntary followers of, 153, 206, 251, 252 ; food of, 169, 176, 184, 214, 215, 239, 281, 349 ; labour at Sakhalin, 274, 275 ; dress of, 288 ; factory, 289-292 ; influence of, 295-297.
Convict barge, 153-159, 164.
Convoy commands, 174.
Correspondence, supervision of, 334.
Criticism, 190, 370, 373-375.
Cuckoo, effect of notes of, on exiles, 178.

Decembrists, the, 299.
Desertion, punishment of, 179, 219.
De Windt, Mr, 195, 329-331, 366.
Dissenters, 14, 53, 230, 289.
Drunkenness, 78, 310, 316.

Emigrants' camp, 46-48.

INDEX.

Emigration, 24-32, 37; regulations of, 27-29.
Étapes, 172-176, 181, 188, 191, 278, 333, 335.
Evolution of the prison, 195.
Ex-convicts, distribution of, 200-202.
Exile by Administrative Process, 201, 331, 332, 336, 337.
Exile system, 197-202, 331, 332; criticism of, 373-375.
Exiles, political, 14, 36, 139, 140, 149, 151, 189, 201, 259, 262, 331-369.
Explosion in Winter Palace, 322.

Fasting, 214.
Ferryboat, 41, 97, 102.
Fertile zone, 7.
Figner, Vera, 340, 341.
Floods, 54, 93-102.
Flora of Siberia, 43, 46, 85, 241.
Forest zone, 6.
"Free-commands," 200, 203, 205, 223, 232-237, 261, 268.
Freedom of Russia, 370-372.

Gilyaks, 274.
Gogol, 300.
Goldenberg, 319.
Gorni-Zerentui, 238; prison at, 242-254, 288.
Great Siberian Iron Road. See Railway, Trans-Siberian.
Guberuski Prison at Tomsk, 292-295.

Herzen, 300-304, 307.
Hospitals, prison, 150, 153, 169, 191, 225, 227, 231, 248, 259, 267, 280, 281, 284, 294, 374.
Hunger strikes, 318, 353.

Identification papers, 164.
Impalement, 196.
Irkutsk, 3, 11, 28, 333; government of, 44; prison at, 227-231.
Irtish, 3, 8, 10, 37, 110-112, 286.

Jelyabov, 323.

Jews, 201, 343, 363, 365.

Kadainsky prison, 237.
Kainsk, 192.
Kamtchatka, 3, 4, 6.
Kansk, 182, 367.
Kara, sea route, 58, 285; prison at, 238, 340, 345-353, 363.
Katkov, 303.
Keane, Professor, 3.
Kennan, Mr, 195, 238, 329-331, 340, 348, 362, 366.
Khalturin, 322.
Khanka, Lake, 12.
Khromov, 119-123; his meeting with Kuzmitch, 124; subsequent story, 125-128, 130-132, 136, 137.
Kirghize, 4, 39.
Knut, 219.
Krasnoyarsk, 49, 285; prison at, 285, 286, 334, 335, 341, 367.
Kurgan, 36, 367.
Kuzmitch, Theodore, his life, 123-131; popular identification of, 136, 137.

Lake Baikal, 3, 4, 11, 13, 24.
Lake Balkhash, 3.
Lake Khanka, 12.
"Land and Liberty" Society, 314, 319, 320.
Lansdell, Dr, 195, 220, 279.
Lavrov, 307-309.
Lena, 8, 9, 112.
Liberal party, the, 299, 300, 302, 303, 305, 321.
Listvinitchnaya, 51, 83.
Littoral, 3.

Manifestoes, 202, 350.
March, on the, 140-142, 172-193.
Mariinsk, 45, 181.
Michailov, 319-321.
Moscow, Peresilni Prison at, 142, 143.
Mountains, Altai, 4; Sayan, *ib.*; Yablonovoi, *ib.*, 54; Ural, 34.

Native races, 12-14.

Nertchinsk, 54, 239, 346, 374; silver mines of, 187, chapter viii. *passim*; prison at, 277-279.
Netchaiev conspiracy, 306-308, 352.
Nihilism, 304-306.

Ob, 2, 8, 9-11, 39, 104, 110, 159.
Ob-Yenisei Canal, 11, 17.
Oblast, meaning of the term, 3.
Okhotsk, 3, 14, 17.
Omsk, 36, 37, 335.
Ossinski, 318.
Ostyaks, 13, 342.
Overland tea-trade, 60, 89.

Peasant life, 42, 76, 78-81, 231.
Penck, 9.
Perm-Kotlass Railway, 59.
Plet, 218, 219.
Pole of cold, 3.
Polish Rebellion, 303.
Political exile, 36, 139, 140, 149, 151, 189, 201, 259, 262, 331-369.
Political "processes," 316, 317.
Population of Siberia, 12-15.
Post-travel, 62-75; cost of, 65; *yamstchik*, 65, 72, 91; stations, 73-75.
Prisons, Tomsk, 138-144, 164, 166-172, 292-295; Nijni-Udinsk, 141: Moscow, 142, 143; overcrowding of, 143-147; Tiumen, 144, 147-153; hospital, 150, 153, 169, 191, 225, 227, 231; evolution of, 195; Alexandrovsky Central, 203-217, 221-226; Peresilni, 225; Irkutsk, 227-231; Akatui, 238, 258-265, 338, 346, 356; Kara, 238, 340, 345-353, 363; Gorni-Zerentui, 242-254, 288; Algatchi, 254-257, 265; Alexandrovsky, 265-269; Nertchinsk, 277-279; Tchita, 279-282; Verkhni-Udinsk, 282-285; Krasnoyarsk, 285, 286, 334, 335, 341, 367; Tobolsk, 286-292.
Punishment of convicts, 149, 152, 196, 197, 217, 221.

Pushkin, 299.

Railway, Perm-Kotlass, 59.
Railway, Trans-Baikalian, 86, 91.
Railway, Trans-Manchurian, 55.
Railway, Trans-Siberian, chap. ii. *passim*, 376; history of, 17-22; Special Commission on, 18; Committee of, 22; working sections of, 23; Tchelyabinsk to river Ob, 35-39: Ob to Irkutsk, 40-51; Irkutsk to Misovskaya, 51-53; Misovskaya to Srjetensk, 53-55; Srjetensk to Khabarovsk, 55, 56; Khabarovsk to Grafskaya, 56; Grafskaya to Vladivostok, 56, 57; present state of, 34; work on, 38, 49-51; convict labour on, 42, 43-45, 243, 244.
Revolutionary movement, 298-324; results of, 326, 327.
River-system of Siberia, 8-12, 51, 103-113.
Robbery, 71, 90.
Romance of political life, 353-356.

Sakhalin, 3, 12, 44, 142, 143, 201, 221, 230, 238, 261, 270-277, 279, 346; climate of, 272; population of, 273, 274; political divisions of, 274; convict labour of, *ib.*, 275.
Sayan Mountains, 4.
Schlusselburg, 340, 346.
Secret printing-press, 324.
Selenga, 11, 86, 87.
Semipalatinsk, 3.
Semirjetchensk, 3, 4.
Serfage, abolition of, 302, 309.
Shamanism, 13, 82.
Shilka, 54, 237, 239, 240.
Siberia, annexation of, 2; area of, *ib.*; political divisions of, 2-4; mountains of, 4; river-system of, 8-12; population of, 12-15; future of, 375, 376.
Slavinski, 259-262, 330.
Socialism, 300-302, 305, 310, 312-314, 321, 358.
Soloviev, 320.

INDEX.

Srjetensk, 23, 54, 188, 239.
Stepanovitch, 315, 316.
Steppe region, 3, 4.
Student life, 307, 309, 313, 338, 354, 356, 363, 364, 369.
Sunday labour, 282.
Sunday-schools, 302, 343.

Taiga, 2, 6, 8, 24, 48.
Tatar, 14, 183.
Tchita, 54, 279; prison at, 280-282.
Tchelyabinsk, 35; railway, 35-39.
Tchernishevski, 301, 302.
Tchuktchi, 12.
Tea trade, 60, 89.
Terrorism, 317-324.
Terrorists, 338-340, 357, 360.
Theodore Kuzmitch, his home, 119-123; his life, 123-137.
Tiumen, 144, 147, 159; Peresilni Prison at, 144, 147-153.
Tobolsk, 2, 7, 28, 31, 286, 287; prison at, 286-292; convict factory at, 289-292.
Tomsk, 2, 7, 28, 45, 114-119, 159; branch line to, 45; legend of, 114-137; Peresilni Prison at, 138-144, 164, 166-172; Gubernski Prison at, 292-295.
Trans-Baikalia, 3, 7, 86, 91, 337, 347.
Trans-Manchurian railway, 55.
Trans-Siberian Railway. See Railway, Trans-Siberian.
Trepov, attempt to assassinate, 217.

Tundra, 2, 4-6, 13.
Tungus, 13, 106, 257, 342.
Turgeniev, 304.

University at Tomsk, 117, 118; at Zurich, 308, 309.
Ural Mountains, 34.
Ussuri, 12, 56, 57.

Vagrancy. See under *Brodyaga*.
Verkhni-Udinsk, 81, 86, 87, 240, 282; prison at, 282-285.
Verkhoyansk, 3.
Village life, 33, 75, 81, 86, 109.
Vladivostok, 55, 57, 60.
Volga, 32, 34, 112, 113.
Voluntary followers of convicts, 153, 206, 251, 252.

Wages, rate of, on railway, 43.
Wheelbarrows, chaining prisoners to, 221.

Yablonovoi Mountains, 4, 54.
Yakutes, 12, 13.
Yakutsk, 2, 8, 12, 335-339, 347, 365, 366.
Yamstchik, 65, 72, 91.
Yana, 3.
Yekaterinburg, 2.
Yenisei, 3, 9-11, 13, 28, 49.
Yeniseisk, 3, 285.
Yermak, 2, 60, 287.

Zasulitch, Vera, 317.
Zurich, University of, 308, 309.

www.ingramcontent.com/pod-product-compliance
Lightning Source LLC
Chambersburg PA
CBHW032138010526
44111CB00035B/609